Table of

Introduction

Beginning in the early 1890's, businessmen and entrepreneurs settled in South Georgia and began to grow a community that became known as Douglas, Georgia. There on that dirt road called Gaskin Avenue, stately homes were built, and they soon became residences for social scenes, business meetings, and Southern graces. It was once labeled "Silk Stocking Row," and aptly so, for these women ushered in an era of beauty and fashion.

Today, many of the homes have been renovated, and their beauty and stature are as strong as ever. Dogwoods now border Gaskin Avenue and usher in the spring with their expansive show of blossoms. Along with the beauty of Gaskin Avenue stands the home for many Christians, First Baptist Church. It is a haven for the lost, a place of rest for the weary, and a cornerstone for the community. Therein is where grace is found, grace that will pardon and cleanse your soul.

Grace on Gaskin is a collection of over 600 recipes from our congregation on Gaskin Avenue. When you turn the pages of this book, you will experience recipes that have been enjoyed time and time again around our tables, at church socials, in homes of the sick, along with many other occasions.

We invite you to experience a part of our heritage,

"*Grace on Gaskin.*"

Contributors

A cookbook is only as good as the recipes that are contained therein, and we have the best. We regret that we were unable to include all that were received due to the amount of space and duplications. Please know that your submissions were greatly appreciated. To those who contributed your time proofing, typing, writing, and selling, we give our heartfelt thanks. To our church family who have waited so patiently for this book to become a reality, we owe a very special thank you.

Grace on Gaskin

First Baptist Church
Douglas, Georgia

by
First Baptist Church
124 North Gaskin Avenue
Douglas, Georgia 31533
fbcdouglas.com

The proceeds from the sale of ***Grace on Gaskin*** will go to further the Ministry of our Annual GEMS Banquet.

Special acknowledgement is due to artist, Toby Smith, for the original watercolor that wraps the collection found within the book.

Photography was provided by Ronald Goodman Photography, Robert Preston, Worth Brown, Allison Cowart, and Stephanie Evans.

ISBN: 978-1-935802-19-8

FATHER
&
SON
PUBLISHING, INC.
4909 North Monroe Street
Tallahassee, Florida 32303-7015
www.fatherson.com
800-741-2712

Choosing the Good Part

Jesus enjoyed a good meal as much as any of us. And he knew that the home of Lazarus and his two sisters, Martha and Mary, was a great place for food and fellowship. The Bible says:

> *Now as they were traveling along, [Jesus] entered a village; and a woman named Martha welcomed Him into her home. She had a sister called Mary, who was seated at the Lord's feet, listening to His word.*
>
> *But Martha was distracted with all her preparations; and she came up to Him and said, "Lord, do You not care that my sister has left me to do all the serving alone? Then tell her to help me."*
>
> *But the Lord answered and said to her, "Martha, Martha, you are worried and bothered about so many things; but only one thing is necessary, for Mary has chosen the good part, which shall not be taken away from her."*
>
> **Luke 10:38-42** (NASB)

The words, "*Mary has chosen the good part*," arrest our attention. What is the "*good part*"? The good part of life is having a real relationship with God. The Bible teaches us that God created the heavens and the earth and God created us. He gave us wonderful minds and a will and freedom of our own. But we used that freedom carelessly and sinned and disrupted our relationship with God, who made us and loved us.

The Bible says that all of us sin, and the consequence of that sin is death and eternal separation from God and all that is good. God was heartbroken to see us destroying ourselves, so about 2000 years ago He came down to this earth on a rescue mission by putting on human flesh and living among us.

God made His grand entrance at a stable in the sleepy village of Bethlehem. Through an amazing miracle of divine conception, He was born into a carpenter's family. His name was Jesus. Jesus grew up to become a teacher and friend of broken hearts. He welcomed the outcasts and healed the sick. Jesus showed us the nature of God by way of the life He lived.

But the world wasn't ready for a humble Savior who was a friend of sinners. So Jesus was arrested and tried as a traitor. Then He was convicted and crucified. A perfectly innocent man was made to suffer because of our sins. The good news is that it was all a part of God's plan.

Jesus Christ died on the cross in our place. He became our substitute. He paid the penalty for our sins. He offered His perfect life in exchange for our sinful life. We deserved to suffer for our sins, but Jesus suffered for us.

Furthermore, Jesus not only took on our sins at the cross, He also offered to clothe us in His perfect righteousness.

Jesus Christ died on the cross, was buried, and three days later He rose from the dead. The resurrection of Jesus proves He has the power to forgive sin and grant eternal life.

The Bible says, "*...God demonstrates His own love toward us, in that while we were yet sinners, Christ died for us. Much more then, having now been justified by His blood, we shall be saved from the wrath of God through Him.*" **Romans 5:8-9** (NASB)

The Bible also says, "*We are made right with God by placing our faith in Jesus Christ. And this is true for everyone who believes, no matter who we are. For everyone has sinned; we all fall short of God's glorious standard. Yet God, with undeserved kindness, declares that we are righteous. He did this through Christ Jesus when He freed us from the penalty for our sins.*" **Romans 3:22-24** (NLT)

You can receive forgiveness and eternal life today by calling on the name of the Lord to be saved. Why not make this your prayer right now:

> Dear Lord, I know I'm a sinner.
> I'm so sorry for what I've done. I was wrong...so very wrong and I am ashamed. Please...please forgive me.
> Jesus, I know You love me.
> I know You died for me...I know You died to pay the penalty for my sin, and You offered me Your perfect righteousness in place of my failures. You took the punishment I deserved,
> and I received Your perfect life.
> Thank you for dying for me and rising from the dead. Please save my soul.
> Please be my Lord and Savior.
> Take control of my life and help me to follow You, and obey You from this day forward.
> In Your Name I pray, AMEN.

When Jesus went to the home of Lazarus, Martha busied herself in the kitchen, but Mary chose the good part. As you enjoy this cookbook and welcome friends and family into your own home, make sure you take time to choose the good part.

The Beginning

First Baptist Church has enjoyed a rich and vibrant history during its 120-year existence. Like so many institutions in Douglas and Coffee County, FBC can trace its presence back to Benajah Peterson, one of the community's most significant early leaders.

On 1890, the Smyrna Baptist Association elected a Baptist preacher named J.R. Tatum to serve as associational missionary for the area surrounding Coffee County. Mr. Peterson owned the courthouse at the time and offered it as a place for Tatum to preach free of charge. As such, Tatum preached the first Baptist message in Coffee County.

Later that year, Dr. William F. Sibbett, a physician of the Baptist faith, moved his family to Douglas. He desperately wanted to bring a Baptist minister to Douglas to preach on a regular basis. He found his pastor just a few miles up the road in Broxton. One morning in 1891, Dr. Sibbett went to hear T.P. O'Neal, a former Confederate soldier, deliver a message. He was pleased with what he heard and offered to pay O'Neal's salary himself if he would come to Douglas. He agreed and the small Baptist congregation, led by O'Neal, continued to meet in Peterson's courthouse until 1893. On Sunday, September 3, 1893, O'Neal preached and thereafter the congregation called the Council for Organization to form First Baptist Church. Nine charter members approved the Church Covenant and Articles of Faith and elected O'Neal pastor.

The first permanent building was constructed in 1896 on the corner of Ward Street and Coffee Avenue. A decade later, the church moved a short distance away to the southwest corner of Ward Street and Gaskin Avenue. Due to economic challenges, construction was a painstaking process, but membership continued to grow, reaching about 400 members during that time. The growth of the church reflected the growth of the community; at the time Dr. Sibbett moved to Douglas, the population was fewer than 100. Construction on the new building was completed on March 10, 1911; on that day, members held the first service in the new building.

By 1946, the church had nearly 800 members and the congregation began searching for property upon which they could construct a new building. Early in 1947, First Baptist Church bought the former home of Dr. Sibbett – the very individual who, by his own courage and vision, had started FBC 56 years earlier – and a new building project began. On Sunday, August 4, 1954, FBC convened in its third and final home.

On the decades since, First Baptist has expanded to meet the spiritual needs of the Douglas-Coffee County Community. Through each and every expansion, each and every pastor, each and every challenge, the church has remained rooted in its love for Christ and its desire to see people establish and develop a relationship with their Savior. Though we like to trace church histories through buildings and construction projects, the true legacy of any church is found in its members – those who utilize the buildings for the glory of God and the growth of His Kingdom.

One of the earliest angels of First Baptist Church and the Coffee County community was a woman named Dollie Freeman. She was a city missionary who tended to her office with the same diligence and fervor as that of someone serving a world away. She was a humble, kind, gentle spirit who glorified Christ in everything she did. W.P. Ward referred to Freeman as "the good angel of Douglas" in his *History of Coffee County.*

Dollie Freeman was one of the first GEMS of First Baptist Church. Today, GEMS stands for Girlfriends Encouraging Ministry and Service. We desire to carry forth the tradition of serving God and serving each other, just like Dollie Freeman and the other selfless women who came before and after her.

There will always be a place set for you should you choose to come and dine with us on the Word. It is now with sincere hearts that we extend to you "Grace on Gaskin."

"O taste and see that The Lord is good!" **Psalm 34:8a** (KJV)

Information regarding the history of First Baptist Church came from "At Work Since 1893" by Thomas Shivers Hubert and Thomas Hubert Frier.

Appetizers and Beverages

"Behold, I stand at the door and knock; if anyone hears My voice and opens the door, I will come in to him and will dine with him, and he with Me."

Revelation 3:20
(NASB)

Appetizers and Beverages

Bacon Appetizer

- 8 slices of bacon, cooked and crumbled or 1 (3 ounce) package Real Bacon Bits
- 3 ounces Swiss cheese, shredded
- 2 medium tomatoes, peeled, seeded, and diced (squeeze out as much liquid as possible)
- 2 cans Hungry Jack flaky biscuits
- 1 teaspoon dried basil
- ½ cup mayonnaise
- 1 small onion, chopped

Mix all together except biscuits and set aside. Spray mini-muffin pan with cooking spray. Separate each biscuit lengthwise in half and press into tins. Fill with bacon mixture. Bake at 325 degrees for 12 minutes. Serves 40.

Note: I sometimes use 2 packages of frozen Athens mini fillo shells in place of the biscuits.

Mary Lou Gillespie

Bacon-Wrapped Chestnuts

- 1 pound bacon
- 1 can water chestnuts, sliced
- 1 cup ketchup
- 1 cup light brown sugar
- 2 tablespoons Worcestershire sauce

Cut bacon strips in half. Roll water chestnuts in bacon and secure with toothpick. Place in 9 x 13 baking dish. Simmer in sauce pan, ketchup, brown sugar, and Worcestershire sauce for 5 minutes. Pour ketchup mixture over bacon and chestnuts. Bake in oven on 350 degrees for 30 minutes or until bacon is crisp.

Pam Gillis

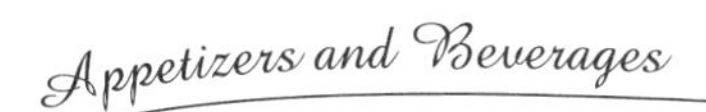

Cranberry-Barbecue Meatballs

2 (16 ounce) packages cooked plain meatballs, thawed
1 (16 ounce) can jellied cranberry sauce
1 cup barbecue sauce

In a 3½- or 4-quart slow cooker, place meatballs. In a medium bowl, combine cranberry sauce and barbecue sauce. Pour over meatballs in cooker, stirring to coat. Cover and cook on low heat setting for 4 to 5 hours or high setting for 2 to 2½ hours. Serve meatballs with toothpicks. If desired, keep warm on low heat setting for up to 2 hours. I use Kraft Original barbecue sauce.

Dot McKinnon

Party Strawberries

1 pound coconut, ground or chopped
¼ pound almonds or pecans, ground or finely chopped
2 packages strawberry Jell-O, dry
1 can Eagle Brand condensed milk , with red food coloring added
½ teaspoon almond extract
Red sugar

Mix all ingredients except red sugar. Shape into strawberries and roll in red sugar. Add leaves (like boxwood). Makes 90-100 depending on size. Freezes well.

Note: Adds color to table and tastes so good!

In Memory of Mrs. Wing Shirley Strickland

Artichoke Dip

- 1 teaspoon garlic powder
- 1 cup mayonnaise
- 1 cup Parmesan cheese
- 2 cans artichoke hearts, chopped
- Dash Tabasco sauce

Combine all ingredients and bake in casserole dish at 300 degrees until bubbly.

Martha Lou Royer

South Georgia Caviar

- ¾ cup balsamic vinegar
- ½ cup extra-virgin olive oil
- ¼ cup sugar
- 2 teaspoons salt
- 1 teaspoon pepper
- 4 (15 ounce) cans black-eyed peas, rinsed and drained
- 1 cup green bell pepper, chopped
- 1 cup yellow bell pepper, chopped
- 1 cup red bell pepper, chopped
- 1 cup red onion, chopped
- 1½ cups cherry tomatoes, quartered
- 1 cup fresh parsley, finely chopped

Combine first 5 ingredients in a jar to make dressing. Cover and shake to dissolve sugar. Set aside. Place peas in a large bowl and add all bell peppers, onions, tomatoes, and parsley. Pour dressing over top and toss well. Transfer to a plastic container, cover, and refrigerate for at least 2 hours before serving. Serve with corn chips or tortilla chips.

Pam Gillis

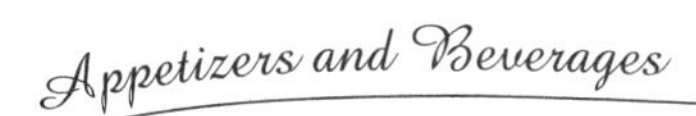

Hoppin' John

- 1 onion, chopped
- 2 stalks celery, chopped
- 2 cups cooked rice
- 2 cups ham, chopped
- 1 to 2 cans black-eyed peas or black beans
- 1 can whole kernel corn, drained
- 2 or 3 cans chopped tomatoes
- Olives, chopped (optional)
- Salt and pepper or other seasonings to taste
- 1 bag of 4 - Mexican cheese blend

Saute onion and celery in small amount of margarine. Add other ingredients. Heat in casserole dish and top with bag of 4-Mexican cheese blend. Serve with tortilla chips.

Dona Christopher

Cheese Pineapple Dip

- 2 (8 ounce) cream cheese, softened
- 1 (8 ounce) crushed pineapple, drained
- ¼ cup green bell pepper, chopped
- 2 tablespoons onion, chopped
- 1 tablespoon seasoned salt
- 1 cup pecans, chopped (optional)

Mix all ingredients thoroughly and refrigerate for a couple of hours or overnight. Serve with your choice of crackers.

Debbie Fender

Fruit Topping

- 1 cup sour cream
- 1 can vanilla frosting
- ⅓ cup lemon juice

Mix all ingredients together. Drizzle over fruit.

Dona Christopher

Ham and Cheese Dip

- ½ cup sour cream
- 2 cups Cheddar cheese
- 1 (8 ounce) cream cheese, softened
- ⅓ cup green onions, chopped
- 4 ounces ham, chopped
- ⅓ cup diced green chilies (canned)
- 1 round loaf of bread
- Dash Worcestershire sauce

Cut off top of bread and hollow out center. Mix all ingredients and pour inside bread. Place top on bread. Wrap in foil. Bake at 350 degrees for 1 hour. Serve with pieces of bread or crackers.

In Memory of Mrs. Geneva Womack

Hot Bacon and Swiss Dip

- 1 (8 ounce) cream cheese, softened
- ½ cup mayonnaise
- 1½ cups Swiss cheese, grated
- 3 tablespoons green onions, chopped
- 8 slices bacon, cooked and crumbled or Real Bacon Bits
- ½ cup Ritz crackers, crumbled

Mix cheeses and mayonnaise together and add onions. Put in 1-quart dish. Top with bacon and Ritz crackers. Bake 20-25 minutes at 350 degrees or until bubbly.

Kelly Lastinger

Hot Crab Dip with Wonton Chips

- 2 (8 ounce) packages cream cheese, cut into cubes
- 2 (6 ounce) cans lump crabmeat, drained and shredded
- 1 (10 ounce) can condensed shrimp bisque
- 1 teaspoon Worcestershire sauce
- 2 teaspoons lemon juice
- 2 teaspoons soy sauce
- 1 scallion, finely chopped
- 1 red pepper, chopped
- 1 package wonton wrappers
- Hot sauce
- Salt and pepper
- Peanut oil

Combine all ingredients in mixing bowl and stir. Place in a broiler-proof serving dish and broil for 10 minutes or until hot and bubbly. Heat 2 inches of peanut oil in a Dutch oven or fryer to 350 degrees. Cut wonton wrappers diagonally. Add them in batches to fry lightly. Remove from oil and let drain on paper towels before serving. Season with salt.

Norma Lynn Hand

Buffalo Chicken Dip

- 2 (10 ounce) cans chicken
- ½ cup Frank's hot sauce or to taste
- 2 (8 ounce) packages cream cheese, softened
- 1 cup ranch dressing
- 1 bag (2 cups) shredded cheese (Monterey/Mexican mix)

Mix chicken and hot sauce. Add cream cheese, ranch dressing, and ½ bag of cheese. Put in 9 × 13 inch baking dish. Top with rest of cheese. Heat in 300 degree oven until cheese melts, approximately 15-20 minutes. Enjoy!

Sherry Patterson

Pizza Dip

- **2 (8 ounce) blocks cream cheese**
- **1 package mini pepperoni**
- **1 jar of pizza sauce**
- **1 cup Cheddar cheese**

Spread cream cheese on bottom of a 9 x 13 baking dish. Layer sauce, then pepperoni, and top with Cheddar cheese. Bake uncovered at 350 degrees until bubbly. This recipe is easily halved for a 9 x 9 baking dish. Serve with your choice of crackers or chips.

Liz Grantham

Tex-Mexican Dip

- **3 avocados**
- **2 tablespoons lemon juice**
- **1 cup sour cream**
- **½ cup mayonnaise**
- **1 package taco seasoning mix**
- **2 (10½ ounce) cans jalapeno bean dip**
- **1 cup green onion, chopped**
- **1 cup tomatoes, chopped**
- **1 large can olives, chopped**
- **1 (8 ounce) package sharp Cheddar cheese**
- **Salt and pepper**

Peel and mash avocados in a bowl, adding salt, pepper, and lemon juice. Combine sour cream, mayonnaise, and taco seasoning in a separate bowl. To assemble, spread jalapeno bean dip in shallow serving dish and top with avocado mixture. Next, layer taco cream mixture. Sprinkle with tomatoes, cheese, onions, and olives. Serve with large tortilla chips.

Jenny Lott

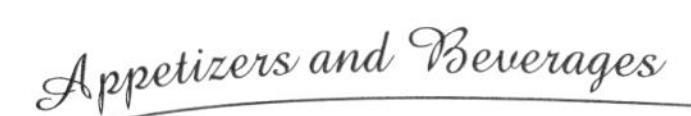

Graham Crackers

1 box Keebler graham crackers
½ cup sugar
1 stick margarine
1 stick butter
Chopped pecans

Line cookie sheet with graham crackers. Bring to a boil the sugar, margarine, and butter and boil for 2 minutes. Pour glaze over crackers. Sprinkle nuts over glaze. Bake in 350 degree oven for 6 minutes. Let slightly cool. Place crackers on a serving dish.

In Memory of Mrs. Othalyne Gillis

Graham Cracker Snack

2 sticks butter
½ cup sugar
1 box graham crackers (will make 2 batches)
Chopped pecans

Spread single layer of crackers on a foil-lined cookie sheet. Boil butter and sugar for 3 minutes. Pour over crackers. Top with nuts sprinkled on all crackers. Bake at 350 degrees for 8 minutes.

In Memory of Mrs. Tess Slowik

Hint: So that you can spend more time with guests, look for appetizers that can be made ahead and require little last-minute fuss.

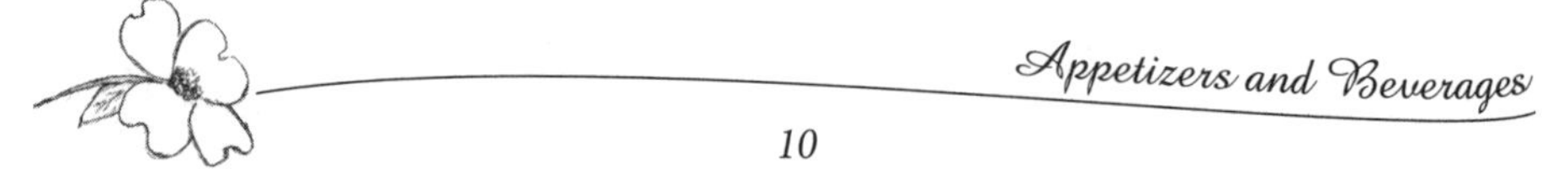

Zesty Party Mix

- 6 ounces Cheddar goldfish
- 6 ounces Parmesan goldfish
- 6 ounces plain goldfish
- 6 ounces pretzel goldfish
- 3 cups wheat Chex cereal
- 3 cups corn Chex cereal
- 3 cups Crispix cereal
- 2 cups regular Cheerios
- 1 tablespoon hot pepper sauce
- 8 to 10 cups peanuts, unsalted
- 2 tablespoons onion powder
- 2 tablespoons celery salt
- 1 tablespoon garlic powder
- 1 tablespoon black pepper
- ½ cup butter
- ½ cup bacon drippings
- 2 tablespoons Worcestershire sauce

Combine goldfish, cereal, and nuts. Mix together onion powder, celery salt, garlic powder, and pepper. Shake over cereal mixture. Let stand eight hours or overnight, shaking occasionally. Melt butter and stir in bacon drippings, Worcestershire sauce, and hot pepper sauce. Pour over seasoned cereal mixture, tossing to coat evenly. Bake at 200 degrees for 1 hour, stirring every 15 minutes.

Betsy Hodges

Oysterette Crackers

- 1 cup Crisco oil
- ½ teaspoon dried dill weed
- ½ teaspoon lemon herb seasoning
- 1 package Hidden Valley dressing mix (original)
- 2 boxes Oysterette crackers

Heat first 4 ingredients until warm. Pour over crackers; mix well. Let cool and then store in airtight containers.

In Memory of Mrs. Othalyne Gillis

Snack Crackers

- 1 package oyster crackers
- ½ cup oil
- 2 teaspoons garlic salt
- 1 package ranch dressing mix
- 2 teaspoons lemon pepper

Mix and let stand overnight in sealed container.

Debbie Slowik

Crispix Snacks

- 4 cups Crispix cereal
- 4 cups Cheez-Its
- 1 cup oil
- 4 tablespoons dill weed
- 1 package Hidden Valley ranch dressing mix

Put Cheez-Its and Crispix into 2 large paper grocery bags (one inside the other). Mix oil, dill weed, and dry dressing. Pour over Crispix and Cheez-Its in bag and shake, shake, shake. Pour onto tray lined with paper towels to drain. Store in an airtight container.

In Memory of Mrs. Wing Shirley Strickland

Spicy Cracker Recipe

- 1 box saltine crackers (whole grain works the best)
- 1 cup vegetable oil
- 1 package ranch dressing mix
- 1 tablespoon dill weed
- 1 tablespoon red pepper flakes
- 1 teaspoon garlic powder

Open whole box of crackers. Dump into a 2-gallon Ziploc bag. Mix oil and remaining ingredients. Pour over crackers, gently tossing to coat. Over the next 24 hours, occasionally toss bag. If serving sooner, spread crackers on cookie sheets and bake on lowest temperature for about an hour, stirring occasionally.

Kim Knight

Pimento Cheese

1 (8 ounce) block mild Cheddar cheese, grated
1 (8 ounce) block sharp Cheddar cheese, grated
1 small tub spreadable cream cheese
1 large jar diced pimentos with juice
¼ teaspoon cayenne pepper or to taste
½ cup Duke's mayonnaise (add more if desired)

Combine all ingredients. Serve with crackers. Keep chilled.

Patsy Herlocker

Pimento Cheese Spread

1 (2 pound) Velveeta cheese, chopped coarsely
1 (8 ounce) package cream cheese
1 (4 ounce) jar chopped pimentos, drained
Mayonnaise (enough to bring to desired consistency)

Mix all ingredients together in mixing bowl at medium speed. Mix thoroughly until smooth.

In Memory of Dr. Arlis Burch

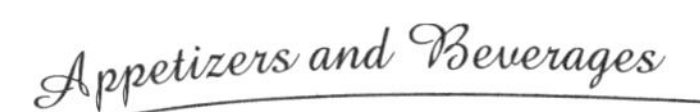

Cheese Ring

1 pound sharp Cheddar cheese, finely grated
1 cup pecans, chopped
¾ cup mayonnaise
1 medium onion, finely chopped
½ teaspoon Tabasco sauce
1 cup strawberry preserves

Combine all ingredients except the strawberry preserves and shape into ring (Tupperware ring). Chill for about 4 hours. Remove from refrigerator and put cheese ring on serving dish. Put strawberry preserves in the center of the ring. Serve with your favorite crackers. Ritz crackers are my favorite.

Liz Grantham

Cheese Balls

1 pound Cracker Barrel cheese
1 (8 ounce) cream cheese, softened
1 medium jar pimentos
1 cup nuts, chopped
1 teaspoon garlic salt
Paprika

Mix and roll into balls. Sprinkle paprika and nuts over balls.

In Memory of Mrs. Tillie Gray

Cheese Dip

1 (8 ounce) cream cheese
1 can Hormel No Bean Chili
1 small can green chilies (mild)
8 ounces Monterey Jack, shredded

Combine in a large microwave safe bowl. Heat about 6 or 7 minutes. Stir once or twice during heating. Serve with favorite chips.

Cindy Ward

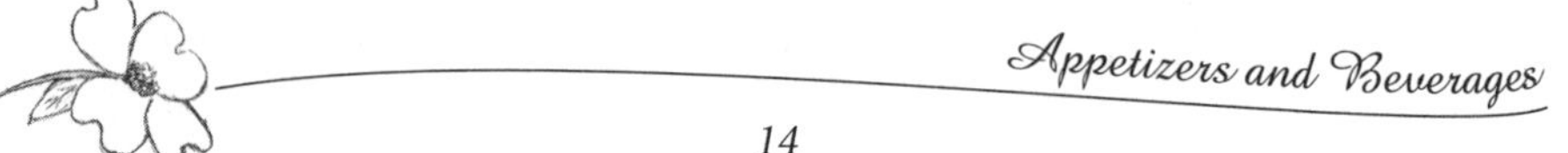

Cheese Straws

1 (8 ounce) sharp Cheddar cheese, shredded
1 stick margarine, softened
1½ cups plain flour, unsifted
Pinch salt
Dash red pepper

Mix all until smooth and rubbery. Spray cookie sheet. Use cookie press to make straws or stars. Bake at 325 degrees for 10 to 12 minutes. If making straws, it is better to cut them before baking.

Wylene Coffee

Cheese Wafers

½ pound butter or margarine, softened
½ pound sharp cheese
2 cups flour (plain)
2 cups Rice Krispies
½ teaspoon cayenne pepper (red pepper)

Mix margarine and cheese by hand. When mixture is soft, add the flour, Rice Krispies, and red pepper. Shape into marble-size balls. Press flat with a wet fork. Bake at 350 degrees for 15 minutes. Makes approximately 90 to 100 wafers.

In Memory of Mrs. Rubye McCarty

Martha Brawner's Cheese Wafers

1 cup flour
1 cup Rice Krispies
1 cup sharp Cheddar cheese, grated
1 stick butter
Pinch of salt
Dash of cayenne pepper

Roll in small balls and mash flat with fork. Bake at 350 degrees for 15 minutes.

Martha Brawner

Cheese Sausage Balls

- **3 cups Bisquick**
- **1 pound hot or mild sausage**
- **10 ounces Kraft cheese, grated**

Add all ingredients and mix well. Form small balls. Bake on ungreased cookie sheet 12 to 15 minutes at 350 degrees. Yields 125.

Virginia Hendrix

Sausage and Cheese Balls

- **2 tubes fresh mild sausage**
- **1½ cups Bisquick mix**
- **8 cups grated, sharp Cheddar cheese**
- **½ teaspoon garlic powder**
- **½ cup onion, finely chopped**
- **½ cup celery, finely chopped**

Preheat oven to 350 degrees. Mix all ingredients together. Place balls on an ungreased cookie sheet. Bake for 10-15 minutes or until golden brown.

Linda Raybon

Spinach Parmesan Balls

- **1 pound frozen chopped spinach, thawed**
- **5 eggs**
- **1 large onion, minced**
- **10 tablespoons margarine, melted**
- **1 cup Parmesan cheese, shredded**
- **2 garlic cloves, minced**
- **½ teaspoon cayenne pepper**
- **1¾ cups breadcrumbs**

Preheat oven to 350 degrees. Squeeze the excess water from the spinach and put it in a large mixing bowl. Add the remaining ingredients and mix well by hand. Form the mixture into 1-inch balls. Place the balls closely together on a sprayed baking sheet. Bake in the top half of the oven until firm to touch, about 20-25 minutes. Let cool 5 minutes before serving. These freeze well.

Wylene Coffee

Ham Spread

1 pound sandwich ham, chopped
11 ounces cream cheese, softened
¼ cup mayonnaise
⅓ cup green onions, chopped
½ cup mayonnaise
Sliced almonds

Mix together ham, 4 ounces cream cheese, ¼ cup of mayonnaise, and green onions. Place into a mold for several hours until firm (Cool Whip container works well). Mix together remaining cream cheese and mayonnaise. Let chill. Remove mixture from mold and spread cream cheese layer over first layer, forming a half ball. Toast sliced almonds for 10 minutes at 350 degrees. Stick almonds onto spread ball in a "porcupine" fashion. Serve with Townhouse or Sociable crackers.

Patsy Herlocker

Shrimp Spread

1 (6 ounce) can tiny cocktail shrimp, rinsed and drained
1 (8 ounce) package cream cheese, softened
1 (10¾ ounce) can cream of shrimp soup, undiluted
¼ cup red bell pepper, chopped
2 tablespoons onion, finely chopped
Dash of hot sauce

Chop shrimp and set aside. Beat cream cheese at medium speed with an electric mixer until fluffy. Gradually add cream of shrimp soup, beating well after each addition. Stir in shrimp and remaining ingredients. Refrigerate at least 2 hours. Serve with crackers or toasted French baguette slices. Yields 2½ cups.

Nell Sturgis

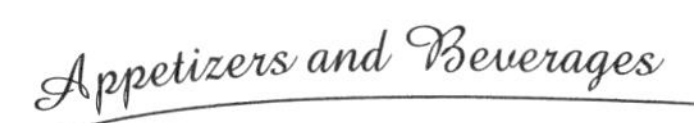

Vegetable Sandwich Spread

2 cups mayonnaise
1½ medium cucumbers, chopped
2 tomatoes, peeled and chopped
½ small onion, grated
1 package unflavored Knox gelatin
Salt and pepper to taste

Drain cucumbers and tomatoes. Grate onion into mayonnaise. Salt and pepper to taste. Dissolve one package of gelatin in ¼ cup of water. Add to mayonnaise. Add drained vegetables. Let stand overnight. Can keep mixture several weeks in refrigerator. Good in spring and summer. Spread on desired bread shape.

Oma Mills

Candy Peanuts

3 cups peanuts
½ cup water
1 cup sugar

Cook all three ingredients on top of stove slowly until water is gone. Bake in a pan at 300 degrees for about 20 minutes. Shake the peanuts about every 5 minutes so they will not stick.

In Memory of Mrs. Mamie Farrar

Fried Pecans

6 cups pecan halves
1 cup granulated sugar
Hot oil for frying

Bring a pot of water to a boil, dropping in 3 cups of pecans at a time. Bring to a rolling boil and boil for 1 minute. Drain, rinse with warm water, and drain again. Roll pecans in sugar. Fry in hot oil until golden brown (10-12 minutes). Drain in colander; spread on paper bag. Do not use paper towels. Salt while hot.

Paula Scott

Sweet and Spicy Pecans

1 stick butter
1 cup sugar
1 tablespoon cayenne pepper
1 teaspoon salt
4 dashes of Worcestershire sauce
1 pound pecans

In a cast iron or nonstick skillet, melt butter and add sugar, cayenne pepper, salt, and Worcestershire sauce. Stir in pecans. Spread pecans on sprayed cookie sheet. Bake in a 350 degree oven for 20-30 minutes. Break into pieces and enjoy.

Liz Grantham

Spicy Nuts

2½ cups nut halves
1 cup sugar
½ cup water
1 teaspoon cinnamon
1½ teaspoons vanilla
½ teaspoon salt

Heat nut halves in 375 degree oven for 5 minutes, stirring once. In a saucepan, combine sugar, water, cinnamon, and salt. Heat and stir mixture until it comes to a boil and sugar dissolves. Cook without stirring to soft-ball stage (236 degrees). Remove from heat. Beat by hand for one minute or until mixture just begins to get creamy. Add vanilla and nuts. Stir gently until nuts are well coated and mixture becomes creamy. Turn out on buttered cookie sheet. Separate while warm. Will make 1 pound.

In Memory of Mrs. Jean Wilson

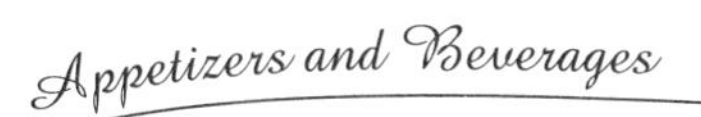

Glazed Pecans

- 6 cups nuts
- 1½ cups sugar
- 1 teaspoon cinnamon
- 3 egg whites
- 3 tablespoons of water

Beat egg whites until frothy. Add other ingredients; mix well. Pour over nuts and stir until they are covered. Bake at 300 degrees for 1 hour. Stir during baking. Let cool completely before storing.

In Memory of Mrs. Othalyne Gillis

Oven-Caramel Corn From 60's

- 15 cups popped corn
- 1 cup packed brown sugar
- ¼ cup light corn syrup
- ½ teaspoon salt
- ½ teaspoon soda
- ½ teaspoon vanilla
- 1 stick margarine

Preheat oven to 200 degrees. Put corn in large baking pan. Mix sugar, syrup, margarine, and salt in saucepan. Cook and stir until it bubbles around edges. Cook 5 minutes more. Remove from heat. Stir in soda and vanilla until foamy. Pour over corn and stir until coated. Bake 1 hour, stirring every 15 minutes. Cool. Break apart. Store in airtight container.

Patsy Herlocker

"Whether, then, you eat or drink or whatever you do, do all to the glory of God."

1 Corinthians 10:31
(NASB)

Tijuana Tidbits

4 cups tortilla chips, broken into 1½ inch pieces
3 cups Crispix cereal
1 (3.5 ounce) bag microwave popcorn, popped
1 (12 ounce) can cocktail nuts
½ cup light corn syrup
½ cup butter
½ cup brown sugar, firmly packed
1 tablespoon chili powder
¼ teaspoon cinnamon or to taste
¼ teaspoon red pepper to taste (optional)

Heat oven to 250 degrees. Combine chips, cereal, popcorn, and nuts in a large roasting pan. Combine corn syrup, butter, brown sugar, chili powder, cinnamon, and pepper in a saucepan. Heat to boiling. Pour over cereal and bake, stirring every 20 minutes or so. Remove from oven and turn onto sheet of waxed paper to cool. Store in airtight container up to 2 weeks. Makes 18 cups.

Variation: Substitute 4 cups of pecans for cocktail nuts and popcorn.

Peggy Hurd
Family Ministry Center Director

Mints

5½ tablespoons butter
1 box 10X sugar
3 tablespoons evaporated milk
13 drops peppermint oil

Soften butter. Add milk, peppermint, and sugar a little at a time. Form into mints and place on wax paper.

Frances Neugent

Creme Puffs

- 1 cup water
- 1 stick butter
- 1 cup sifted plain flour
- ½ teaspoon salt
- 4 eggs

Bring water and butter to boil in saucepan. Add flour and salt all at once. Stir until mixture forms balls. Remove from heat and cool slightly. Add eggs one at a time. Beat after each egg until smooth and glossy. Drop on ungreased cookie sheet. Bake at 400 degrees for 30 minutes. Cool and fill with tuna or chicken salad or anything you choose.

Audrey Wilkerson

Hallelujah Ham Rolls

- 1 cup butter
- 3 tablespoons poppy seeds
- 1 teaspoon Worcestershire sauce
- 3 tablespoons prepared mustard
- 1 medium onion, minced
- 1 pound ham, minced
- 1 (12 ounce) Swiss cheese, grated
- 60 small party rolls

Preheat oven to 400 degrees. Cream first 4 ingredients. Add onion, ham, and Swiss cheese and mix well. Halve rolls lengthwise. Return bottom half of rolls to pan. Spoon ham mixture on top. Cover with top half of rolls. Seal and freeze or bake immediately. To bake, sprinkle lightly with water and cover with foil. Bake 10 minutes or until thoroughly heated.

Jan Tyre

Salsa

- 2 cans whole or diced tomatoes
- 1 onion, cut into big chunks
- 1 can original Ro-tel
- 3 tablespoons vinegar
- 1 tablespoon salt
- 1 tablespoon Accent seasoning
- 2 teaspoons garlic, minced
- 2 teaspoons ground cumin

Put ingredients in blender and blend well. Place in container and chill overnight or at least 6 hours.

Amanda Morgan

Pina Colada

- 2 cups vanilla ice cream
- ½ cup pineapple juice
- ¼ cup cream of coconut

Combine all ingredients in an electric blender. Process until smooth. Serve immediately.

Audrey Wilkerson

Wild Purple Smoothie

- 1¼ cups fresh or frozen blueberries
- 1 cup orange juice
- 2 cups fat-free plain yogurt
- ¼ cup 1 percent milk

Blend in blender until smooth. Makes 2 large glasses.

In Memory of Mrs. Lou Ann Walker

Almond Punch

- 1 gallon water
- 1 large can pineapple juice
- 1 (1 ounce) bottle almond flavoring
- 1 (8 ounce) bottle lemon juice
- 3½ cups sugar
- 1 large bottle of ginger ale
- Food coloring (optional)

Heat water until warm and add sugar, mixing well; add other ingredients. Add ginger ale just before serving. One recipe makes 1½ gallons. Will serve 64 (3 ounce) servings.

Alice Ward

Banana Punch

- 6 ripe bananas
- 6 cups warm water
- 4 cups sugar
- 1 (6 ounce) can of frozen lemonade concentrate
- 1 (12 ounce) can of frozen orange juice concentrate
- 1 (46 ounce) can of pineapple juice
- 1 (6 pack) of Sprite

Blend bananas and add lemonade, orange, and pineapple juice; stir well. Bring 6 cups of water to a low boil and add 4 cups of sugar. Stir until sugar is completely dissolved. Let cook and add to fruit juice and banana mix. Freeze. Place frozen mixture in punch bowl, pour Sprite over mixture, and serve as a slush.

Cathalene Taylor

Christmas Punch

- **1 quart cranberry juice, chilled**
- **1 (6 ounce) can orange juice concentrate, thawed**
- **1 (6 ounce) lemonade concentrate, thawed**
- **1 large can (1 quart, 2 ounces) unsweetened pineapple juice**
- **1 quart ginger ale**

Mix all ingredients together. Pour over ice cubes and add ginger ale.

In Memory of Mrs. Lou Ann Walker

Coffee Frappe

- **5½ gallons of vanilla ice cream**
- **1½ ounces instant decaffeinated coffee (dissolve in ½ gallon of hot water)**
- **1 cup of sugar (dissolve in coffee mixture)**
- **1 pint whipping cream**

Mix coffee, water, and sugar. Set aside and let come to room temperature. Cut ice cream into large chunks. Put into large punch bowl. Pour coffee mixture and whipping cream over ice cream. Let stand 45 minutes before serving. Yield: 40 servings.

Cathalene Taylor

Hint: In order to appeal to everyone's tastes and diets, have a balance of hearty and low-calorie appetizers as well as hot and cold choices.

Coffee Punch

- 2 ounces instant coffee (Folgers and Sanka make a 2 ounce container)
- 2 cups boiling water
- 2 cups sugar
- 1 tablespoon vanilla extract
- 1 gallon milk (whole)
- Vanilla ice cream

Bring water to boil and turn off. Add coffee, vanilla, and sugar, stirring until dissolved. Let cool. Before serving, mix gallon of milk with mixture and add scoops of ice cream.

Note: Mixture can be refrigerated for a several days or frozen in a double-lined Ziploc bag for a month or two. Thaw frozen mixture before adding milk and ice cream.

Amanda Morgan

Holiday Punch Bowl

- 1 package frozen sliced strawberries
- 3 cans frozen lemonade concentrate
- 1 quart ginger ale
- 2 limes, sliced

Partially thaw berries. Reconstitute lemonade as label directs. In punch bowl, combine lemonade, strawberries, and ginger ale. Float lime slices on top. Makes 4 quarts.

In Memory of Mrs. Julia Ann Elliott

Louise Duncan's Punch

1 (48 ounce) bottle cranberry juice cocktail
1 sparkling white grape juice
1 (2 liter) bottle of lemon-lime soda or ginger ale

Ice ring (made with extra Sprite or ginger ale)

Prepare ice ring using desired liquid. Combine all other ingredients, chilling before mixing. Add ice ring to punch bowl. Pour punch into bowl.

Note: This was Louise Duncan's recipe. Louise's name could usually be found on the hostess list for the many showers back then. She always made the punch, and this is the one she served. Her secret was to make sure the ingredients were thoroughly chilled and poured over an ice ring. Being diabetic, the beverages (except the sparkling white grape juice) were usually sugar free. It is still a favorite of mine, and I think of Louise every time I serve it.

Mary Lou Gillespie

Percolator Punch

1 (32 ounce) bottle of apple juice or cider
1 (16 ounce) bottle of cranberry juice cocktail
1 (3 inch) cinnamon stick, broken in pieces
½ cup brown sugar
6 whole cloves

Put apple juice or cider and cranberry juice in bottom of percolator and the remaining ingredients in basket on top. Perk for 10 minutes or until percolator stops. This is a great drink for winter parties.

Audrey Wilkerson

Punch

- 6 quarts weak tea
- 1 large can pineapple juice
- 1 large can frozen orange juice concentrate
- 1 large can frozen lemonade concentrate
- 6 cups sugar
- Food coloring for desired color

Prepare orange juice and lemonade per directions on can. Combine all ingredients. Freeze overnight in milk jugs or any large plastic container. Makes 3 gallons.

Note: Thaw punch and serve cold or break up frozen and serve as a slush.

Terry B. Cook

Ruby's Fabulous Punch

- 1 (1 quart, 14 ounce) can pineapple juice
- 1 (12 ounce) can frozen lemonade
- 1 (12 ounce) can apricot nectar
- 1 quart ginger ale, chilled
- 1 can strawberry soda, chilled

In a punch bowl, mix together pineapple juice, frozen lemonade, and apricot nectar. At serving time, add ginger ale and strawberry soda. Keep chilled with a frozen ring.

Frozen fruit ring:

- 1 small package of frozen strawberries (whole or sliced)
- 2 to 3 lemons, sliced

The day before serving, add slices of lemons and slices of frozen strawberries (overlapping slightly) in the bottom of a ring mold. Add water to cover slices. Freeze.

Shelby Waldron

Strawberry Punch

- 3 cups sugar
- 2 cups boiling water
- 2 packages strawberry Kool-Aid
- 1 large can pineapple juice
- 1 cup bottled lemon juice
- 3 quarts water
- 1 package frozen strawberries

Dissolve sugar in boiling water and let cool. Combine all ingredients in punch bowl except frozen strawberries. Mix thoroughly and add frozen strawberries, breaking them up as they thaw.

Note: If you prepare the sugar water in advance, this punch can be easily assembled in large quantities.

Glennis Coleman
Wife of Bro. Ray Coleman
Smyrna Baptist Association

Wedding Punch

- 1 ounce citric acid, dissolved in ½ gallon of boiling water (prepare night before serving)
- 8 cups sugar, dissolved in ½ gallon of warm water
- 2 large cans pineapple juice
- 1 large can frozen condensed orange juice
- 1 small can frozen condensed lemonade
- 2 gallons water

Combine all ingredients. Makes 4½ gallons of delicious punch!

Charlotte Bacon

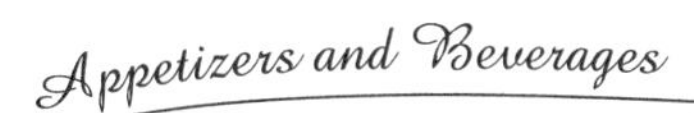

White Christmas Punch

- 2 cups sugar
- 1 cup water
- 1 (12 ounce) can evaporated milk
- 1 tablespoon almond extract
- 3 (½ gallon) containers vanilla ice cream, softened
- 6 (2 liter) bottles lemon-lime carbonated beverage, chilled

Combine sugar and water in a saucepan. Cook over medium heat until sugar dissolves, stirring constantly. Remove from heat. Add evaporated milk and almond extract; let cool. Chill until ready to serve. Combine milk mixture and remaining ingredients in punch bowl just before serving, stirring to break ice cream into small pieces. Yields 3½ gallons.

Note: Serve White Christmas Punch in glass punch cups tied with Christmas ribbon for a festive occasion.

Mollie Morgan

Instant Spiced Tea

- 1 jar Tang
- 1 to 2 cups sugar
- ¾ cup instant tea
- 1 teaspoon cinnamon
- ½ teaspoon ground cloves
- Dash of salt

Combine all ingredients. Serve 2 teaspoons of mixture per 1 cup boiling water or ⅔ cup of mixture per 1-quart boiling water.

Martha Lou Royer

Russian Tea

- **3 quarts water**
- **7 tea bags or 2 Lipton family-size bags**
- **2 teaspoons of cloves**
- **1½ cups sugar**
- **½ cup pineapple juice**
- **½ cup lemon juice, freshly squeezed**
- **1½ cups orange juice, fresh**

In a pot, heat 1-quart water, 7 tea bags (or 2 big ones), and 2 teaspoons of cloves. Strain. In another pot dissolve sugar in 2-quarts water. Add pineapple, lemon, and orange juice. Do not let come to a boil. Combine together with first mixture.

Note: We like to have this on Christmas Eve.

Lori Bradner

Spiced Tea Mix

- **18 ounces powdered Tang**
- **1 quart package sweetened lemonade mix**
- **2½ cups sugar**
- **2 teaspoons cinnamon**
- **¾ cup instant tea granules**
- **½ teaspoon cloves**

Mix. Use several spoonfuls in cup of hot water.

Susan Cox
Wife of Bro. John Cox
Former Minister of Music

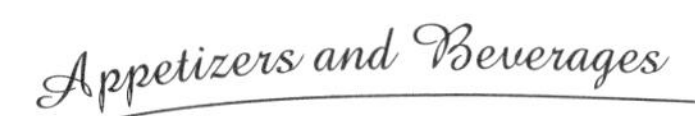

Wassail

- 1 gallon apple cider
- 1 quart orange juice
- 1 quart pineapple juice
- 8 ounces lemon juice
- 1 cup sugar
- 24 whole cloves
- 4 cinnamon sticks

Mix all ingredients and simmer for 10 minutes. Remove cinnamon and cloves. Serve warm in punch cups.

Note: Put ingredients in crockpot to keep warm and serve. Tie cloves and cinnamon sticks in cheesecloth for easy removal.

Jane Ann Simmons

Anytime Punch

- 1 small can frozen orange juice
- 1 small can frozen lemonade
- 1 (46 ounce) can pineapple juice
- ½ - 1 cup sugar (according to taste)
- 1 ounce almond flavoring
- 1 (2 liter) ginger ale

Mix all together in a gallon container except the ginger ale. Add water to make a full gallon. Add the ginger ale when ready to serve. Use food coloring to color the punch any color you wish. For red, omit the almond flavoring and add 1 package of cherry Kool-Aid. We serve this at holidays!

Lynn Meeks

Breakfast and Brunch

"Let me hear Your lovingkindness in the morning;
For I trust in You; Teach me the way in which I should walk;
For to You I lift up my soul."

Psalm 143:8
(NASB)

Breakfast and Brunch

Cream Cheese Danish

- 2 packages crescent rolls
- 2 (8 ounce) packages cream cheese
- ¾ cup sugar
- 1 egg, separated

Roll out one package of rolls in bottom of 9 x 13 pan. Beat together cream cheese, sugar, and egg yolk until creamy. Smear over rolls in pan. Cover cream cheese mixture with other package of crescent rolls. Glaze with egg white and sprinkle with sugar. Bake for 30 minutes at 350 degrees.

Donya Gillespie

Mini Cinnamon Rolls

- 1 package refrigerated crescent rolls
- ¼ cup margarine, softened
- 2 teaspoons cinnamon
- ¼ cup sugar

Preheat oven to 375 degrees. Separate rolls into 4 rectangles. Press perforations to seal. Spread with margarine. Sprinkle with cinnamon and sugar mixture. Roll into rectangles, beginning with the long edge. Cut each rectangle into 4 to 6 rolls. Place rolls on greased cookie sheet. Bake for 12 to 15 minutes or until lightly browned.

Glaze:

- 1 cup powdered sugar
- 2 tablespoons milk

Combine powdered sugar and milk; stir until smooth. Drizzle over warm cinnamon rolls immediately after they come out of oven.

Renee Roberson

Cinnamon Rolls

- **3 cups all-purpose flour**
- **6 tablespoon shortening, melted**
- **3 tablespoons sugar**
- **1 teaspoon salt**
- **1 egg**
- **1 package yeast**
- **1 cup water**
- **½ cup powdered milk**
- **Cinnamon sugar to taste**

Dissolve sugar in water. Sprinkle yeast on top. Let stand until foamy. Place yeast mixture and egg in mixing bowl. Add shortening; mix well. Add flour, salt, and dry milk and allow dough to rise. Roll out dough, sprinkle with cinnamon sugar, and roll up. Cut in ½-inch slices and place them in greased pan. Let rise. Bake in 350 degree oven until brown, about 15 minutes.

Icing:

- **½ box powdered sugar**
- **¼ cup milk**
- **½ teaspoon vanilla extract**

Mix together. Pour over cinnamon rolls.

Susan O'Steen

Pecan-Cinnamon Breakfast Rolls

- **1 cup pecans, chopped**
- **2 loaves frozen bread dough, thawed**
- **1 stick butter, melted**
- **1 large Cook & Serve vanilla pudding (not instant)**
- **1 tablespoon milk**
- **1 tablespoon cinnamon**
- **1 cup light brown sugar**

Defrost bread dough until soft. Grease 9 x 13 Pyrex dish. Sprinkle pecans in the bottom of dish. Pull bread dough into walnut-size pieces and roll into balls. Fill your Pyrex dish with a single layer of balls leaving a small space between each to allow for rising. Heat remaining ingredients until boiling. Pour this over dough balls. Cover and refrigerate overnight. Bake uncovered at 350 degrees for 30 minutes. Flip the rolls over immediately onto a new dish. Serve. Makes approximately 24 rolls.

Bari Sims

Sausage Pinwheels

1 (1 pound) hot sausage
1 (8 ounce) cream cheese
1 Pillsbury Big & Flaky crescent rolls

Brown sausage and drain grease. Place sausage back in pan and mix with cream cheese until it melts. Unroll crescent rolls onto waxed paper but leave intact, pushing the edges together and flattening out the dough. Spread mixture on flattened dough with hands because it is hard to spread. Roll it up and put into refrigerator until the next day. Preheat oven to 350 degrees. Slice the long roll thin and lay on a baking pan. Bake in oven until crescent rolls are brown.

Bari Sims

Baked French Toast

1 (1 pound) loaf French bread, cut diagonally into slices
8 eggs
2 cups milk
1½ cups half-and-half cream
2 teaspoons vanilla extract
¼ teaspoon ground cinnamon
1⅓ cups light brown sugar
3 tablespoons corn syrup
Butter

Butter a 9 x 13 inch baking dish. Arrange bread on the bottom. In a large bowl, beat together eggs, milk, cream, vanilla, and cinnamon. Pour over bread slices. Cover and refrigerate overnight. The next morning, preheat oven to 350 degrees. Combine butter, brown sugar, and corn syrup and heat until bubbling. Pour over bread and egg mixture. Bake uncovered for 40 minutes.

Paula Scott

Praline French Toast Casserole

- 8 eggs
- 1½ cups half-and-half
- ⅓ cup maple syrup
- ⅓ cup light brown sugar, packed
- 10 - 12 slices soft bread, 1 inch thick (Texas Toast)

Topping:

- ½ cup (1 stick) butter
- ½ cup light brown sugar, packed
- ⅔ cup maple syrup
- 2 cups pecans, chopped

Generously butter a 9 × 13 inch casserole dish. Mix the eggs, half-and-half, maple syrup, and sugar in a large bowl. Place the bread slices in the prepared casserole dish and cover with the egg mixture. Cover with plastic wrap and let soak overnight in the refrigerator.

Preheat the oven to 350 degrees and remove the casserole from the refrigerator. In a saucepan, melt the butter and add the sugar and maple syrup and cook for 1 to 2 minutes. Stir in the pecans and pour the mixture over the bread and bake for 45 to 55 minutes. Allow to sit for 10 minutes before serving.

Note: You can make 2 layers of bread so it would fit in casserole dish. Topping goes on the next morning.

Cindy Williams

Breakfast Special

10 slices bacon
1 package crescent rolls
1 cup cheese, grated
3 eggs
1 cup milk

Preheat oven to 425 degrees. Fry bacon and crumble. Unroll crescent rolls and press into bottom of greased 9 x 13 casserole dish. Sprinkle grated cheese and bacon over dough. Slightly beat eggs and combine with milk; pour over bacon. Bake for 20 minutes.

Teresa Holliday
Wife of Bro. B.J. Holliday
Minister of Music

Breakfast Casserole

2 tubes of crescent rolls, almost room temperature
3 cups Cheddar cheese, shredded
1 or 2 packages of ground sausage
3 - 5 eggs (depending on how egg-y you like it)

Cook sausage meat in pan; drain. Scramble eggs. Lay dough from 1 crescent roll in bottom of medium baking pan. Flatten out the edges. Put cooked sausage and egg on top of dough. Sprinkle 3 cups of cheese on top. Place other crescent dough on top working it to the edges. (It doesn't have to pinch to the bottom dough.) Bake according to the crescent roll directions and an extra 3 to 5 minutes.

Note: You can add salsa or different cheeses for extra flavor.

Kelly Lastinger

Brunch Casserole

- 2 pounds link sausage
- ¾ pound Cheddar cheese, grated
- 2¼ cups milk
- 1 (8 ounce) can sliced mushrooms, drained (optional)
- 1 (10¾ ounce) can cream of mushroom soup (or cream of chicken)
- ½ soup can of milk
- 8 slices bread, trimmed and cubed
- 4 eggs
- 2 teaspoons dry mustard
- 2 tablespoons butter

Fry sausage and cut into bite-size pieces. Arrange bread in greased 9 x 13 inch pan. Cover with cheese. Scatter sausage over cheese. Beat eggs with milk and mustard and add mushrooms. Pour over the sausage. Cover and refrigerate overnight. Let stand at room temperature for 1 hour before baking. Dilute soup with milk and pour over top. Dot with butter and bake at 325 degrees for 1 hour.

Bro. Shep Johnson
Senior Pastor

Mexican Breakfast Casserole

- 1 pound Jimmy Dean sausage (regular or hot)
- 2 cans of crescent dinner rolls
- 1 (8 ounce) block cream cheese
- 1 (4 ounce) can chopped green chiles, drained
- Shredded cheese to cover top (Colby, Monterey Jack, or sharp Cheddar)

Preheat oven to 375 degrees. Spray casserole dish with cooking spray. Spread one can of crescent rolls on the bottom of casserole dish and bake for 5 to 7 minutes. Brown sausage and drain excess fat. Add cream cheese and drained green chiles to sausage in skillet. Mix together. Spread sausage mixture over slightly cooked crescent rolls and top with second layer of rolls. Bake casserole for approximately 12 to 15 minutes. After top layer of crescent rolls have slightly cooked, add shredded cheese for the last 5 minutes of baking time.

Amanda Morgan

Mother's Day Brunch Casserole

- 2 packages of Jimmy Dean regular flavor pork sausage
- 12 eggs, lightly beaten
- 4 cups milk
- 1 tablespoon plus 1 teaspoon dry mustard
- 2 teaspoons salt
- 2 pounds (30 ounces) frozen hash browns
- 4 cups sharp Cheddar cheese, shredded
- 1 teaspoon black pepper
- 1 cup mushrooms, sliced (optional)
- 2 medium tomatoes, seeded and chopped (optional)
- 1 cup green onion, thinly sliced (optional)

Preheat oven to 325 degrees. In large skillet, cook sausage over medium-high heat, stirring frequently until thoroughly cooked and no longer pink. In a large mixing bowl, combine eggs, milk, mustard, salt, and pepper. Add in hash browns, cheese, and optional ingredients of your choice. Mix well. Pour into greased 9 x 13 baking dish. Bake uncovered for 55-60 minutes or until eggs are set. Tent with foil if top browns too quickly.

Jan Tyre

Quick and Easy Breakfast Casserole

- 4 slices bread
- 1 pound ground or link sausage
- 1 cup Cheddar cheese, grated
- 6 eggs
- 2 cups milk
- 1 teaspoon dry mustard
- 1 teaspoon salt
- ½ teaspoon pepper

Tear slices of bread into small pieces into a 9 x 13 x 2 inch greased baking dish. Brown, drain, and spoon sausage over bread. Sprinkle with cheese. Beat eggs, milk, and seasonings and pour over mixture in baking dish. Bake in preheated oven at 350 degrees for 35 to 40 minutes.

Note: Onion, green peppers, or other ingredients can be added, if desired. The casserole can be prepared and refrigerated ahead of time and then baked when needed.

Kate Walker

Southern-Fried Grits

- 1 cup grits
- 5 cups water
- 1 teaspoon salt
- Vegetable oil

Cook grits in cold water with salt added. Stir continuously until thickened. Let cook (covered) for 20 to 25 minutes until done. Put in suitable mold, cover with Saran Wrap, and place in refrigerator. On the following morning, cut grits in slabs, sprinkle with salt and pepper, and fry the slabs in vegetable oil.

In Memory of Mrs. Merle A. Parker

Jesus taught us to pray this way:

Our Father which art in heaven, Hallowed be Thy name.
Thy kingdom come, Thy will be done in earth as it is in heaven.
Give us this day our daily bread. And
forgive us our debts, as we forgive our debtors.
And lead us not into temptation, but deliver us from evil:
For Thine is the kingdom, and the power and the glory, for ever.
Amen.

Matthew 6:9-13
(KJV)

Steeplechase Brunch

- **12 slices white bread**
- **2-3 tablespoons butter, softened**
- **½ cup butter**
- **½ pound mushrooms, sliced**
- **2 cups yellow onions, thinly sliced**
- **1½ pounds Jimmy Dean mild sausage**
- **¾ pound Cheddar cheese, grated**
- **5 eggs**
- **2⅓ cups milk**
- **1 tablespoon Dijon mustard**
- **1 teaspoon dry mustard**
- **1 teaspoon nutmeg**
- **1 teaspoon salt**
- **⅛ teaspoon pepper**
- **2 tablespoons parsley, finely chopped**
- **Salt and pepper to taste**

Remove crust from bread. Butter one side of bread slices with softened butter and set aside. Melt butter (½ cup) and add mushrooms and onions. Sauté over medium heat for 5 to 8 minutes or until tender. Season with salt and pepper. Drain and set aside. Cook sausage, drain, and break in bite-size pieces. Butter a 7 x 11 shallow pan and layer half the bread with buttered side down. Next, add mushrooms, onions, sausage, and cheese. Repeat layers. In a bowl, mix the eggs, milk, Dijon mustard, dry mustard, nutmeg, salt, and pepper. Pour over sausage and cheese. Cover and refrigerate overnight. Remove from refrigerator 1 hour before baking. Sprinkle parsley over the top. Bake uncovered in preheated 350 degrees oven for 1 hour.

Note: Must be prepared a day in advance.

Jean Bowlin

Tomato and Bacon Grits

1 (16 ounce) box quick grits
1 can chicken broth
1 pint heavy cream
1 (8 ounce) block pepper jack cheese (cubed)
1 can Ro-tel tomatoes
8 pieces of crumbled bacon or 1 (3 ounce) package Real Bacon Bits

Cook grits according to package instructions. Add chicken broth and stir. Add remaining ingredients, stirring until all ingredients are melted. Simmer for 15 minutes or transfer to crockpot and set to low. Garnish with fresh tomatoes and crumbled bacon.

Benita Lott

Sausage Muffins

1 pound sausage
1 (16 ounce) sour cream
1½ cups Cheddar cheese, grated
2 cups self-rising flour
1 stick butter, melted

Brown sausage and drain. Combine ingredients with spoon. Bake at 350 degrees for 25 to 30 minutes. Makes 12 large muffins.

Jackie Wilson

"The Lord be with your Spirit. Grace be with you."
2 Timothy 4:22
(NASB)

Brunch Pizza Squares

1 pound bulk pork sausage
1 (8 ounce) tube refrigerated crescent rolls
4 eggs
2 tablespoons milk
⅛ teaspoon pepper
¾ cup Cheddar cheese, shredded

Cook sausage until no longer pink; drain. Unroll dough into lightly greased 9 x 13 x 2 baking dish. Press dough ½ inch up sides; seal seams. Sprinkle with sausage. In a bowl beat the eggs, milk, and pepper; pour over sausage. Sprinkle with cheese. Bake uncovered at 400 degrees for 15 minutes or until crust is golden brown and cheese is melted.

Cindy Ward

Hash Brown Quiche

3 cups shredded fresh russet potatoes
4 tablespoons (½ stick) butter, melted
3 large eggs, beaten
1 cup half-and-half
¾ cup cooked ham, diced
½ cup green onions, diced
1 cup Cheddar cheese, shredded
Salt and pepper to taste

Preheat oven to 450 degrees. Gently press the potatoes between paper towels to dry them as best as possible. In a 9-inch pie plate, toss the potatoes with the melted butter into the plate. Press them into the bottom and up the sides to form a crust. Bake for 20 to 25 minutes until golden brown and starting to crisp. Meanwhile in a large mixing bowl, combine the remaining ingredients. When the hash brown crust is ready, pour the egg mixture over it and return to the oven. Lower the oven temperature to 350 degrees. Bake for about 30 minutes until the quiche is light brown on top and puffed.

Betty Mullis

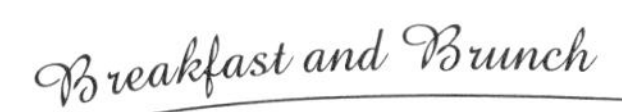

Bobbie's Breakfast Surprise Pie

- 1 (9-inch) pie crust
- 6 ounces bulk sausage
- ¾ cup milk
- 4 ounces mozzarella cheese, chopped
- ½ teaspoon salt
- ¼ teaspoon pepper
- 4 eggs

Sprinkle cheese in pie crust. Cook and stir sausage until done; drain. Sprinkle on top of cheese. Beat eggs and add milk, salt, and pepper. Pour milk mixture over cheese and sausage. Bake in preheated oven 375 degrees for 25 or 30 minutes until center of pie is set. Do not overcook!

Note: I like to jazz it up with a dash of red pepper, mushrooms, onions, and oregano leaves—use any or all of these. Be sure to cook mushrooms and onions before adding or there will be too much juice!

Joan Raulerson

Isn't it amazing how many recipes there are for us to try? Some of us have more cookbooks than we can count. Thank God right now for the wonderful variety of foods we are blessed to enjoy day after day.

"Then God said, 'Behold, I have given you every plant yielding seed that is on the surface of all the earth, and every tree which has fruit yielding seed; it shall be food for you...'"

Genesis 1:29
(NASB)

Spinach-Sausage Quiche

- 1 9-inch frozen pastry shell
- 1 (8 ounce) bulk pork sausage
- ¼ cup green onion, chopped
- 1 garlic clove, minced
- ½ (10 ounce) package frozen chopped spinach, cook and drain well
- ½ cup herb seasoned stuffing mix
- 2 tablespoons Parmesan cheese, grated
- 1 (6 ounce) Monterey Jack cheese, shredded
- 3 eggs, slightly beaten
- 1½ cups half-and-half
- Paprika

Preheat oven to 400 degrees. Let frozen pastry shell stand at room temperature for 10 minutes. Do not prick shell. Bake 7 minutes and set aside. Reduce oven to 375 degrees. In medium skillet, cook sausage, onion, and garlic over medium-high heat until sausage is done. Drain and stir in spinach and stuffing mix. Sprinkle Monterey Jack cheese, and then sausage mixture into pastry shell. In a medium bowl, combine eggs and half-and-half with whisk. Pour egg over sausage mixture in pastry shell. Bake 30 minutes. Sprinkle with Parmesan cheese and paprika, and then bake 15 minutes. Let stand 10 minutes before serving.

Cathalene Taylor

Waffles

- 3 cups self-rising flour
- ⅔ cup margarine, melted
- 2 teaspoons sugar
- 2 cups milk
- 4 eggs, separated

Beat 4 egg whites separately until stiff. Combine flour, margarine, sugar, milk, and egg yolks; mix well. Carefully fold in stiffly beaten egg whites. Preheat waffle iron. Spray with cooking spray; add batter. The amount depends on the size of the waffle iron. Leftover batter can be refrigerated. It makes great pancakes the next day.

Susan O'Steen

Quiche

1 deep-dish pie shell
2 cups cheese, shredded
2 tablespoons flour
1¼ cups milk
3 eggs
½ teaspoon salt
1 (10 ounce) package frozen spinach or chopped broccoli
Pepper to taste

Toss flour and cheese and sprinkle over crust. Cook broccoli or spinach per instructions on package. Drain and place on top of cheese. (You may not use all of the vegetables; probably ¾ of package). Beat together with fork, milk, eggs, salt, and pepper. Pour into crust. Bake at 350 degrees for 55-60 minutes. Let cool 15 minutes.

Kim Arnett

Mushroom Quiche

1 unbaked pie crust
½ pound Italian sausage
1 tablespoon butter
½ pounds fresh mushrooms, sliced or 4 ounce can, drained
⅔ cup half-and-half
3 eggs, slightly beaten
¼ teaspoon salt
1 cup Monterey Jack cheese
Dash of pepper

Preheat oven and cookie sheet to 375 degrees. In a skillet, brown sausage and drain. Meanwhile, sauté mushrooms in butter. Mix together half-and-half, eggs, salt, and pepper. Combine sausage and mushrooms with egg mixture. Sprinkle cheese on bottom of pie crust. Gradually pour meat mixture over cheese. Bake on preheated cookie sheet for 35 to 40 minutes or until knife inserted in center comes out clean.

Peggy Hurd
Family Ministry Center Director

Add-What-You-Like Quiche

2 cups (½ pound) Swiss cheese, grated
½ cup milk
½ cup mayonnaise
2 tablespoons flour
¼ cup onions, minced
2 eggs
1 optional ingredient listed below
9 or 10 inch baked pie shell

Combine cheese, milk, mayonnaise, flour, onions, eggs, and one of the optional ingredients, if you wish. Pour into pie shell. Bake at 350 degrees for 40 to 50 minutes or until well browned and set in the middle. (Check by inserting knife blade into center. If it comes out clean, the quiche is finished). Allow quiche to stand for 10 minutes before slicing and serving.

Variations:
Mix first 6 ingredients in a blender. Do not use a pie crust. Instead, place ¾ cup all-purpose baking mix, along with the first 6 ingredients, in a blender and mix. Stir in optional ingredient, if you wish, and pour into greased pie plate. Follow baking directions above.

Optional Ingredients:
4 ounces crabmeat
4 ounce can fully cooked ham chunks
1½ cups fresh broccoli
6 strips bacon, cooked and crumbled
1½ - 2 cups fresh spinach, chopped

Jenny Lott

Hint: Store dried herbs and spices in the freezer. They will stay fresh for up to a year.

Quiche

- 1 pastry crust
- ½ cup onion, chopped
- ½ teaspoon minced garlic or ¼ teaspoon powdered garlic
- 2 teaspoons liquid Butter Buds or 2 teaspoons margarine
- 4 Egg Beaters (1 carton) or 4 slightly beaten eggs
- 1 cup skim milk
- 1 tablespoon flour
- 1 teaspoon basil leaves
- ¾ teaspoon Tabasco sauce
- 1 cup Alpine Lace non-fat mozzarella cheese, grated (or cheese of choice)

Optional Additions:

- 1 cup frozen chopped spinach, thawed and drained
- 6 slices bacon, fried and crumbled
- ½ cup ham, chopped

In a nonstick skillet over medium heat, cook onion and garlic in the liquid Butter Buds until golden brown. Add spinach, bacon or ham, if desired, and spoon into bottom of crust; set aside. In a bowl, combine milk and flour until flour is dissolved. Add Egg Beaters, basil, Tabasco sauce, and grated cheese. Pour over onion mixture in crust. Bake at 350 degrees for 45 to 50 minutes or until a knife inserted comes out clean. Let stand 10 minutes before serving.

Toby Smith

Pancakes for Two

- 1 cup self-rising flour
- 1 egg
- 1 tablespoon vegetable oil
- 2 tablespoons sugar
- 1 teaspoon vanilla
- Buttermilk
- Water

Mix all ingredients above except buttermilk and water until blended with a fork. Add enough buttermilk to make a thick batter. Add water until mixture is runny. Cook on a griddle.

Patsy Herlocker

Salads and Dressings

"As each one has received a special gift, employ it in serving one another as good stewards of the manifold grace of God."
1 Peter 4:10
(NASB)

GEMS Annual Ladies' Banquet

Salads and Dressings

Chicken Salad Amandine with Frozen Fruit Salad

3½ pounds chicken breasts
6 stalks celery, diced
2 tablespoons salt
½ tablespoon white pepper
2 cups mayonnaise
½ cup pickle relish

Garnish: ½ cup toasted almond slices

To make chicken salad, boil chicken breasts in lightly salted water until meat is tender. Reserve stock for future use. Let chicken cool. Separate meat from bones and skin. Leave chicken in medium-size strips. Toss remaining ingredients, except almonds, with chicken. Cover and refrigerate until serving. Garnish with almonds and serve with Frozen Fruit Salad.

Frozen Fruit Salad:

1 (8 ounce) package cream cheese
½ cup powdered sugar
⅓ cup mayonnaise
2 teaspoons vanilla extract
1 (6½ ounce) can sliced peaches, well drained
½ cup maraschino cherry halves, well drained
1 (26 ounce) can fruit cocktail, well drained
1 (13 ounce) can crushed pineapple, well drained
2 cups miniature marshmallows
½ cup whipping cream, whipped
Food coloring, if desired

Put cream cheese in mixer. Add powdered sugar and blend in mayonnaise. Add vanilla extract. Fold in fruit and marshmallows gently. Whip cream separately and gently fold into fruit mixture. Add a few drops of food coloring if desired. Ladle into large paper soufflé cups or muffin liners. Freeze immediately. Defrost about 15 minutes before serving. Do not allow to get soft. Remove soufflé cups or muffin liners before serving.

Note: This dish was served in the old Rich's Magnolia Room in downtown Atlanta.

Norma Preston

Chicken Salad

- ¾ cup mayonnaise
- ½ teaspoon ground ginger
- ½ teaspoon salt
- 3 cups chicken, cooked and cubed
- 1½ cups red seedless grapes
- 1 cup celery, sliced
- ⅓ cup green onion, sliced
- ½ cup walnuts, chopped

Mix all together in large bowl. Cover and chill before serving.

Lola Burch

Pecan Chicken Salad

- 5 cups chicken, cooked and diced
- 1 cup celery, diced
- 2 cups Miracle Whip
- 1½ cups Red Delicious apple with peel, chopped
- 2 cups Georgia pecan halves
- 1 (10 ounce) jar sweet pickle relish
- 4 hard-boiled eggs, diced

In a large bowl, combine chicken, celery, and Miracle Whip. Add remaining ingredients; mix until well blended. Serving suggestions: Spoon salad into baked puff pastry shells or serve over a bed of mixed salad greens.

June Cowart

Heart-Healthy Chicken Salad

- 4 skinless chicken breasts, cooked and diced
- 1 green apple, chopped
- 1 red apple, chopped
- ½ cup celery, chopped
- 1 cup seedless green grapes, cut in half
- Hellmann's Light mayonnaise

Mix with Hellmann's Light mayonnaise until desired consistency.

In Memory of Mrs. Doris Elrod

Chicken Cashew Salad

- ⅔ cup wild rice, cooked
- 2½ cups chicken, cooked and chopped
- 1 (8 ounce) can sliced water chestnuts
- 2 tablespoons onion, grated
- ⅔ cup mayonnaise
- ⅓ cup milk
- ⅓ cup lemon juice
- 1 cup cashew nuts, chopped
- 2 cups seedless grapes, halved

Mix rice with chicken, chestnuts, and onion. Blend together mayonnaise, milk, and lemon juice. Add to chicken mixture and toss well. Refrigerate at least one hour. Add grapes and nuts just before serving.

Dona Christopher

Hot Chicken Salad

- 4 skinless chicken breasts, cooked and shredded
- 1 can cream of chicken soup
- 1 (8 ounce) container sour cream
- 1 stick butter
- 1 sleeve Ritz crackers, crushed

Mix chicken, soup, and sour cream. Place in casserole dish. Top with mixture of Ritz crackers and butter. Bake 30 minutes at 350 degrees.

Benita Lott

Buttermilk Congealed Salad

- **2 (3 ounce) boxes lemon gelatin**
- **1 (16 ounce) can crushed pineapple in heavy syrup**
- **1 (8 ounce) carton frozen whipped topping, thawed**
- **2 cups buttermilk**
- **½ cup pecans, chopped**

In a heavy saucepan, mix dry gelatin with can of crushed pineapple in heavy syrup. Bring to boil to dissolve gelatin. Remove from heat and cool to room temperature. In a large bowl, mix whipped topping with buttermilk. Fold in pineapple mixture; add pecans. Pour into an 8 x 8 x 2 inch dish and chill until firm. Cut into squares.

Jane Simmons

Frozen Cheese and Pineapple Salad

- **½ cup Cheddar cheese**
- **¼ cup salad dressing or mayonnaise**
- **½ pound marshmallows, finely cut**
- **1 small can crushed pineapple**
- **½ pint whipping cream**

Cream Cheddar cheese with ¼ cup salad dressing; fold in marshmallows and crushed pineapple. Beat whipping cream until stiff and fold into mixture. Freeze. Serve with salad dressing or mayonnaise and a maraschino cherry on top of each portion.

Ann Sheppard

Congealed Salad

- 1 (8 ounce) carton cottage cheese
- 1 (8 ounce) carton Cool Whip
- 1 (3 ounce) package orange Jell-O
- 1 regular size can pineapple chunks, drained and cut into small pieces
- 1 small can Mandarin oranges, drained and cut into small pieces

Mix cottage cheese, Cool Whip, and orange Jell-O. Add pineapple and Mandarin oranges. Refrigerate until ready to serve.

Dot McKinnon

Congealed Salad

- 1 (20 ounce) can pineapple
- ½ cup sugar
- 2 envelopes of Knox gelatin
- 1 cup cold water
- 1 (2 ounce) jar pimentos
- 2 cups cheese, grated
- 1 cup pecans, chopped
- 1 cup mayonnaise

Boil pineapple and sugar for 3 minutes. Set aside to cool. Dissolve 2 envelopes of Knox gelatin in 1 cup cold water. Add the following to pineapple and sugar mixture: 1 small jar diced pimentos, 2 cups grated cheese, 1 cup chopped pecans, 1 cup mayonnaise, and Knox gelatin mixture. Refrigerate to congeal. This is good with ham.

Lola Warnock
Wife of Rev. Charles Warnock

Delicious Congealed Salad

- 2 small packages orange Jell-O
- 1 large can crushed pineapple
- 1 cup pecans, chopped
- 2 packages Dream Whip
- 1 (8 ounce) cream cheese
- 1 cup cold milk
- 1 cup sugar
- 2 tablespoons flour
- 2 eggs

Squeeze juice out of pineapple and reserve for later. Dissolve Jell-O in 2 cups of boiling water. Add 1½ cups of cold water and pineapple. Pour into oblong dish and let mold. Chop nuts and sprinkle over molded Jell-O. Mix 2 packages of Dream Whip, 1 cup cold milk, and soft cream cheese. Whip until stiff. Spread over nuts and Jell-O. Take reserved pineapple juice and enough water to make 1 cup. Put into pot. Add sugar, flour, and eggs. Cook slowly until thick. Let cool and spread over Dream Whip. Refrigerate.

Cindy Williams

Cranberry Congealed Salad

- 1 can whole berry cranberry sauce
- 1 large can crushed pineapple, drain juice and reserve
- 1 small package lemon Jell-O
- 1 small package strawberry Jell-O
- 1 cup ginger ale
- 1 cup boiling water
- 1 cup celery, chopped
- 1 cup pecans, chopped

Heat pineapple juice and water and dissolve both packages of Jell-O. Mix cranberry sauce, crushed pineapple, celery, and pecans together. Pour in Jell-O mix, and then pour in the ginger ale; mix together. Pour into salad bowl or mold and refrigerate until congealed.

Elizabeth White

Frozen Cranberry Salad

- 1 (8 ounce) package cream cheese
- 1 medium to large container Cool Whip
- 4 tablespoons mayonnaise
- 1 can whole cranberry sauce
- 1 cup toasted nuts, cut small
- 1 large can crushed pineapple

Blend together cream cheese, Cool Whip, and mayonnaise. Fold remaining ingredients into creamed mixture. Freeze until ready to serve.

In Memory of Mrs. Lois Meeks

Frozen Salad

- 1 can cherry pie filling
- 1 (20 ounce) can crushed pineapple, drained
- 1 can condensed milk
- 1 large tub of whipped topping
- 1 cup nuts, chopped

Combine ingredients. Pour into 9 x 13 inch dish. Freeze.

Mirt Dockery

Frozen Fruit Salad

- 1 (16 ounce) Cool Whip
- 1 (8 ounce) carton sour cream
- 1½ cups sugar
- 1 large can crushed pineapple, drained
- 1 cup nuts, chopped
- ½ cup cherries, drained and chopped
- 5 bananas, mashed

Mix well and freeze. Will keep several weeks.

Gina Gibbs

Frozen Fruit Salad

- 2 cups sour cream
- 1 (9 ounce) can crushed pineapple, drained
- 1 banana, mashed
- ⅓ cup walnuts, finely chopped
- ½ cup red maraschino cherries, quartered
- ½ cup green maraschino cherries, quartered
- ½ cup coconut
- 2 tablespoons fresh lemon juice
- ½ cup sugar

Mix all ingredients together and spoon into lined muffin tins or silicone molds. Makes 12 servings. Freeze. Will keep for one month in freezer. Take out of freezer 15 minutes before serving and unmold on a bed of lettuce.

Dotty Hutchinson

Frozen Orange Sherbet Salad

- 1 cup boiling water
- 1 (6 ounce) package orange gelatin
- 1 pint orange sherbet
- 1 cup miniature marshmallows
- 1 cup crushed pineapple, drained
- 1 cup whipping cream, whipped
- 1 (11 ounce) can Mandarin oranges, drained

Dissolve gelatin in hot water. Add sherbet, stirring until melted. Add marshmallows. Allow mixture to cool. Stir fruit into gelatin mixture. Fold in whipped cream. Spoon into individual molds or a 5-cup mold. Freeze. Unmold to serve.

Mirt Dockery

Lime-Fruit Congealed Salad

- 2 packages lime Jell-O
- 1 (20 ounce) can crushed pineapple
- 1 cup pecans, finely chopped
- 1 (8 ounce) cream cheese, beaten
- ½ pint sweet cream, whipped
- 12 large marshmallows
- Cherries

Drain pineapple; add enough water to the pineapple juice to make 2 cups liquid. Bring liquid to a boil and add Jell-O and marshmallows; let cool. Add pineapple, whipped cream, cream cheese, and nuts. Pour into mold. Add cherries for color.

In Memory of Mrs. Virginia Norris

Holiday Cream Cheese Salad

- 1 cup cold water
- 2 (8 ounce) packages cream cheese
- 2 cups crushed pineapple
- 1 package lemon Jell-O
- 1 tablespoon gelatin
- 2 tablespoons cold water
- Juice of 1 lemon
- ½ cup nuts, chopped
- 1 celery rib, finely chopped
- 20 small marshmallows
- ½ pint whipped cream
- ¼ teaspoon salt
- ½ cup mayonnaise
- 1 small jar cherries, chopped (used mostly for color)

Drain crushed pineapple. Add water to juice to make 2 cups. Heat juice and add to lemon Jell-O. Mix gelatin with 2 tablespoons cold water; add to Jell-O mixture. Add lemon juice and ¼ teaspoon salt. Cool until partially set. Mix together cream cheese, mayonnaise, cherries, nuts, and celery; add to mixture. Whip ½ pint whipping cream. Fold in whipped cream and marshmallows. Pour into mold and chill.

Marvelyne Fletcher

Lime Salad

- 16 large marshmallows
- 1 cup milk
- 1 large package lime Jell-O
- ⅔ cup mayonnaise
- 1 (8 ounce) package cream cheese
- 1 (9 ounce) carton Cool Whip
- ½ to 1 cup pecans, chopped
- 1 large can crushed pineapple, undrained

Melt marshmallows in milk in double boiler. Pour over lime Jell-O in large bowl and stir until dissolved. Blend mayonnaise and cream cheese together and stir into Jell-O mixture. Stir in undrained pineapple . Fold in Cool Whip. Add pecans, if desired. Pour into 9 x 12 dish. Chill or freeze.

In Memory of Mrs. Sara Betty Durham

Deborah's Orange Salad

- 1 (3½ ounce) box orange Jell-O
- 1 cup cottage cheese
- 1 (8 ounce) carton Cool Whip
- 1 can Mandarin oranges, drained

Process cottage cheese in food processor or blender until smooth. Mix dry Jell-O, cottage cheese, Cool Whip, and oranges. Spoon into mold and refrigerate until set. May use low-fat cottage cheese and nonfat Cool Whip, if desired. May double.

In Memory of Mrs. Merle A. Parker

Mandarin Orange Salad

1 small can Mandarin oranges, drained
½ cup sugar
1 (3 ounce) package orange Jell-O
1 cup boiling water
1 small can crushed pineapple, drained
1 cup sour cream

Mix sugar and Jell-O. Add boiling water and stir until dissolved. Add oranges and pineapple. Stir in sour cream until dissolved. Chill.

Sue Brantley

Orange Jell-O Salad

1 container cottage cheese
1 small Cool Whip
1 small box powdered orange Jell-O
1 can fruit cocktail, drained
1 can crushed pineapple, drained
Optional: crushed pecans

Mix cottage cheese, Cool Whip, and powdered orange Jell-O until smooth. Add fruit cocktail, pineapple, and pecans. Refrigerate overnight.

Betty Bates

Peach Salad

1 (8 ounce) cream cheese, softened
½ cup mayonnaise
½ cup pecans, chopped
½ cup cherries, chopped
1 cup Cool Whip
1 can peach halves

Blend cream cheese and mayonnaise. Fold in Cool Whip, nuts, and cherries. Put topping onto peach halves.

Sally Deems

Pistachio Salad

- 1 package pistachio pudding mix
- 1 large can crushed pineapple, drained
- ½ cup nuts, chopped
- 1 cup miniature marshmallows
- 1 cup Cool Whip

Dissolve pistachio pudding mix with crushed pineapple. Add all other ingredients. Place in a closed container. Refrigerate.

In Memory of Mrs. Anita Thompson

Three-Layer Salad

- 1 large box orange Jell-O
- 1 (20 ounce) can crushed pineapple, drained

Prepare Jell-O by box directions. Drain pineapple well. Save juice for top layer. Add drained pineapple to Jell-O. Pour into glass serving dish approximately 9 x 13. Refrigerate until firm.

Middle layer:

- 1 (8 ounce) cream cheese
- ½ cup powdered sugar
- 1 (8 ounce) Cool Whip

Mix cream cheese and powdered sugar with electric mixer. Gradually add Cool Whip, mixing until fluffy. Spread over firm Jell-O. Return to refrigerator.

Top layer:

- Reserved pineapple juice (about 1 cup)
- 2 tablespoons flour
- ⅔ cup sugar
- 2 eggs, beaten well

Combine all top layer ingredients in heavy pot. Cook over medium-high heat until thick, stirring constantly. Cool. Spread over cream cheese layer. Refrigerate. Sprinkle top with finely chopped nuts, if desired.

Susan O'Steen

Strawberry Salad

- 2 small or 1 large package frozen strawberries, thawed
- 3 bananas
- 2 small packages strawberry Jell-O
- 1 large can crushed pineapple, drained
- 1 cup nuts, chopped
- 1 carton Cool Whip

Dissolve Jell-O in 1¼ cups boiling water; let cool. Add berries, bananas, pineapple, and nuts. Chill until firm. Top with Cool Whip and serve!

Joyia Lanier

Strawberry Salad

- 1 cup sugar
- 1 (8 ounce) cream cheese
- 1 large can crushed pineapple, drained
- 1 carton frozen strawberries, thawed
- 3 medium bananas, sliced
- 1 cup pecans, chopped
- 1 medium carton Cool Whip

Mix sugar and cream cheese. Add the other ingredients except bananas; refrigerate. Add bananas just before serving.

Linda Raybon

Pretzel Strawberry Congealed Salad

- **1½ cups margarine, melted**
- **½ cup sugar**
- **2 cups thick pretzels, crushed**
- **2 cups pineapple juice, heated**
- **1 large strawberry Jell-0, dissolve in pineapple juice**
- **2 (10 ounce) cartons strawberries, thawed**
- **1 large tub Cool Whip**
- **1 cup sugar**
- **1 (8 ounce) package cream cheese**

Stir together first three ingredients and place in baking dish and bake at 350 degrees for about 10 minutes. Let cool completely. Mix together juice, Jell-0, and strawberries and chill in refrigerator while the pretzel mixture is cooking. Mix together cream cheese, Cool Whip, and sugar. Set aside. Layer cream cheese mixture on pretzel layer and top with strawberry mixture. Refrigerate for several hours before serving.

Denise Purvis

Cornbread Salad

- **1 box Jiffy cornmeal, baked**
- **2 cups tomatoes, chopped**
- **1 cup bell pepper, chopped**
- **1 medium onion, chopped**
- **1 cup mayonnaise**
- **½ cup pickle relish**
- **9 slices bacon, cooked and crumbled**

In serving dish, place a layer of crumbled cornbread, layer of bacon, and layer of vegetables. Drizzle some of mayonnaise and pickle relish combination on top. Repeat with another sequence of these layers. Top with rest of mayonnaise mixture and bacon for final layer. Keep refrigerated.

Emma Lou C. Aughinbaugh

Vickers' Salad

1 sleeve of saltine crackers
1 can diced tomatoes, drained
1 tablespoon sweet pickle relish
Mayonnaise
Salt and pepper to taste

Coarsely crumble crackers. Pour ½ can of tomatoes over cracker crumbs. Add relish, mayonnaise, salt, and pepper until salad is desired consistency. Add more tomatoes if desired.

Oma Mills

Apple Salad

1 large can crushed pineapple, undrained
⅓ cup self-rising flour
1 cup sugar
⅓ stick butter
1 tablespoon lemon juice
3 or 4 cups apples (Granny Smith or Golden Delicious)
Cool Whip
Toasted nuts, chopped

On medium heat, cook pineapple, flour, and sugar until thick. Take off heat and add butter and lemon juice. Cool completely. Peel and chop apples; stir into mixture. Put in 9 x 13 dish. Cover with Cool Whip. Sprinkle chopped toasted nuts on top.

Carolyn Norris

"Like apples of gold in settings of silver is a word spoken in right circumstances."

Proverbs 25:11
(NASB)

Cherry Salad

- 1 (6 ounce) package cherry Jell-O
- 16 ounces Coca-Cola
- 1 (8 ounce) can crushed pineapple
- 1 (16 ounce) can sweet Bing cherries
- 1 tablespoon lemon juice
- ½ cup nuts, chopped

Dissolve Jell-O in hot Coca-Cola. Add other ingredients. Pour in mold and refrigerate. Do not drain anything.

Joyia Lanier

Christmas Salad

- 1 (20 ounce) can crushed pineapple, drain and save juice
- 4 slices American cheese
- 4 cups miniature marshmallows
- 1½ cups pecans, chopped
- 2 large Red Delicious apples, peeled and diced

Drain pineapple in bowl and save juice. Cut cheese into small pieces and add marshmallows, pecans, and apples.

Christmas Salad Sauce:

- 2 eggs, beaten
- 2 tablespoons flour
- 1 cup sugar
- 2 tablespoons butter
- Juice from drained pineapple

Combine all ingredients in saucepan; cook over low heat, stirring constantly until thick. Pour over apple mixture while very hot. Let cheese and marshmallows melt before stirring. Cover bowl and keep refrigerated. Better the next day.

Suzanne Goodman

Cranberry-Pineapple Salad

- 1 (20 ounce) can of Dole crushed pineapple in juice
- 2 (3 ounce) packages Jell-O raspberry flavor gelatin
- 1 (16 ounce) can whole berry cranberry sauce
- ⅔ cup walnuts, chopped
- 1 large red apple, chopped and unpeeled

Drain pineapple, reserving juice. Add enough water to juice to measure 2½ cups; pour into saucepan. Bring to a boil. Add to gelatin mixes in larger bowl, stirring 2 minutes until completely dissolved. Stir in pineapple, cranberry sauce, nuts, and apples. Place in desired container. Refrigerate 2½ hours or until firm.

Note: To make fancy, spoon gelatin mixture into 24 paper lined muffin cups. Remove muffin cup liners before serving.

Betty Taylor

Cranberry Waldorf Salad

- 2 cups fresh cranberries
- 3 cups miniature marshmallows
- ¾ cup sugar
- 2 cups apples, diced
- ½ cup green grapes
- ½ cup walnuts, chopped
- ¼ teaspoon salt
- 1 cup whipping cream, whipped

Grind cranberries and combine with marshmallows and sugar. Cover and chill overnight. Add apples, grapes, walnuts, and salt. Fold in whipped cream. Chill. Serve in large bowl.

Ann Sheppard

Sparkling Citrus Salad

- **1 (1 pound) can grapefruit sections**
- **1 (9 ounce) can crushed pineapple**
- **¼ cup sugar**
- **2 envelopes unflavored gelatin**
- **½ cup pecans or walnuts, broken**
- **2 (7 ounce) bottles chilled ginger ale**
- **Dash salt**

Drain fruits, reserving syrups. Combine sugar, gelatin, salt, and syrups; heat and stir over low heat until gelatin dissolves. Chill until cold but not set. Stir in fruits and nuts. Pour ginger ale carefully down sides. Stir gently with up and down motion. Chill until partially set. Turn into a 5-cup mold. Chill until firm set. Unmold on salad greens.

Ruby S. Harper

Diet Coke Salad

- **2 cups canned, crushed pineapple (no sugar added)**
- **2 cups canned cherries packed in water, drained**
- **1 small box sugar-free lime gelatin**
- **1 small box sugar-free cherry gelatin**
- **1 (20 ounce) Diet Coke**

Cut up cherries in a colander and drain. Set aside. Heat pineapple (with juice) until boiling and dissolve gelatins in it. Remove from heat and add cherries and Diet Coke. Pour into plastic container or mold and chill until firm.

Aggie Pat Dockery

Fruit Salad

- **2 cans chunk pineapple, drain and reserve one cup of juice**
- **1 can Mandarin oranges, drained**
- **1 cup maraschino cherries, drained**
- **3 bananas, sliced**
- **½ cup pecans or walnuts, chopped**
- **1 package instant vanilla pudding**

Mix one cup pineapple juice with pudding and beat for 1 minute. Combine pineapple, oranges, cherries, nuts, and bananas. Pour pudding over fruit and chill.

Sherry Patterson

Summer Fruit Salad with Blueberry Vinaigrette

- **2 cups fresh or frozen blueberries**
- **1 cup fresh strawberries, halved**
- **2 nectarines, sliced**
- **8 cups mixed salad greens**
- **½ cup slivered almonds, toasted (optional)**
- **Blueberry Vinaigrette**

Combine first 4 ingredients in a large bowl. Cover and chill 1 hour. Drizzle ⅓ cup Blueberry Vinaigrette over blueberry mixture, tossing to coat. Sprinkle with almonds. May add 2 cups chopped, cooked chicken to salad.

Blueberry Vinaigrette:

- **¼ cup Blueberry Chutney (Recipe in "All the Rest")**
- **⅓ cup onion, minced**
- **⅓ cup balsamic vinegar**
- **1 teaspoon salt**
- **½ teaspoon pepper**
- **⅔ cup vegetable oil**

Whisk together first 5 ingredients. Gradually whisk in oil until blended.

In Memory of Mrs. Geneva Womack

Burkes' Thanksgiving Grape Salad

- **2 cups red seedless grapes, halved**
- **6 cups Gala apples, cubed and unpeeled**
- **1½ cups sugar**
- **½ cup all-purpose flour**
- **½ cup water**
- **1 teaspoon butter**
- **1 teaspoon vanilla**
- **1 cup walnuts, chopped**
- **Sprite**

Apples can be cut and cubed ahead of time. Put in a bowl of Sprite and refrigerate. Drain before using. Combine sugar and flour in a saucepan; stir in water. Bring this to a boil. Cook and stir until mixture thickens. Remove from heat. Stir in butter and vanilla flavoring. Cool to room temperature. In a large bowl, combine fruit and nuts; add dressing from above and toss gently. Refrigerate until ready to serve.

Lynn Meeks

Grape Salad

- **2 pounds red seedless grapes, washed, stemmed, and left whole**
- **2 pounds white seedless grapes, washed, stemmed, and left whole**
- **1 (8 ounce) cream cheese, softened**
- **1 (8 ounce) sour cream**
- **½ cup brown sugar**
- **1 cup Cheddar cheese, shredded (reserve small amount for topping)**
- **1 cup pecans, chopped (optional)**

Blend brown sugar, cream cheese, and sour cream with mixer. Fold in the cheese, grapes, and ½ cup nuts. Pour into a pretty glass dish for serving. Sprinkle the top with a small amount of cheese and the remaining nuts. Chill.

Note: This makes a "ton!" I usually halve the recipe. DO NOT use all of the sour cream mixture. Use just enough to hold salad together. Freeze the rest of this mixture. I usually use red grapes as green ones are not usually sweet.

Sara Allen

Pineapple Salad

- 1 cup pineapple, crushed
- ¼ cup sugar
- 1 cup water
- 1 cup cheese, grated
- ½ cup cream, whipped
- 1 envelope gelatin
- Juice of ½ lemon

Heat pineapple (juice and all). Add lemon and sugar. Heat until dissolved. Dissolve gelatin in cup of cold water. Add to mixture while hot. Cool until thickened. Fold in cheese and cream. Congeal.

In Memory of Mrs. Lois Meeks

Cold Spiced Fruit

- 1 to 2 unpeeled oranges, sliced and seeded
- 1 (20 ounce) can unsweetened pineapple chunks, drained
- 1 (16 ounce) can sliced peaches, drained
- 1 (16 ounce) can apricot halves, drained
- 1 cup sugar
- ½ cup apple cider vinegar
- 3 sticks cinnamon
- 5 whole cloves
- 1 (3 ounce) package cherry flavored gelatin
- Juice from drained fruit

Cut orange slices in half; place in a saucepan and cover with cold water. Simmer until rind is tender. Drain well and set aside. Remove orange slices and add juice to next batch. Drain canned fruits well, reserving all of the pineapple juice and half of the peach and apricot juices. Combine reserved juices, sugar, vinegar, cinnamon, cloves, and gelatin. Simmer for 30 minutes. Combine fruits in a 9-cup container and pour hot juice over fruit. Refrigerate for at least 24 hours before serving.

In Memory of Judy Evans

Pear Ambrosia

- 8 to 10 raw pears, peeled and cored
- 1 (10 ounce) can frozen orange juice concentrate
- 1 large can crushed pineapple
- 1 or 1½ cups sugar or less
- 1 jar maraschino cherries
- Coconut, optional

Place pears in food processor and pulse until consistency of applesauce. Mix together all other ingredients and add to pears. Chill.

Marie Harrell

Tangerine Tossed Salad

- ½ cup almonds, sliced
- 3 tablespoons sugar, divided
- 2 medium tangerines or navel oranges
- 6 cups torn lettuce
- 3 green onions, chopped
- 2 tablespoons cider vinegar
- 2 tablespoons olive oil
- ¼ teaspoon salt
- ¼ teaspoon pepper

In skillet, cook and stir almonds and 2 tablespoons sugar over medium-low heat for 20-25 minutes until sugar is melted and almonds are toasted. Remove from heat. Peel and section tangerines, reserving 1 tablespoon juice. In large bowl, combine lettuce, onions, tangerines, and almonds. In a small bowl, whisk the vinegar, oil, salt, pepper, reserved juice, and remaining sugar. Drizzle over salad and toss to coat.

Sandy Borland Cason

Layered Salad

Base:

- **1 head lettuce, chopped**
- **1 cup celery, chopped**
- **½ cup red or green bell pepper, chopped**
- **½ cup corn (optional)**
- **1 small can Le Sueur English peas, drained**

Topping:

- **10 tablespoons Duke's mayonnaise**
- **1 tablespoon sugar**
- **1 or 1½ cups sharp Cheddar cheese, shredded**
- **1 cup bacon, crumbled**

Layer base ingredients in a large bowl. Top with mayonnaise and sprinkle 1 tablespoon sugar over mayonnaise. Cover this with 1 to 1½ cups shredded sharp Cheddar cheese and top with crumbled bacon (or bacon bits). Cover and refrigerate. Let stand overnight or several hours before serving. Mix just before serving.

Cathy Tatum

Deviled Eggs

- **6 boiled eggs, peeled and halved**
- **2 tablespoons homemade sweet pickles, finely chopped**
- **2 to 3 heaping tablespoons mayonnaise**
- **1 to 2 teaspoons mustard**
- **Salt and pepper**
- **Paprika**

Boil eggs. They peel easier if a little vinegar is added to the water and if you start peeling at the fat end of the egg under running water. Halve each egg and reserve the yolk. Mash the yolks with a fork and add the remaining ingredients. Stir until fluffy. Fill each egg white with the mixture using a small spoon. Paprika may be sprinkled on top. Keep refrigerated until ready to serve.

Dawn Burch Moore

Hint: The freshness of eggs can be tested by placing them in a large bowl of cold water. If they float, do not use them.

Romaine Salad

4 tablespoons unsalted butter
1 cup pecans, chopped
1 package Ramen noodles, broken up

Cook on medium heat until toasted. Cool. Can prepare ahead and put in Ziploc bag.

Dressing:
1 cup canola oil
1 cup sugar
½ cup red wine vinegar
3 teaspoons soy sauce

Cook on medium heat until sugar is melted. Let cool. Keep in refrigerator until chilled. Can prepare day before.

Salad: romaine lettuce, spring greens, broccoli florets, green onions

Wash and cut lettuce. Mix with spring greens and add broccoli and green onions. I keep the ingredients separate until serving. I usually use one head of broccoli and one package of romaine lettuce hearts. Use as many spring greens as needed for color. Pour dressing over greens just before serving and toss lightly. Add pecans and noodles.

Pam Gillis

Spinach Salad

1 large bag spinach
1 dozen boiled eggs, sliced
1 pound bacon, fried
1 package frozen English peas
2 small cans water chestnuts, sliced
1 cup mayonnaise
1 cup sour cream
1 package zesty Italian or ranch seasoning mix

In a large bowl, layer spinach, sliced eggs, bacon pieces, cooked peas, and sliced water chestnuts in that order. Mix mayonnaise, sour cream, and dressing mix in separate bowl. Then spread on top of salad. Best made one day early.

Alice Ward

Strawberry Spinach Salad

- 2 bags of spinach
- 1 pint of strawberries, washed and sliced

Dressing:

- ½ cup sugar
- ¼ teaspoon paprika
- ¼ teaspoon Worcestershire sauce
- 1 tablespoon sesame seeds
- 1½ tablespoons poppy seeds
- 1½ teaspoons onion, minced
- ½ cup apple cider vinegar
- ¼ cup olive oil

Whisk dressing together and toss with spinach and strawberries. Serve immediately.

Benita Lott

Strawberry Pecan Salad

- Romaine lettuce
- Boston lettuce
- Sliced strawberries
- Monterey Jack cheese
- Roasted pecans

Preheat oven to 350 degrees. Place pecans on baking sheet and bake for 5 minutes. Prepare lettuce for salad. Toss together lettuce, strawberries, cheese, and pecans. Add dressing and toss before serving.

Dressing:

- 1 cup canola oil
- ¾ cup sugar
- ½ cup red wine vinegar
- ½ teaspoon salt
- ¼ teaspoon paprika

In a saucepan, cook dressing on medium heat until sugar is dissolved. Let chill before adding to salad.

Cheryl Skipper

Strawberry Salad

Romaine lettuce
Toasted pecans
Real Bacon Bits
Sliced strawberries

Prepare salad by mixing lettuce, pecans, bacon bits, and strawberries together in salad bowl.

Dressing:

1 cup apple cider vinegar
⅓ cup canola oil
½ cup sugar
1 teaspoon poppy seeds

Make dressing by mixing vinegar, oil, sugar, and poppy seeds together.

Note: Dressing is best made a day ahead for better flavor. Add to salad when ready to serve.

Teresa Holliday
Wife of Bro. B.J. Holiday
Minister of Music

Taco Salad

1 pound ground beef
1 package taco seasoning
¾ cup water
1 head lettuce, cut
2 tomatoes, cubed chunks
¾ cup Colby cheese, shredded
1 bag tortilla chips

Dressing:

2 cups mayonnaise
1 bottle of mild taco sauce

Brown ground beef in a large skillet. Drain off excess fat. Add taco seasoning and water. Bring to boil and simmer 10 minutes. Place tortilla chips in bottom of plate. Next, layer lettuce, follow by tomatoes, and then meat. While meat is still warm, sprinkle cheese on top so it melts. Serve with dressing.

Mary Lou Gillespie

Loaded Baked Potato Salad

- 4 large Russet or Yukon Gold potatoes
- ¼ cup mayonnaise
- ½ cup sour cream
- ½ cup Cheddar cheese, shredded
- ¼ cup chives, freshly chopped and divided
- 8 strips of thick bacon, cooked and crumbled (6 for the salad and 2 for the topping)
- 1 teaspoon black pepper
- Salt to taste

In a small bowl, mix together mayonnaise and sour cream. Make sure the two are completely combined, and then add half of the chives, cheese, and pepper. Taste mixture to see if you prefer some salt. Let chill in fridge. Peel and cube potatoes into bite-size pieces. Put in a large pot, cover with water, and boil until fork tender (about 20 minutes). Keep an eye on them because if they boil too long, you'll end up with more of a mashed-potato consistency when you mix them with the sauce. When potatoes are ready, drain and let cool just a bit. Put potatoes in a large bowl and combine with sour cream mixture. Fold in most of your crumbled bacon (6 slices). Top with remaining half of chives and remaining crumbled bacon (2 slices).

Kathy Stone

Macaroni Salad

- 2 cups cooked and drained macaroni noodles
- 1 small can green peas, drained
- 1 medium onion, diced
- 1 cup carrots, chopped
- ½ cup green bell pepper, diced
- ⅓ cup mayonnaise
- ⅓ cup ranch dressing
- 2 tablespoons white vinegar

Put the macaroni and vegetables into a large mixing bowl. Combine the mayonnaise, dressing, and vinegar together. Pour over macaroni mixture; toss. Cover tightly and refrigerate until ready to serve.

Brenda Lycett
Wife of Bro. Ed Lycett
Former Minister of Education

Asian Broccoli Slaw

- 1 pound bag broccoli slaw
- 1 bunch green onions, chopped
- 1 cup sunflower seeds
- ½ cup almonds, toasted
- 2 packages chicken flavor Ramen noodles, uncooked and broken into small pieces

Dressing:

- 1 cup vegetable oil
- ½ cup sugar
- ⅓ cup vinegar
- 2 flavor packs out of chicken Ramen noodles

Mix the first 5 ingredients together. In a separate bowl, mix the dressing and pour over the broccoli mixture. Toss and refrigerate.

Liz Grantham

Coleslaw

- 1 bag of cabbage slaw
- ½ cup of sugar
- ½ cup of mayonnaise
- 4 squirts of mustard

Mix all ingredients and store in refrigerator overnight for best results.

Theresa Wiggins

"Therefore let us draw near with confidence to the throne of grace, so that we may receive mercy and find grace to help in time of need."

Hebrews 4:16

(NASB)

Three-Week Coleslaw

- **3** **pounds white cabbage**
- **1** **green pepper, finely chopped**
- **1 or 2 white onions, finely chopped**
- **1 or 2 carrots, grated**
- **1** **cup yellow cider vinegar**
- **1** **cup sugar**
- **½** **cup salad oil**
- **1** **tablespoon salt**
- **1** **tablespoon celery seeds**

Combine cabbage, pepper, onion, carrots, and sugar in a large bowl and mix well. Mix oil, vinegar, celery seeds, and salt in a saucepan. Bring to boil and pour over cabbage mixture. Store in airtight container. Let stand three days as flavor improves. Will keep refrigerated for 3 to 4 weeks or more.

Note: To be classified as white cabbage the outer very-green leaves have been removed. The remainder of the cabbage may be used.

Bro. Shep Johnson
Senior Pastor

Kraut Salad

- **1** **(2 pound) package sauerkraut (from refrigerator section in grocery is best)**
- **2** **stalks celery, chopped**
- **4** **green onions, chopped**
- **1** **bell pepper, chopped**

Mix above ingredients. Cover with marinade and chill before serving.

Marinade:

- **½** **cup cider vinegar**
- **½** **cup vegetable oil**
- **½** **cup water**
- **1½** **cups sugar**

Pour above marinade ingredients into a pot. Heat until all ingredients are dissolved. Pour over salad and refrigerate. Great with barbecue!

Becky Miller

Bok Choy Salad

Dressing:

- ¾ cup vegetable oil
- ½ cup sugar
- ¼ cup red wine vinegar
- 2 tablespoons soy sauce

Mix well and chill.

Greens:

- 1 large head Bok Choy, (including green part) chopped diagonally
- 4 or 5 green onions, chopped

Crunch:

- ½ cup butter
- 2 tablespoons sugar
- ½ cup sesame seeds
- 3 ounces sliced almonds
- 2 (3 ounce) packages Ramen noodles (do not use seasoning)

In saucepan, combine and stir constantly over medium heat until golden brown. Watch carefully! Cool. Just before serving, combine dressing, greens, and crunch.

Jan Tyre

Broccoli Salad

- 4 cups broccoli florets
- ¼ cup purple or Vidalia onions, chopped
- ¼ cup pecans, chopped
- ¼ cup raisins, soaked in water and drained
- 8 slices of fried bacon or ½ cup bacon bits
- ¾ cup mayonnaise
- ¼ cup sugar
- 2 tablespoons cider vinegar

Whisk mayonnaise, sugar, and vinegar and toss with remaining ingredients. Cover and refrigerate.

Janet Wade

Broccoli and Cauliflower Salad

1 head of broccoli
1 head of cauliflower
1 cup purple onion, chopped
1 bottle of Real Bacon Bits
1 cup raisins
1 cup nuts, chopped (pecans, almonds, or walnuts)
Cheddar cheese, shredded

Dressing:
1 cup mayonnaise
¼ cup sugar or Splenda
1 tablespoon lemon juice

Wash and cut the fresh broccoli and the cauliflower into florets and discard the rest. Mix together all the ingredients except the cheese. Sprinkle the top with shredded Cheddar cheese. Refrigerate until ready to serve.

Cynthia Deal

Carrot Salad

1 small bag carrots, grated
1 (8 ounce) package cream cheese, softened
1 small can coconut
½ box raisins
1 large can crushed pineapple, drained (reserve 2 tablespoons juice)
A few small marshmallows

Add 2 tablespoons pineapple juice to cream cheese and beat until smooth. Combine all ingredients; mix well. Chill and serve.

In Memory of Mrs. Tish Overstreet

Cucumber Salad

- 4 cucumbers, pared
- 1 sweet onion, sliced
- 1 cup sugar
- 1 cup water
- ½ cup vinegar
- ½ cup oil
- Celery seed

Score lengthwise with tines of fork all around cucumbers. Slice thinly. Put in salted ice water. Add sliced onion. Let stand 1 to 2 hours. Cook 1 cup sugar and 1 cup water over low heat until sugar is dissolved. Drain and rinse cucumbers and onion slices. Combine sugar and water mixture with vinegar and oil; pour over cucumbers and onions. Sprinkle with celery seed. Refrigerate overnight.

Sherry Patterson

Vegetable Salad

- 1 can tiny green peas
- 2 cans white shoepeg corn
- 1 can French-cut green beans
- 1 medium jar chopped pimentos
- 1 medium onion, chopped
- ½ cup bell pepper, chopped
- ½ cup sugar
- ¼ cup vegetable oil
- ½ cup vinegar
- ½ teaspoon pepper
- ½ teaspoon salt

Drain peas, corn, green beans, and pimentos together in colander. Pour drained vegetables into a large container. Add onion and bell pepper. In medium sauce pan, mix together the sugar, vegetable oil, vinegar, salt, and pepper. Bring to a boil to dissolve the sugar. Pour over vegetables. Seal in container. Chill overnight before serving.

Mary Lou Gillespie

Raspberry Vinaigrette Dressing

- 1/3 cup raspberry balsamic vinegar
- 1 tablespoon dry mustard
- 1 tablespoon salt
- 1/2 cup sugar
- 1 cup extra-virgin olive oil
- 1 tablespoon poppy seed

Mix all ingredients except poppy seed in blender; add poppy seed.

Note: Best when poured over mixed baby greens right before serving. Add sliced strawberries or Mandarin orange slices and chopped nuts (pecans, walnuts, or sunflower seeds). Toss and serve immediately.

Susan O'Steen

Celery Seed Dressing

- 1/3 cup sugar
- 1 teaspoon dry mustard
- 1 teaspoon salt
- 1 teaspoon paprika
- 1 teaspoon onion, grated
- 1 heaping teaspoon celery seed
- 1 teaspoon white vinegar
- 1 cup vegetable oil
- 3 tablespoons white vinegar

Place first six ingredients in a bowl. Mix in 1 teaspoon vinegar. Add alternately, beating well, 1 cup vegetable oil and 3 tablespoons vinegar. Beat until smooth and thick. Refrigerate. Delicious over fruit!

Martha Brawner

Balsamic Vinaigrette

- 2 tablespoons balsamic vinegar
- 1 tablespoon honey
- 2 teaspoons Dijon mustard
- 1 clove garlic, finely minced
- ¼ cup extra-virgin olive oil
- Salt and pepper

Whisk together vinegar, honey, mustard, and garlic; add salt and pepper. Slowly whisk in olive oil. Keep refrigerated.

Pam Gillis

Honey Mustard Dressing

- 1¼ cups fat-free mayonnaise
- ¼ cup honey
- ¼ cup yellow mustard
- ⅓ cup apple cider vinegar
- 2 tablespoons water
- 1 medium garlic, finely minced
- ¼ teaspoon cayenne pepper
- 2 teaspoons ground stone mustard (optional)

Whisk together all ingredients and chill.

Hattie Harkleroad

Thousand Island Dressing

- 1 small onion
- 3 celery stalks or celery seed
- 3 teaspoons pickle relish
- 1½ teaspoons mustard
- 1 cup mayonnaise
- ¼ cup chili sauce
- 1 teaspoon lemon juice
- 1 teaspoon paprika
- 1 teaspoon vinegar

In a food processor, add all ingredients and process until smooth. Keep refrigerated.

Kellie Lingenfelter

Soups

"My faith looks up to Thee, thou Lamb of Calvary, Savior divine!"
Song written in 1830 by hymnist and minister, Ray Palmer

Soups

Italian Pasta and Bean Soup

- 1 tablespoon olive oil
- 1 medium onion, chopped
- 1 clove garlic, finely chopped
- 6 cups low-sodium chicken broth
- 1½ cups farfallini (small bowtie pasta)
- Kosher salt and pepper
- 2 cans cannellini beans, rinsed
- 1 can diced tomatoes in juice
- ½ cup fresh flat-leaf parsley, chopped
- ¼ cup Parmesan cheese, grated

Heat the oil in a large saucepan over medium-high heat. Add the onion and ¼ teaspoon each of salt and pepper and cook, stirring until beginning to soften, 4 to 5 minutes. Add the garlic and cook, stirring for 1 minute (do not let it brown). Add the broth and pasta and bring to a boil. Reduce heat and simmer until the pasta is just tender, 8 to 10 minutes. Stir in the beans and tomatoes and cook until heated through, about 2 minutes. Remove from heat and stir in the parsley. Serve with the Parmesan cheese.

Andrea Bassett

Autumn Harvest Vegetable Beef Soup

- 1½ pounds lean ground beef
- 1 cup onion, chopped
- 4 cups beef broth or water
- 1 cup carrots, diced
- 1 cup potatoes, diced
- 1 cup celery, diced
- 1 quart canned tomato juice
- ½ - 1 teaspoon basil to taste
- ½ teaspoon pepper
- ¼ cup cabbage, chopped (optional)
- 1 teaspoon salt, or to taste

Brown ground beef and onion; drain, if needed. Add remaining ingredients. Simmer 2 hours.

Brenda Lycett
Wife of Bro. Ed Lycett
Former Minister of Education

Spicy Sausage and Bean Soup

- **1 teaspoon olive oil**
- **1 pound bulk hot sausage**
- **1 small onion, chopped**
- **2 garlic cloves, minced**
- **4 (15½ ounce) cans Great Northern beans, undrained**
- **2 (14½ ounce) cans ready-to-use chicken broth**
- **1 (14½ ounce) can diced tomatoes, undrained**
- **1 teaspoon dried basil**
- **½ teaspoon black pepper**

In a large soup pot, heat the oil over medium-high heat. Add the sausage, onion, and garlic; cook for 5 to 6 minutes or until no pink remains in the sausage, stirring frequently to break up the meat. Add the remaining ingredients and bring to a boil. Reduce the heat to medium-low and simmer, uncovered, for 30 minutes.

Note: I like this soup spicy, but if you prefer to use a mild sausage or even turkey, go ahead. Make it your own!

Mary Lou Gillespie

L. L.'s Beef and Cabbage Soup

- **½ head cabbage, chopped**
- **1 large onion, diced**
- **1½ pounds hamburger meat**
- **1 can sliced carrots**
- **2 cans kidney beans**
- **2 cans tomatoes**
- **2 packages onion mushroom soup mix**
- **3-4 bouillon cubes**

Boil cabbage until tender. Brown hamburger meat and onions. Mix all ingredients and simmer 45 minutes.

Jean Bowlin

Broccoli Soup

- 1 can broccoli soup
- 1 can cream of chicken soup
- 2 cans homogenized milk or evaporated milk
- 1 small package frozen broccoli

Mix in saucepan on stove and heat through and through.

Marion Boyd

Brunswick Stew

- 1 (2 ½ pound) fryer
- 1 pound hamburger meat, cooked and drained
- 1 (28 ounce) can crushed tomatoes, sweetened with ⅓ cup sugar
- 2 large potatoes, cut up
- 1 (16 ounce) can creamed corn
- ½ bag frozen green peas
- 1 cup ketchup
- ½ cup barbecue sauce
- 2 cups chicken broth (or more as needed)
- 1 tablespoon liquid smoke
- 1 onion, chopped
- 1 tablespoon vinegar
- 1 tablespoon Worcestershire sauce
- Salt and pepper
- Celery salt
- Water

In a large pot, place the chicken and enough water to cover it and bring to a boil. Cook chicken until meat falls off the bone, approximately 45 minutes. Drain the chicken and reserve 2 cups of stock. Remove the skin and bones and chop meat. In a separate pot, mix the chicken, hamburger meat, and remaining ingredients. Simmer slowly for 30 minutes or until potatoes are tender, stirring often to prevent sticking. Add more chicken broth if the stew becomes too thick.

Betty Mullis

Easy Brunswick Stew

- 1 (24 ounce) can Brunswick Stew
- 1 (10 ounce) can barbecue beef
- 1 (10 ounce) can barbecue pork
- 2 (17 ounce) cans cream-style corn
- 1 (16 ounce) can tomatoes, cut
- 1 tablespoon vinegar
- 1 tablespoon lemon juice
- 1 tablespoon Worcestershire sauce
- 1 teaspoon onion salt
- ½ teaspoon salt
- ¼ teaspoon black pepper (or to taste)

Optional: 1 can butterbeans and 1 can English peas

Mix all ingredients in a large pot or Dutch oven. Heat and serve.

Charlotte Bacon

Allen Spivey's Brunswick Stew

- 7 pounds course ground lean beef, browned and drained
- 2 pounds course ground lean pork, browned and drained
- 3 large onions, finely chopped
- 1 tablespoon salt
- 1 tablespoon red pepper
- 2 sticks butter
- 1 (8 ounce) bottle lemon juice
- 2 (15 ounce) cans Le Sueur peas
- 2 (15 ounce) cans Le Sueur corn
- 4 tablespoons sugar
- 1 cup vinegar
- 4 tablespoons hot sauce
- 2 (26 ounce) bottles catsup
- ½ gallon water
- 5 pounds potatoes, cut up

Add meat and water and let come to boil. Add onions and cook until done. Add potatoes and cook until tender. Add corn, peas, and other ingredients; cook slowly. Stir to keep from sticking until well done. Recipe can be halved.

Note: Every time this recipe was cooked, we always took half to Mr. Tom Frier, a long-time member of this church and owner and editor of our local newspaper, *The Douglas Enterprise.*

Eloise Spivey

Grandmother Preston's Brunswick Stew

- 4 (51 ounce) cans tomatoes
- 3 large Irish potatoes
- 3 large onions (can use more)
- 1 (20 ounce) can corn (don't grind)
- 1 (5 pound) hen, boiled
- 1 quart chicken stock from hen
- 2 pounds lean pork (plus some juice!)
- 2 pods hot pepper
- 3 tablespoons salt
- 1 tablespoon black pepper
- 3 tablespoons mustard
- 2 tablespoons Accent
- 3 tablespoons Durkee's meat sauce

Debone hen and grind all ingredients except corn. May add catsup for desired color. Stir frequently. Cook for 2 hours.

In Memory of Mrs. Minnie Preston

Zuppa Toscana

- 1 pound hot Italian sausage
- 3 large russet potatoes, thinly sliced
- 1 large onion, diced
- 3 strips of bacon
- 2 garlic cloves, diced
- 2 cups kale, washed and chopped
- 2½ cups water
- 2 (8 ounce) cans of chicken broth
- 1 cup heavy cream

Remove casing from sausage and brown in skillet; drain and set aside. Fry bacon in sausage grease, crumble, and set aside. Sauté diced onions and garlic in sausage grease. Put sliced potatoes, sautéed onions, and garlic in pot with chicken broth and water; boil for 30 minutes until potatoes are tender. Lightly mash potatoes. Add sausage and crumbled bacon and simmer for 10 minutes. Add kale and simmer until tender; add heavy cream. Delicious with Parmesan cheese sprinkled on top.

Rosemary Brown

Cincinnati-Style Chili

1 pound chorizo sausage
½ teaspoon ground nutmeg
1 pound lean ground beef
½ teaspoon allspice
1 cup yellow onions, diced
¼ teaspoon cloves
2½ cups tomato sauce
2 pounds thin spaghetti pasta
1¼ cups beef broth
Dash cardamom (optional)
2 tablespoons cider vinegar
1 tablespoon unsweetened cocoa powder
2 teaspoons paprika
4 teaspoons cumin
2 teaspoons cayenne pepper
2 teaspoons oregano
4 teaspoons garlic powder
½ tablespoon ground cinnamon

Preheat stockpot on medium 2 to 3 minutes. Add chorizo, beef, and onions; cook, stirring and crumbling meat until thoroughly cooked. Combine all dry powders and spices and add to meat. Cook for 1 to 2 minutes to blend flavors. Stir in tomato sauce, broth, and cider vinegar. Cook 8 to 10 minutes or until chili thickens and liquid reduces. Cook pasta, following package instructions. Serve chili over pasta. Top with additional onions and shredded cheese, if desired.

Note: This chili is our favorite condiment for hotdogs, but may also be lathered on baked potatoes or added to cheese to make a dip. After our first meal, we freeze the leftovers into small portions for our "hotdog" days. This recipe is as close as I can get to the special chili topping I enjoyed at Rudy's Hotdogs growing up in downtown Toledo, Ohio.

Jennifer Butler
Wife of Bro. John Butler
Associate Pastor

Chili

- **2 pounds ground round beef**
- **1 pound ground venison**
- **1 small onion, chopped**
- **2 (14 ½ ounce) cans petite diced tomatoes**
- **1 can Ro-Tel tomatoes**
- **1 can tomato soup**
- **1-2 packages McCormicks mild chili seasoning mix**
- **1 can light red kidney beans**

Sprinkle meat with Charlie's Choice (or seasoning of choice) and brown in a large skillet on medium-high heat with onion. Drain fat. Put meat in crockpot and sprinkle with seasoning mix and stir. Add tomatoes, soup, and kidney beans. Stir. Cover and cook on low for 4 to 6 hours.

Note: Anytime I make a dish that has a lot of tomatoes in it, I will always add molasses to the dish. My grandmother taught me that little trick. It seems to take the strong tomato bite away. YUMMY!!

Helen Mercer

White Chicken Chili

- **5 chicken breasts**
- **1 stick butter**
- **1 onion, chopped (sauté in butter, add ¼ cup plain flour to make a roux)**
- **2 cups chicken broth**
- **2 cups heavy cream**
- **2 cans chopped green chilies, drained**
- **2 cans Great Northern beans, drained**
- **1½ teaspoons chili powder**
- **1 teaspoon cumin**
- **1 teaspoon white pepper**
- **1 teaspoon salt**
- **1½ teaspoons hot sauce (Texas Pete or Tabasco)**
- **2 cups pepper jack cheese, shredded**

Boil chicken, cool, and debone (if necessary). Save 2 cups chicken broth or use canned broth. Sauté onion in 1 stick butter. Add flour to make roux. Add all other ingredients except for pepper jack cheese. Let simmer for 20 minutes and add pepper jack cheese. Top with sour cream and tortilla chips.

Terri and Steve Bailey

White Chicken Chili

- ½ pound dried navy beans, picked over
- 1 large onion, chopped
- 1 stick unsalted butter
- ¼ cup all-purpose flour
- ¾ cup chicken broth
- 2 cups half-and-half
- 1 teaspoon Tabasco (or to taste)
- 1½ teaspoons chili powder
- 1 teaspoon ground cumin
- ½ teaspoon salt (or to taste)
- ½ teaspoon white pepper (or to taste)
- 2 (4 ounce) cans mild green chilies, drained and chopped
- 5 boneless, skinless chicken breast halves (about 2 pounds), cooked and cut into ½ inch pieces
- 1½ cups Monterey Jack, grated
- ½ cup sour cream

In a large kettle, add enough cold water to cover beans by about 2 inches. Soak overnight. Drain beans in a colander, return to kettle, and cover with cold water by 2 inches. Cook beans in a bare simmer until tender, about 1 hour, and drain in colander. In a skillet, cook onion in 2 tablespoons butter over moderate heat until softened. In a 6- to 8-quart heavy kettle, melt remaining 6 tablespoons butter over moderately low heat and whisk in flour. Cook roux, 3 minutes, whisking constantly. Stir in onion and gradually add broth and half-and-half, whisking constantly. Bring mixture to a boil and simmer 5 minutes or until thickened, stirring constantly. Stir in Tabasco, chili powder, cumin, salt, and white pepper. Add beans, chilies, chicken, and Monterey Jack and cook mixture over moderately low heat, stirring 20 minutes. Stir sour cream into chili. Garnish chili with coriander and serve with salsa.

Lynn Graham

Southwest White Chili

- 1 tablespoon olive oil
- 1½ pounds chicken breast, cut in cubes
- ¼ cup onion, chopped
- 1 cup or can of chicken broth
- 1 (4 ounce) can chopped green chilies
- 1 can white (navy) beans, undrained
- 2 green onions, sliced (optional)
- Shredded cheese (Mexican 4-blend, Monterey Jack, etc.)
- Tony Chachere's seasoning
- Fritos

Heat oil over medium-high heat. Add chicken, seasoned with Tony Chachere's (Cajun seasoning) and onion. Cook 4-5 minutes. Stir in broth, chilies, and spice blend. Simmer 15 minutes. Stir in beans; simmer 5 minutes. Top with green onions. May garnish with shredded cheese and Fritos.

Spice Blend:

- 1 teaspoon garlic powder
- 1 teaspoon ground cumin
- ½ teaspoon oregano leaves
- ½ teaspoon cilantro leaves
- Tony Chachere's or ⅛ teaspoon ground red pepper

Amanda Morgan

Chili Soup

- 1½ pounds lean ground beef
- 1 medium onion, chopped
- 3 (10¾ ounce) cans Campbell's condensed minestrone soup
- 1 (14½ ounce) can stewed tomatoes
- 1 (10 ounce) can Ro-tel tomatoes
- 1 (15½ ounce) can chili beans
- 3 (10¾ ounce) cans water

Brown together beef and chopped onion. Drain thoroughly. Add remaining ingredients together. Simmer for 10 minutes. Serves 16.

Note: I serve Sour Cream Cornbread with the Chili Soup.

Paula Thomas

French Onion Soup

- **4 cups onions, thinly sliced (Vidalia, if possible)**
- **¼ cup butter, melted**
- **2 (10½ ounce) cans beef broth**
- **1 (10¾ ounce) can chicken broth**
- **2 tablespoons all-purpose flour**
- **1 can water (soup can)**

Sauté onions in butter until limp but not brown. Blend in flour and add broths and water. Stir until smooth. Simmer about 30 minutes. Serve with puffy cheese croutons or dry toasted French bread.

Puffy Cheese Croutons:

- **¼ cup butter**
- **2 egg whites**
- **1 tablespoon milk**
- **French bread**
- **1 cup cheese, grated**

Melt butter over very low heat, add milk and cheese, stirring constantly until smooth. Remove from heat. Beat egg whites until stiff but not dry; gently fold into cheese mixture. Cut 30 bite-size cubes of bread and dip into cheese mixture. Bake on ungreased cookie sheet at 400 degrees for 10 to 15 minutes until lightly browned. Remove from heat immediately.

Catherine Moodie

Hint: A hamhock is the knuckle above the pig's foot that has meat, fat, and bone. It is cured, smoked, and used to flavor foods such as dried beans, soups, stews, and vegetables.

French Vegetable Potage (Stew) with Pistou

- 2 cups cannellini beans, undrained
- 2 cups fresh tomatoes, peeled and cubed
- 1 cup carrots, sliced
- 1 cup zucchini, unpeeled and cubed
- 1 (14.5 ounce) can French-style green beans, drained
- ⅛ teaspoon cayenne pepper
- 2 cups potatoes, peeled and cubed
- 1 cup green onions and tops, sliced
- Salt to taste
- 1 cup onion, sliced
- 1 cup butternut squash, peeled and cubed
- 1 teaspoon dried thyme
- 2 large cloves garlic, crushed and finely minced
- 6 chicken bouillon cubes
- 2 ounces vermicelli, broken in pieces
- 2 tablespoons fresh parsley, chopped
- Black pepper, freshly ground
- French bread
- Pistou or Pesto

In a large stockpot, add the above vegetables, seasonings, and bouillon cubes. Add cold water to cover vegetables by about 2 inches. Bring to a boil and then reduce heat and simmer, partially covered, for about 40 minutes or until vegetables are almost tender. Add the broken vermicelli and cook for another 10 minutes or until pasta is cooked. Add the fresh chopped parsley. Ladle the potage (stew) into large soup bowls. Serve with 1 tablespoon of Pistou or Pesto stirred into the hot stew and pass the French bread.

Sherry Patterson

Mushroom Soup

½ cup butter
2 (8 ounce) packages fresh mushrooms, sliced
1 large onion, sliced
2 (10¾ ounce) cans cream of mushroom soup, undiluted
2 (10½ ounce) cans beef consommé, undiluted

Melt butter in saucepan over medium high heat. Add mushrooms and onions. Cook, stirring often, 5 minutes or until onions are tender. Stir in mushroom soup and remaining ingredients, stirring often. Bring to a boil. Reduce heat and simmer for 25 minutes.

Norma Lynn Hand

Tomato Rice Soup

2 tablespoons olive oil
½ cup onion, chopped
½ cup long grain rice
1 (28 ounce) can diced tomatoes
2 cups chicken broth
Salt and pepper to taste

Heat oil in a large saucepan over medium heat. Add onion and cook until soft, about 2-3 minutes. Add rice and cook, stirring until rice is evenly coated in oil, 1-2 minutes. Stir in undrained tomatoes, broth, salt, and pepper. Bring to a boil. Reduce heat, cover, and simmer for 15 minutes. Continue to simmer until rice is tender, about 5-10 minutes. Season to taste with salt and pepper.

Lisa Williams

Tomato Florentine Soup

- 3 tablespoons olive oil
- ½ cup onion, diced
- 3 cloves garlic, minced
- ⅓ cup apple juice
- 1 bay leaf
- 2 teaspoons celery salt
- 2 teaspoons dried basil
- 2 teaspoons Italian seasoning
- 1 teaspoon salt
- 1 teaspoon black pepper
- 2 tablespoons sugar
- ¼ teaspoon nutmeg
- 1 tablespoon chicken base
- 3 tablespoons flour
- 3 cups V-8 vegetable juice
- 2 (28 ounce) cans tomatoes, chopped with juice
- 6 cups milk
- 1 cup heavy cream
- 1 (10 ounce) package fresh spinach
- 2 tablespoons fresh basil, chopped

In a large soup pot, heat the oil and sauté onions and garlic until light in color. Add apple juice, bay leaf, celery salt, basil, Italian seasoning, salt, and pepper. Bring to a boil and let mixture reduce for 10 minutes. Next, add sugar, nutmeg, and chicken base; stir well. To thicken this onion herb mixture, stir in 3 tablespoons flour. Slowly add V-8 juice, stirring over medium heat until you have a smooth sauce. Add chopped tomatoes and milk; simmer soup for 30 minutes. Add heavy cream, spinach, and basil. Simmer another 10 to 15 minutes and serve. Yields 1 gallon. Really good.

Dot McKinnon

Many of us say a blessing before each meal. The Bible instructs us to offer thanks following a delicious meal as well.

"When you have eaten and are satisfied, you shall bless the Lord your God for the good land which He has given you."

Deuteronomy 8:10
(NASB)

Sausage Corn Chowder

- 6 medium potatoes, cubed
- 1 pound ground hot sausage
- 1 (14 ounce) can chicken broth
- 1 (15 ounce) can cream-style corn
- 1 (11 ounce) can niblet corn, undrained
- 1 (10¾ ounce) can cream of mushroom soup or cream of chicken soup, undiluted
- 1 pint half-and-half

Boil cubed potatoes in salted water until done; drain. Brown and drain sausage. Combine all ingredients except half-and-half. Heat chowder mixture until hot. Add half-and-half and simmer until hot. Makes about 3 quarts.

Eleanor Sammons

Turkey Gumbo Soup

- 3 cups turkey or chicken broth
- ½ medium onion, chopped
- ¼ cup celery, chopped
- 1 (10 ounce) package frozen okra, cut
- 1 (16 ounce) can tomatoes, chopped
- ½ teaspoon salt
- ⅛ teaspoon pepper
- ¼ cup rice, uncooked
- 2 cups turkey, cooked and diced

Heat broth to boiling. Add vegetables, seasonings, rice, and turkey. Cover and cook slowly, 15 minutes, until vegetables and rice are tender. Serve with green salad and garlic bread.

In Memory of Mrs. Julia Ann Elliott

Easy Chicken Noodle Soup

- 2 quarts water
- 8 chicken bouillon cubes
- 6½ cups wide egg noodles, uncooked
- 2 cans condensed cream of chicken soup
- 3 cups chicken, cooked and cubed
- 1 cup sour cream
- Minced fresh parsley

In a large saucepan, bring water and bouillon to a boil. Add noodles and cook uncovered until tender (about 10 minutes). Do not drain. Add soup and chicken; heat through. Remove from heat and stir in sour cream. Sprinkle with parsley.

Janet Pridgen

Homemade Chicken Noodle Soup

- 1 whole chicken, cut into pieces
- 5 quarts water
- 6 sprigs fresh parsley
- 6 bay leaves
- 3 large carrots (2-inch pieces)
- 3 stalks celery (2-inch pieces)
- 4 cloves garlic
- 1 large onion (2-inch pieces)
- 2 tablespoons butter
- 2 cups carrots, diced
- 2 cups celery, diced
- 1 cup onion, diced
- 2 tablespoons salt
- 1 teaspoon black pepper
- 8 ounces dried egg noodles

In a large Dutch oven or stockpot, combine chicken, water, parsley sprigs, bay leaves, carrots, celery, garlic, and onion. Bring to a boil over high heat; reduce heat and simmer, uncovered, for 1 hour or until chicken is tender. Cool chicken slightly; remove and discard skin and bones. Chop chicken into bite-size pieces; set aside. Strain broth, discarding solids; set aside. In a Dutch oven, melt butter over medium heat. Add diced carrot, diced celery, and diced onion. Cook for 8 minutes, stirring frequently until vegetables are tender. Add reserved broth, salt, and pepper. Bring to a boil over medium-high heat. Add noodles and cook for 10 minutes or until noodles are tender; add chicken. Cook for 2 minutes or until heated thoroughly.

Pam Gillis

Baked Potato Soup

- **4 large baking potatoes**
- **⅔ cup butter**
- **⅔ cup all-purpose flour**
- **6 cups milk**
- **¾ teaspoon salt**
- **½ teaspoon pepper**
- **4 green onions, chopped and divided**
- **12 slices bacon, cooked, crumbled, and divided**
- **1¼ cups Cheddar cheese, shredded and divided**
- **1 (8 ounce carton) sour cream**

Wash potatoes and prick several times with fork; bake at 400 degrees for 1 hour or until done. Let cool. Cut potatoes in half lengthwise; scoop out pulp. Melt butter in heavy saucepan over low heat; add all-purpose flour, stirring until smooth. Cook 1 minute, stirring constantly. Gradually add 6 cups milk; cook over medium heat, stirring constantly until mixture is thickened and bubbly. Add potato pulp, salt, pepper, 2 tablespoons green onions, ½ cup bacon, and 1 cup cheese. Cook until thoroughly heated; stir in sour cream. Add extra milk if necessary for desired thickness. Serve with remaining onion, bacon, and cheese.

Note: I always triple this recipe and use a huge pot to cook the soup in. I also bake my potatoes ahead of time, scoop out pulp, mash and store in refrigerator for several days. This allows the potatoes to mellow. If you double or triple the recipe, plan to have a stool to sit on when stirring the roux. Your arm will get tired stirring, but you don't want the roux to scorch. This recipe was given to me by my sister-in-law, Kathy, who has often taken this soup to the sick. They called it "Saved my Life Soup" and claimed that it was her soup that brought them back. Every year on Christmas Eve my family attends the Candlelight Service at First Baptist Church and then comes home to enjoy a bowl of Baked Potato Soup!

Rosemary Brown

Potato Soup

- 5 potatoes, peeled
- 1 medium onion, chopped
- 4 tablespoons butter
- 1 can celery or chicken soup
- 1 large can evaporated milk or regular milk
- 4 ounces sour cream
- ½ teaspoon sugar
- ½ teaspoon salt
- ¼ teaspoon pepper
- Charlie's Choice seasoning (or seasoning of choice)

Cover potatoes with water. Boil until tender. Add onion, butter, soup, milk, sugar, salt, and pepper. Mix and simmer. Before serving top with sour cream and sprinkle with Charlie's Choice Seasoning.

In Memory of Mrs. Mary Lee Daniel

Taco Soup

- 2 pounds ground beef
- 1 to 2 cups onions, chopped
- 1 or 2 (15.5 ounce) cans pink kidney beans
- 1 or 2 (15 ounce) cans niblet corn, drained
- 1 (14.5 ounce) can Del Monte Mexican tomatoes
- 1 or 2 (14.5 ounce) cans diced tomatoes
- 1 (14.5 ounce) can Del Monte tomatoes with chilies
- 2 (15.5 ounce) cans pinto beans
- 1 package taco seasoning mix
- 1 package Hidden Valley original ranch salad dressing mix
- ½ tablespoon Worcestershire sauce
- Dash ground red cayenne pepper
- Salt and pepper to taste
- Olives (desired amount)

Brown the ground beef and onions in a large skillet. Drain the excess fat and transfer the browned beef and onions to a large crockpot or stockpot. Add the beans, corn, tomatoes, chilies, olives, and seasoning. Cook on low setting all day (6 to 8 hours) in crockpot. If cooking on stove, cook for 1 hour in a large stockpot. To serve, place corn chips in each bowl and ladle soup over them. Top with sour cream, cheese, and onions.

Kelly Lastinger

Taco Soup

- 2 pounds ground chuck
- 1 small onion, finely chopped
- 1 can mild chili beans
- 1 small can green chiles
- 1 can kidney beans (light or dark)
- 1 can shoepeg corn
- 1 can Mexican corn
- 3 cans stewed tomatoes, chopped (with basil, green chiles, etc.)
- 1 packet mild taco mix
- 1 packet ranch salad dressing

Brown chuck and onion; pour off excess liquid. Combine meat mixture with rest of ingredients and heat thoroughly on medium heat.

Jan Tyre

Taco Stew

- 2½ pounds lean ground beef, browned
- 2 tablespoons vegetable oil
- 1 large onion, chopped
- 1 tablespoon minced garlic
- 1 (10 ounce) can Ro-Tel
- 1 (15¼ ounce) can white niblet corn, undrained
- 1 (15½ ounce) can chili beans in zesty sauce, undrained
- 1 (10¾ ounce) can tomato soup, undiluted
- 1 can diced tomatoes
- 1½ - 2 cups water
- 4 ounces Cheddar cheese, shredded
- 1 (1.25 ounce) envelope taco seasoning
- Sour cream
- Salt to taste
- Baked tortilla chips

In a Dutch oven, brown beef and onion in oil. Drain, if needed. Add other ingredients except chips, cheese, and sour cream. Mix well, cover, and simmer on low 45 minutes for flavors to blend and stew to heat thoroughly. To serve, crumble tortilla chips in a bowl and cover with stew. Sprinkle with grated cheese. Add a "dollop" of sour cream if so desired. Can be made a day ahead, refrigerated and reheated for serving.

Angie O'Steen

Breads

"…this do in remembrance of Me."

I Corinthians 11:24

(KJV)

Breads

Yeast Rolls

- ½ cup instant potato flakes
- 2 cups hot water
- ½ cup sugar
- 1½ teaspoons salt
- 2 packages yeast
- 3 eggs, beaten
- 7 cups all-purpose flour, divided
- ½ cup vegetable oil

Stir together instant potatoes, hot water, sugar, and salt until sugar is dissolved. Cool to lukewarm. Add yeast and let soften. With spoon, add beaten eggs and beat in 3½ cups flour until elastic. Beat in ½ cup oil. Add 3½ cups flour and work dough with hands until no longer sticky. Knead a few minutes and place in a greased bowl. Cover with plastic wrap and let rise until doubled (about 1 hour). Push down dough and work in a little flour, if needed. Shape in rolls and place in greased tins. Bake at 400 degrees until brown. Optional: Brush honey on top of rolls when hot.

Maudine Wright

Angel Biscuits

- 1 package active dry yeast
- 2 tablespoons lukewarm water
- 5 cups all-purpose flour
- 1 teaspoon baking soda
- 3 teaspoons baking powder
- 2 tablespoons sugar
- 1½ teaspoons salt
- 1 cup vegetable shortening
- 2 cups buttermilk

Dissolve yeast in warm water. Sift all dry ingredients into a large bowl. Cut in shortening with a pastry blender. Add buttermilk, then the yeast mixture, and stir until thoroughly moistened. Turn dough onto a floured board and knead a minute or two. No rising is required. Roll out to desired thickness; ½ inch is a good thickness. Cut into rounds of desired diameter. Place on a lightly greased baking sheet, brush with melted butter, and bake at 400 degrees for 12 to 15 minutes or until lightly browned.

Bro. Shep Johnson
Senior Pastor

Cheesy Sausage Biscuits

- 1 pound pork sausage
- 1 small onion, finely chopped
- 1 can Cheddar cheese soup, undiluted
- ½ cup water
- 3 cups biscuit mix

Crumble sausage into a large skillet. Add onion and cook until sausage is browned. Drain well on paper towels. Combine all ingredients, stirring well. Drop by heaping tablespoons about 2 inches apart on lightly greased baking sheets. Bake at 425 degrees for 10 to 15 minutes.

Sue Bordeaux

Crisp Corn Biscuits

- ¾ stick butter (no substitutes)
- 2 cups Bisquick baking mix
- 1 can cream-style corn

Melt butter in oven on a cookie sheet with sides. Mix together Bisquick and corn, and drop by teaspoonfuls onto cookie sheet which contains the butter. Turn biscuits over once to coat with butter. Bake at 400 degrees for 20 minutes or until golden and edges are brown. Yields 2 to 3 dozen biscuits.

Allison Cowart

Garlic Cheese Biscuits

2 cups Bisquick baking mix
⅔ cup milk
½ cup sharp Cheddar cheese, grated
½ cup butter, melted
¼ teaspoon garlic salt

Mix Bisquick, milk, and cheese until a soft ball forms. Beat vigorously for 30 seconds. Drop by balls onto an ungreased baking sheet and bake at 450 degrees for 8 to 10 minutes. Mix melted butter and garlic salt and brush on hot biscuits while still on the pan.

Catherine Moodie

Madie's Iron Skillet Biscuits

Cast iron skillet
1 stick butter
2 cups self-rising flour
1 cup buttermilk

Preheat oven to 425 degrees. Melt butter in skillet in oven as it preheats. Mix buttermilk and flour together. Drop batter by rounded spoonfuls into the butter. It is easier to go around the outer edge of the skillet first and work toward the middle. Bake about 10 minutes or until lightly browned. Let biscuits sit for about 2 minutes before serving to let them soak up the butter!

Trina Wilkerson

Sour Cream Biscuits

2 cups Bisquick baking mix
8 ounces sour cream
1 stick butter

Melt butter and mix all ingredients. Mixture will be thick and lumpy. Spoon in greased muffin tins. Fill mostly full because batter will not rise much. Bake at 425 degrees for 15 minutes. Makes about 6 biscuits.

Lisa Williams

Apple Bread

- 1 cup apples, peeled and diced
- ½ cup pecans, chopped
- 1½ cups self-rising flour
- 1 cup sugar
- 2 eggs
- ½ cup vegetable oil
- 1 teaspoon vanilla

Mix oil, eggs, sugar, and vanilla. Add apples, nuts, and flour to other mixture. Bake in ungreased loaf pan at 350 degrees for 40 to 45 minutes.

Joan Raulerson

Banana Bread

- ½ cup Crisco shortening
- 1 cup sugar
- 2 eggs
- 2 large or 3 small bananas, mashed
- 1 teaspoon vanilla
- 1 teaspoon baking soda
- ½ cup pecans, chopped
- 2 cups all-purpose flour

Cream Crisco and sugar well and add eggs. Sift together flour and baking soda and add to Crisco mixture. Fold in bananas, nuts, and vanilla. Pour batter in a greased and slightly floured pan and bake at 350 degrees for almost an hour. Makes 1 regular loaf or 4 tea loaves.

June Cowart

"They were continually devoting themselves to the apostles' teaching and to fellowship, to the breaking of bread and to prayer."
Acts 2:42
(NASB)

Cranberry Banana Bread

- 2 cups fresh cranberries
- 1 cup sugar
- 1 cup water
- ⅓ cup shortening
- ⅔ cup sugar
- 2 eggs
- 1¾ cups plain flour
- 2 teaspoons baking powder
- ½ teaspoon salt
- ¼ teaspoon baking soda
- 1 cup bananas, mashed
- ½ cup pecans, chopped

Combine cranberries, 1 cup sugar, and water; cook over medium heat about 5 minutes or until cranberries begin to pop. Drain and set aside. Cream shortening; gradually add ⅔ cup sugar, beating until light and fluffy. Add eggs one at a time, beating well after each addition. Combine dry ingredients; add to creamed mixture, alternating with banana, mixing well after each addition. Fold in cranberries and nuts. Grease and flour a 9 x 5 x 3 inch loaf pan. Spoon batter into pan. Bake at 350 degrees for 60 to 65 minutes. Cool for 10 minutes in pan. Yield: 1 loaf.

Renee Roberson

Geneva's Bread

- 1 cup warm water
- 2 packages of dry yeast
- 1 cup bread flour
- 1 cup whole wheat flour
- ½ cup rye flour
- 2 tablespoons honey
- 1 teaspoon salt

Whisk together water and yeast. Let yeast sit until it starts bubbling. Mix together flours, yeast water, honey, and salt. Knead, adding more flour as needed, until dough can be easily handled. Let rise two hours. Divide dough into loaves and let rise until they are approximately double in bulk. Bake at 350 degrees for 40-45 minutes or until the loaves are lightly brown and sound hollow when tapped down on them.

In Memory of Mrs. Geneva Womack

Blueberry Gingerbread

- ½ cup canola oil
- 1 cup sugar
- ½ teaspoon sea salt
- 3 tablespoons molasses
- 1 egg
- 2 cups all-purpose flour
- ½ teaspoon ginger
- 1 teaspoon cinnamon
- ½ teaspoon nutmeg
- 1 teaspoon baking soda
- 1 cup fresh or frozen blueberries
- 1 cup buttermilk
- 2 tablespoons sugar

Beat together in mixer oil, sugar, salt, and molasses; beat in egg. Combine flour, spices, and baking soda. Coat blueberries with 2 tablespoons of flour mixture. Alternate flour mixture and buttermilk, beating after each addition. Stir in blueberries. Pour into a greased and floured 12 x 7½ x 2 inch baking dish and sprinkle sugar over top. Bake in a 350 degree oven for 35-40 minutes. Cut into squares and serve warm with butter.

Ann Freeman

Blueberry Corn Muffins

- 1 cup Jiffy corn muffin mix
- 1 cup self-rising flour
- 1 egg
- 2 tablespoons mayonnaise
- Milk
- Blueberries

Mix all ingredients with milk to cake consistency. Put in muffin cups and bake at 350 degrees for 10 to 12 minutes.

Note: These were made with my great-grandmother, Luell Brown.

Jenna Spivey

My Mother's Gingerbread with Lemon Sauce

- ⅓ cup shortening
- ½ cup sugar
- 1 egg
- 1 cup molasses
- 1 cup boiling water
- 2½ cups all-purpose flour
- 1½ teaspoons baking soda
- 1 teaspoon cinnamon
- ½ teaspoon cloves
- 1 tablespoon ginger
- ¼ teaspoon salt

Cream shortening and sugar; add egg and beat well. Add molasses, to which soda has been added. Combine spices with flour, sift, and add to shortening mixture. Add boiling water and salt. Pour into greased baking pan. Bake at 350 degrees for 20 to 30 minutes or until desired doneness. Overcooking will result in dry gingerbread. Cool and cut into squares.

Lemon Sauce:

- 2 eggs
- 1½ cups sugar
- 2 tablespoons flour
- 1½ cups boiling water
- 1 tablespoon butter
- ⅛ teaspoon salt
- Grated rind of 1 lemon
- Juice of 2 lemons

In a saucepan, beat eggs until light. Add sugar and flour gradually. Add salt and boiling water. Cook over low heat until mixture begins to thicken. Add lemon juice and lemon rind and cook until it reaches desired thickness. Remove from heat and stir in butter until melted. Serve warm or cold on gingerbread squares.

Allison Cowart

Hint: When substituting self-rising flour for all-purpose flour, omit salt, baking soda, and baking powder.

Lemon Pecan Bread

- ¾ cup butter or margarine, softened
- 1½ cups sugar
- 3 eggs
- 2¼ cups all-purpose flour
- 1 teaspoon grated lemon rind
- ¼ teaspoon baking soda
- ¼ teaspoon salt
- ¾ cup buttermilk
- ¾ cup pecans, chopped

Cream butter and gradually add sugar, beating well. Add eggs one at a time, beating well after each addition. Combine flour, baking soda, and salt; add to creamed mixture alternately with buttermilk, beginning and ending with flour mixture. Stir in pecans and lemon rind. Pour batter into greased and floured 9 x 5 x 3 loaf pan. Bake at 350 degrees for 1 hour and 15 to 20 minutes or until wooden pick inserted in center comes out clean. Cool for 10 minutes and remove loaf from pan. Cool completely.

Frances Neugent

Nutty Monkey Bread

- ½ cup pecans, chopped
- ½ cup sugar
- 1 teaspoon ground cinnamon
- 1 (10 ounce) can refrigerated buttermilk biscuits
- 1 cup light brown sugar, firmly packed
- ½ cup butter or margarine, melted

Sprinkle pecans in bottom of well-greased 10-inch Bundt pan. Set aside. Combine sugar and cinnamon. Cut biscuits into quarters. Roll each piece in sugar mixture and layer in pan. Combine brown sugar and butter. Pour over dough. Bake at 350 degrees for 30 to 40 minutes. Cool bread for 10 minutes in pan and invert onto serving platter.

Kathy Stone

Olive Bread

- 1 regular can whole black olives
- 1 (6 ounce) jar pimento-stuffed green olives
- 2 green onions
- ¾ - 1 pound Monterey Jack cheese, shredded
- ½ cup real mayonnaise
- 1 stick butter, softened
- 1 loaf French bread

Chop black olives, green olives, and green onions. Combine olives and onions with butter, mayonnaise, and cheese. Mix thoroughly. Slice bread in half lengthwise and spread mixture on top of each half. Bake at 325 degrees for 25 minutes or until done. Cut into diagonal slices.

Amanda Morgan

Praline Pull-Apart Bread

- 1 cup granulated sugar
- 4 teaspoons ground cinnamon, divided
- 1 (2 pound) package frozen bread roll dough (Rhodes Rolls)
- ½ cup butter, melted
- 1 cup pecans, chopped
- ¾ cup whipping cream
- ¾ cup brown sugar, firmly packed

Stir together granulated sugar and 3 teaspoons cinnamon. Coat each frozen roll in butter and dredge rolls in sugar mixture. Arrange in a lightly greased 10-inch tube pan; sprinkle with pecans. Cover and chill 8 to 18 hours. Preheat oven to 325 degrees. Beat whipping cream at high speed with an electric mixer until soft peaks form. Stir in brown sugar and remaining 1 teaspoon of cinnamon. Pour mixture over dough. Place pan on an aluminum foil-lined baking sheet. Bake at 325 degrees for 1 hour or until golden brown. Cool on a wire rack 10 minutes. Invert onto a serving plate and drizzle with any remaining glaze in pan.

Kim Knight

Praline-Apple Bread

- 1½ cups pecans, chopped and divided
- 1 (8 ounce) container sour cream
- 1 cup granulated sugar
- 2 large eggs
- 1 tablespoon vanilla extract
- 2 cups all-purpose flour
- 2 teaspoons baking powder
- ½ teaspoon baking soda
- ½ teaspoon salt
- 1½ cups Granny Smith apples (about ¾ pound), peeled and finely chopped

Sauce:

- ½ cup butter
- ½ cup light brown sugar, firmly packed

Preheat oven to 350 degrees. Bake ½ cup pecans in a single layer in a shallow pan 6 to 8 minutes or until toasted and fragrant, stirring after 4 minutes. Beat sour cream and next 3 ingredients at low speed with an electric mixer 2 minutes or until blended. Stir together flour and next 3 ingredients. Add to sour cream mixture, beating just until blended. Stir in apples and ½ cup toasted pecans. Spoon batter into a greased and floured 9 x 5 inch loaf pan. Sprinkle with remaining 1 cup chopped pecans. Lightly press pecans into batter. Bake at 350 degrees for 1 hour until a wooden pick inserted into center comes out clean. Shield with aluminum foil after 50 minutes to prevent excessive browning. Cool in pan on a wire rack 10 minutes. Remove from pan to wire rack.

Bring butter and brown sugar to a boil in a 1-quart heavy saucepan over medium heat, stirring constantly. Boil for 1 minute. Remove from heat and spoon over top of bread. Let cool completely (about 1 hour).

Note: To freeze, cool bread completely. Cover with plastic wrap and aluminum foil. Freeze up to 3 months. Thaw at room temperature before serving.

Sara Allen

Strawberry Bread

- 3 cups self-rising flour
- 1 tablespoon cinnamon
- 3 eggs, well beaten
- 2 cups sugar
- 1¼ cups vegetable oil
- 2 (10 ounce) packages frozen strawberries, drained (save juice)
- 1¼ cups pecans, chopped

Combine flour, cinnamon, and sugar. Make a well in dry ingredients and add oil and eggs. Stir only until dry ingredients are moistened. Stir in strawberries and pecans. Spoon batter into 2 floured 8-inch bread pans. Bake 350 degrees for 1 hour and let sit overnight before slicing.

Note: For a spread, mix together 1 (8 ounce) package cream cheese, ¾ cup powdered sugar, 1 teaspoon cinnamon, and juice from strawberries.

Faye Ray

Stuffed French Bread

- 1 large loaf French bread
- 2 (8 ounce) packages cream cheese, softened
- 1 pound Cheddar cheese, shredded
- 1 tomato, chopped
- ½ bell pepper, chopped
- ½ onion, chopped
- 2 cups meat, cooked and diced
- ½ teaspoon onion powder
- ½ teaspoon garlic
- 1 dash hot sauce
- Salt and pepper to taste

Preheat oven to 400 degrees. Slice bread lengthwise and core out. Mix ingredients and stuff into bread shell. Wrap in foil and bake for about an hour. Serve with nachos or crackers. You may toast the bread that was removed from center and use for dipping.

Note: I use whatever meat I have on hand. Leftover ham or beef roast works well. You may also use packaged corned beef, ham, chicken, or turkey. I have also used a variety of cheeses. One cup of mayonnaise can be substituted for one cup of cream cheese.

Wylene Coffee

Zucchini Bread

- 3 eggs
- 1 cup cooking oil
- 2 cups sugar
- 1 teaspoon vanilla extract
- 2 cups raw zucchini, peeled, grated, and drained
- 3 cups all-purpose flour
- 1 teaspoon salt
- 1 teaspoon baking soda
- 3½ teaspoons cinnamon
- ¼ teaspoon baking powder
- ⅔ cup pecans, chopped

Beat eggs until foamy. Add oil, sugar, and vanilla. Mix well and stir in grated zucchini. Sift dry ingredients together and add to egg mixture. Fold in nuts. Pour into 2 greased 9 x 5 x 3 inch loaf pans or 2 ungreased foil loaf pans. Bake in a 325 degree oven for 1 hour. Freezes well

In Memory of Mrs. Tish Overstreet

Cinnamon-Walnut Coffee Cake

- ¾ cup butter, softened
- 1½ cups sugar
- 3 eggs
- 1 teaspoon vanilla flavoring
- 1 teaspoon lemon flavoring
- 3 cups self-rising flour
- 1½ cups sour cream

Heat oven to 350 degrees. Grease tube pan. In large mixer bowl, combine butter, sugar, eggs, vanilla, and lemon flavoring. Beat on medium speed 2 minutes. Mix in flour alternately with sour cream. Spread ⅓ of batter in pan and sprinkle with ⅓ of filling. Repeat twice. Bake about 60 minutes or until wooden pick inserted in center comes out clean. Cool slightly in pan before removing. Dust with powdered sugar.

Filling:

- ½ cup light brown sugar, packed
- ½ cup walnut halves
- 1½ teaspoons cinnamon

Mix ingredients together.

Ann Freeman

Orange Coffee Cake

- 2 tablespoons butter, melted
- 1 (16.3 ounce) can refrigerated biscuits (Pillsbury Grands)
- ¼ cup walnuts, minced
- ⅓ cup granulated sugar
- 2 teaspoons orange zest

Glaze:

- ½ cup confectioners' sugar
- 2 ounces cream cheese, softened
- 2 tablespoons orange juice (or more, if needed)

Preheat oven to 350 degrees. Butter a 9-inch round cake pan. Separate the biscuit dough into 8 biscuits. Place 1 biscuit in the center of the pan. Cut the remaining biscuits in half and arrange the pieces around the center biscuits with cut sides facing in the same direction. Brush melted butter over the tops of the biscuits. In a small bowl, combine the walnuts, granulated sugar, and orange zest. Mix well and sprinkle over the biscuits. Bake for 20 minutes or until golden brown. Meanwhile in a small bowl, combine confectioners' sugar, cream cheese, and orange juice. Blend until smooth, adding more juice if needed to thin. Drizzle glaze over the warm coffee cake.

Brenda Lycett
Wife of Bro. Ed Lycett
Former Minister of Education

Hint: Hot water kills yeast. One way to test for the correct temperature is to pour the water over your wrist. If you cannot feel hot or cold, the temperature is just right.

Phil's Coffee Cake

- 1 box yellow cake mix
- ¾ cup plus 2 tablespoons water
- 4 eggs
- 1 (3 ounce) box instant vanilla pudding
- ¾ cup Crisco oil

Topping:

- ⅓ cup light brown sugar
- ¼ cup sugar
- 1 teaspoon cinnamon
- 1 cup pecans, chopped
- 2 tablespoons butter, melted

Mix together first 5 ingredients for 4 minutes with mixer. Pour half of the batter into a greased and floured 9 x 13 pan. Combine all topping ingredients and sprinkle ¾ of topping on top of batter. Pour rest of batter over and spread with knife. Sprinkle rest of topping on top. Bake 50-60 minutes at 350 degrees.

Sue Bordeaux

Broccoli Cornbread

- 1 stick butter, melted
- 1 (10 ounce) package frozen broccoli, chopped into small pieces
- 1 box Jiffy corn mix
- 4 eggs
- 1 small onion, chopped
- 1 cup Cheddar cheese, shredded

Mix all ingredients and place in a greased 9 x 13 pan. Bake 25-30 minutes on 400 degrees.

Kay Fletcher

Frances Gillis' Crackling Cornbread

- 1½ cups cornmeal
- ¼ cup all-purpose flour
- 1 teaspoon baking soda
- 1 teaspoon salt
- 1 large egg, beaten
- 1 cup cracklings, presoaked in broth or milk
- 2 cups buttermilk

Preheat oven to 450 degrees. Combine first 4 ingredients. Add egg and buttermilk. Stir in cracklings. Pour into a greased and preheated cast iron skillet. Bake for 30 minutes or until inserted toothpick comes out clean.

Pam Gillis

Cornbread

- 1 cup cornmeal
- ½ cup self-rising flour
- 1 can cream corn
- 1 cup mayonnaise
- 1 tablespoon sugar
- 1 egg, beaten

Mix all ingredients and bake for 30 minutes in a small cast iron skillet at 350 degrees until done.

Norma Lynn Hand

Mexican Cornbread

(Old Family Recipe)

- 1½ cups self-rising meal
- 1½ cups onions, finely chopped
- ½ cup Wesson oil
- ½ cup buttermilk
- 3 eggs
- Dash garlic salt
- 1 medium can cream-style corn
- 1 cup sharp cheese, grated
- 3 pods hot pepper, seeded and chopped
- ¼ teaspoon salt

Mix all ingredients well. Fill muffin or cornstick pans ½ full and bake at 350 degrees until done.

Charline McElroy

Jalapeno Cornbread

- 1 cup yellow cornmeal
- ½ cup vegetable oil
- 2 eggs, beaten well
- 1 cup sour cream
- 1 cup sharp Cheddar cheese, grated
- 3 teaspoons baking powder
- 1 teaspoon salt
- 1 cup cream-style canned corn
- 1 tablespoon jalapeno pepper, finely chopped

Mix all ingredients except jalapeno pepper and grated cheese. Pour half of the batter into greased 9 x 13 inch casserole pan. Sprinkle the jalapeno pepper and cheese over batter; pour remaining batter on top. Bake in a preheated 350 degree oven for about an hour.

Bro. Shep Johnson
Senior Pastor

Mexican Cornbread

- 1½ cups cornmeal
- ¼ cup self-rising flour
- 1 (16-17 ounce) can creamed corn
- ½ teaspoon baking soda
- ½ cup vegetable oil
- 1 medium bell pepper, chopped
- 1 cup buttermilk or sour cream (either is good)
- 1 teaspoon salt
- 2 eggs
- 1 medium onion, chopped
- ½ pound cheese, grated

Combine all ingredients and pour into oiled pan and bake at 350 degrees for about 45 minutes or 1 hour. Can serve with baked beans and tossed salad.

In Memory of Mrs. Tish Overstreet

Skillet Cornbread

- ¼ cup vegetable oil
- 1¼ cups yellow cornmeal
- ¾ cup all-purpose flour
- ¼ cup sugar
- 1 tablespoon baking powder
- ½ teaspoon salt
- 1 cup milk or buttermilk
- 1 egg, beaten

Pour oil into a 8-inch cast iron skillet and place in a 425 degree oven for 5 minutes or until hot. Combine cornmeal, flour, sugar, baking powder, and salt in a medium bowl and stir well. Add milk and egg, stirring just until dry ingredients are moistened. Remove skillet from oven and pour oil into cornmeal mixture. Stir until combined. Pour batter into skillet and bake at 425 degrees for 22 to 26 minutes or until golden brown.

Note: If you prefer a thinner cornbread, bake in a 10-inch cast iron skillet and reduce cooking time.

Cathalene Taylor

Sour Cream Cornbread

- 1 cup self-rising flour
- 1 teaspoon baking powder
- 3 eggs
- 1 (7 ounce) can cream corn
- 1 cup sour cream
- ½ cup vegetable oil
- ½ tablespoon sugar

Mix all ingredients together. Pour into a greased 9 x 9 baking pan. Bake at 350 degrees in a preheated oven for 20 minutes. Check to be sure it is done. Cornbread will be moist inside when done.

Paula Thomas

Blueberry Muffins

- 1 egg
- ½ cup milk
- 1½ cups all-purpose flour
- ½ cup sugar
- ¼ cup vegetable oil
- 2 teaspoons baking powder
- ½ teaspoon salt
- 1 cup blueberries (fresh is best)

Beat the egg and add milk and oil. Blend in dry ingredients and stir until just moistened. The batter will be lumpy. Gently fold in berries. Fill greased muffin cups ⅔ full. Bake at 400 degrees for 25 minutes. Makes 1 dozen.

Ann Sheppard

Fudge Muffins

- 2 sticks margarine
- 4 (1 ounce) blocks semi-sweet chocolate
- 1½ cups sugar
- 1 cup self-rising flour, sifted
- 4 eggs (one at a time)
- 1 teaspoon vanilla
- 2 cups pecans, chopped
- Pinch salt

In a double boiler, melt margarine and semi-sweet chocolate until fully combined. In a separate bowl, mix together sugar, flour, and salt. Add eggs one at a time to dry mixture until blended well. Add chocolate mixture, vanilla, and nuts. Pour into individual paper muffin molds and bake at 325 degrees for 25 to 30 minutes. Makes 24 large or 48 small muffins.

Martha Brawner

Garlic Parmesan Pull-Apart Bread

- 1 can refrigerated Grands biscuits (not flaky)
- ½ stick of butter
- 3 cloves garlic, minced
- ½ cup Parmesan cheese, grated

In a greased fluted or tube pan, place biscuits around pan. Mix butter, garlic, and cheese in small bowl and pour on top of biscuits. Bake biscuits according to directions on package.

Kellie Lingenfelter

Lemon Blossoms

- 4 large eggs
- 3½ ounce package instant lemon pudding mix
- 1 (18½ ounce) package yellow cake mix
- ¾ cup vegetable oil

Glaze:

- 4 cups confectioners' sugar
- ⅓ cup fresh lemon juice
- Grated zest of 1 lemon
- 3 tablespoons vegetable oil
- 3 tablespoons water

Preheat the oven to 350 degrees. Spray miniature muffin tins with cooking spray. Combine the cake mix, pudding mix, eggs, and oil and blend well with electric mixer until smooth (about 2 minutes). Pour a small amount of batter, filling each muffin tin halfway. Bake for 12 minutes. Turn out onto a tea towel.

To make the glaze, sift the sugar into a mixing bowl. Add the lemon juice, zest, oil, and 3 tablespoons water. Mix with a spoon until smooth.

With fingers, dip the cupcakes into the glaze while they're still warm, covering as much of the cake as possible or spoon the glaze over the warm cupcakes, turning them to completely coat. Place on wire racks with waxed paper underneath to catch any drips. Let the glaze set thoroughly, about one hour, before storing in containers with tight-fitting lids. Yields: 5 dozen.

Nell Sturgis

Pecan Pie Muffins

- **1 cup pecans, chopped into small pieces**
- **1 cup dark brown sugar, packed**
- **½ cup all-purpose flour**
- **2 eggs**
- **1 stick butter, melted**

Combine the pecans, brown sugar, and flour in a bowl and mix well. Beat the eggs with the butter in a small bowl, add to the pecan mixture, and stir just until mixed. Spoon into greased muffin cups. Bake at 350 degrees for 20 minutes for regular-size muffins or 10 minutes for miniature muffins. Makes 12 regular-size or 20 miniature muffins.

Rosemary Brown

Pumpkin Muffins

- **¾ cup brown sugar, firmly packed**
- **½ cup butter or margarine, softened**
- **¼ cup molasses**
- **1 egg, beaten**
- **1 cup canned pumpkin**
- **1¾ cups self-rising flour**
- **½ cup pecans, chopped**

Combine sugar, butter, and molasses. Beat well. Add egg and pumpkin, beating until smooth. Stir together remaining ingredients and add to pumpkin mixture, stirring only until moistened (the batter should be lumpy). Fill lightly greased muffin pans half full. Bake at 375 degrees for 20 minutes. Makes approximately 15 muffins.

Ann Freeman

Sweet Green Tomato Cornmeal Muffins

- **2 cups green tomatoes, seeded and diced**
- **½ cup sugar, divided**
- **½ cup butter, melted and divided**
- **2 cups self-rising white cornmeal mix**
- **2 teaspoons lemon zest**
- **5 large eggs**
- **1 (16 ounce) container sour cream**
- **Vegetable cooking spray**

Preheat oven to 450 degrees. Sauté tomatoes and 2 tablespoons sugar in 2 tablespoons melted butter in a large skillet over medium-high heat for 10 to 12 minutes (until tomatoes begin to caramelize and turn light brown). Stir together cornmeal mix, lemon zest, and remaining 6 tablespoons sugar in a large bowl and make a well in the center of mixture. Whisk together eggs, sour cream, and remaining 6 tablespoons butter. Add to cornmeal mixture, stirring just until dry ingredients are moistened. Fold in tomatoes.

Generously coat small (¼ cup size) brioche molds or muffin pans with vegetable spray. Spoon batter into molds, filling two-thirds full. Bake at 450 degrees for 15 to 17 minutes or until wooden pick inserted in center comes out clean.

Betty Dees

Mini Sour Cream Muffins

- **1 cup butter or margarine, softened**
- **1 (8 ounce) carton sour cream**
- **2 cups self-rising flour**

Combine butter and sour cream. Mix until smooth. Gradually stir in flour and blend well. Spoon into ungreased miniature muffin pans, filling each with 1 tablespoon of batter. Bake at 350 degrees for 25 to 30 minutes.

Jane Simmons

Hush Puppies

- 1 cup cornmeal
- ½ cup all-purpose flour
- 1 teaspoon salt
- 1 teaspoon baking powder
- 1 medium onion, chopped
- 1 cup milk

Combine all ingredients. Heat deep fat to 350 to 400 degrees. Drop by teaspoon into hot fat. Fry until brown on both sides. Drain on folded paper towels.

Valeria Plymale

Okra Hushpuppies

(Family Favorite)

- 1 egg, whisked
- 1 cup young okra, chopped
- 1 large firm tomato, chopped
- ½ cup onion, chopped
- ½ cup green bell pepper, chopped
- ⅔ cup self-rising cornmeal
- ⅓ cup self-rising flour
- Salt and pepper to taste

Mix all ingredients together and let stand for ½ to 1 hour. Drop by spoonfuls into deep fat and fry until golden brown on both sides.

Lola Burch

Aunt Gladys' Hushpuppies

- 1 cup cornmeal
- 1 egg
- ½ cup all-purpose flour
- 1 teaspoon salt
- 1 cup milk
- 1½ teaspoons baking powder

Mix together cornmeal, egg, and flour until blended well. Add salt and baking powder. Stir in milk. Fry in hot oil until done. If batter is too stiff, dip spoon in water to dip out.

Janice Preston

Make - Ahead Dinner Rolls

- 1 package of yeast (or 2 teaspoons loose)
- ½ cup sugar
- 1 cup warmed milk (at least 110 degrees)
- 2 eggs, beaten
- 1 teaspoon salt
- ½ cup butter, melted
- 2 cups whole wheat flour
- 2 cups all-purpose flour and extra flour

Mix together first 3 ingredients. Let stand 30 minutes. Add eggs, salt, and butter and stir until smooth. Add flour 2 cups at a time, using additional flour if needed to keep dough from being too sticky. It should feel sticky without sticking to your fingers. Cover and chill until ready to bake or use right away. Divide dough in half and roll each half into a 9-inch circle. Cut each circle into 12 wedges and roll from the wide end. Place on a greased cookie sheet and let rise until doubled in size. Bake at 375 degrees for 12-15 minutes.

Cass Collins

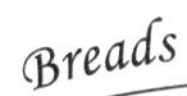

Sourdough Bread Starter

- **1 package yeast**
- **2 cups warm water**
- **½ cup sugar**
- **2 teaspoons salt**
- **½ cup instant potatoes**

Dissolve yeast in ½ cup of the water; add remaining ingredients and stir well. Keep at room temperature for 24 hours. Put starter in refrigerator 3 to 5 days. Take out and feed with the following:

- **¾ cup sugar**
- **3 tablespoons instant potatoes**
- **1 cup warm water**

Mix well and add to starter. Let stand out of refrigerator all day (8 to 12 hours). Mixture will be very bubbly. Take out 1 cup to make bread and return to refrigerator. Keep in refrigerator 3 to 5 days and feed again. If not making bread after feeding starter, throw away 1 cup. This is to avoid deflating your starter.

Rosemary Brown

"Ordering the people to sit on the grass, He took the five loaves and the two fish, and looking up toward heaven, He blessed the food, and breaking the loaves He gave them to the disciples, and the disciples gave them to the crowds, and they all ate and were satisfied. They picked up what was left over of the broken pieces, twelve full baskets. There were about five thousand men who ate, besides women and children."

Matthew 14:19-21
(NASB)

Sourdough Bread Recipe

Begin by feeding your 'Sourdough Starter' that you have received from a friend. Feed every 3 to 5 days.

Remove starter from the refrigerator and add 3 tablespoons of instant potato flakes, ¾ cup of sugar, and 1 cup of hot water. Mix very well and let it sit for 12 hours without a lid. During the 12-hour period you will see the starter work. The potato flakes will work up and down the mixture. It will become somewhat bubbly. Between feedings keep starter in the refrigerator. (I use a quart jar and keep a lid on it while in the refrigerator.) Once you remove from the refrigerator, feed immediately but do not put the lid back on until you have removed your starter for the bread. Put lid back on and refrigerate immediately.

Bread recipe:

- **6 cups of bread flour**
- **½ cup sugar**
- **1 tablespoon salt**
- **1 cup starter**
- **1½ cups lukewarm water**

Combine the first 3 ingredients and mix well in a very large bowl. Stir your starter well. Add 1 cup starter to the dry ingredients. Add lukewarm water to mixture and mix well. I begin mixing with a spoon, and then I have to finish it with my hands. Leave the mixture in the same large bowl, cover loosely with plastic wrap, and let rise for 12 hours. Keep away from draft. After 12 hours punch down and separate into 3 sections. Knead each section well. Put each section in a greased loaf pan, cover with plastic wrap, and let stand for 12 more hours. Keep away from draft.

Bake at 350 degrees for approximately 25 to 28 minutes. Remove from oven and immediately rub each loaf with butter so that the top crust does not become hard.

These loaves can be put in a plastic bag and stored in the freezer for up to a month.

Marsha Gilliard

Dedication Hymn

First Baptist Church, Douglas, Georgia

April Seventh, Nineteen Hundred Eighteen

Pasta

"See, I lay a stone in Zion, a chosen and precious cornerstone, and the one who trusts in Him will never be put to shame."

1 Peter 2:6

(NIV)

Pasta

Mexican Lasagna

- **1½ pounds lean ground beef**
- **1 (1.25 ounce) package taco seasoning mix**
- **1 teaspoon Lawry's seasoned salt**
- **1 cup diced tomatoes, (canned or fresh)**
- **2 (8 ounce) cans tomato sauce**
- **1 (4 ounce) can green chiles, diced**
- **1 cup ricotta cheese**
- **2 eggs, beaten**
- **10 corn tortillas**
- **2½ cups Monterey Jack cheese, grated**

Brown beef in a large skillet, stirring until cooked through. Drain and add next 5 ingredients; blend well. Bring to a boil. Reduce heat and simmer uncovered for 10 minutes. In a small bowl combine ricotta cheese and eggs. In bottom of a 9 x 13 x 2 inch baking dish, spread ½ of meat mixture. Top with ½ of tortillas, spread ½ of ricotta cheese mixture, and top with ½ of the grated cheese. Repeat layering ending with grated cheese. Bake uncovered at 350 degrees for 20 to 30 minutes or until hot and bubbly. Let stand 10 minutes. Cut into squares.

Note: This may be assembled early in the day. Refrigerate covered until ready to bake. Add 10 to 15 minutes to baking time. It freezes well. Defrost completely before baking.

Sue Bordeaux

Hint: Save time with pasta leftovers – double your favorite recipes and freeze the extra servings for later use. This works especially well with sauces and baked pasta dishes like lasagna.

Sausage and Beef Lasagna

- **1 tablespoon olive oil**
- **1 medium onion, finely chopped**
- **6 medium garlic cloves, minced**
- **1 pound ground beef**
- **½ pound ground sausage**
- **½ teaspoon salt**
- **½ teaspoon ground pepper**
- **¼ cup heavy cream or half-and-half**
- **1 (28 ounce) can tomatoes, diced**
- **1 (28 ounce) can tomatoes, pureed**
- **1¾ cups ricotta cheese**
- **1¼ cups Parmesan cheese, grated**
- **½ cup fresh basil, chopped (dried, purchased basil will substitute)**
- **1 large egg, beaten**
- **½ teaspoon salt**
- **½ teaspoon ground black pepper**
- **12 lasagna noodles, cooked according to package directions**
- **4 cups mozzarella cheese, shredded**

Preheat oven to 375 degrees. Brown onion in oil until softened; add garlic. Add ground meats and cook lightly but not completely browned. Add cream and stir over low to medium heat until some of liquid has cooked off. Add all tomatoes and simmer, stirring occasionally.

For layers: Mix ricotta, 1 cup Parmesan, basil, egg, salt, and pepper. Set aside.

In a 9 x 13 pan or baking dish, smear bottom with ¼ cup sauce, with no chunks of meat. Lay 3 noodles in a row across bottom of pan. Drop 3 tablespoons of ricotta mix down each noodle and flatten slightly with back of spoon. Next, layer the following: 1 cup mozzarella, meat sauce, noodles, ricotta, mozzarella, and sauce 2 more times. Top with sauce, remaining mozzarella, and Parmesan. Spray foil with nonstick spray and cover lasagna. Bake 15 minutes, remove foil, and bake 25 minutes longer. Cool 10 minutes and serve. Freezes well.

Becky Miller

Lasagna

6 lasagna noodles
2 cloves garlic, minced
1 medium onion, chopped
2 tablespoons butter
1 to 1½ pounds ground beef
2 teaspoons salt
¼ teaspoon pepper
1 tablespoon basil
1 tablespoon oregano
1 tablespoon parsley
1 large can tomato paste
1¼ cups water
¼ cup sugar
1 tablespoon vinegar
2 tablespoons Worcestershire sauce
8 ounces mozzarella cheese, grated

Cook noodles according to package. Sauté garlic and onion in butter. Add beef and cook until done. Drain. Add all other ingredients (with the exception of mozzarella cheese). Simmer until warm.

Cheese Mixture:

½ carton cottage cheese
3 ounces cream cheese, softened
1 egg
1 tablespoon parsley

Mix cheeses, egg, and parsley together. Set aside. In a 9 x 13 x 2 casserole dish, put ⅓ sauce, 3 noodles (side by side), all of cheese mixture, ½ mozzarella cheese (4 ounces), ⅓ sauce, 3 noodles, and rest of sauce. Top with rest of mozzarella cheese. Bake uncovered for 30 to 35 minutes.

In Memory of Mrs. Jonell Garrett

Homemade Lasagna

- 2 pounds ground beef
- 1 heaping teaspoon garlic salt
- 1 (10 ¾ ounce) can tomato soup
- 1 can water (size of soup can)
- 2 tablespoons white vinegar
- 1 tablespoon oregano
- 1 tablespoon Italian seasoning
- 1 can tomato sauce
- 8 large lasagna noodles
- 2 eggs
- 1 medium carton of small curd cottage cheese
- 2 medium onions, grated
- 2 packages mozzarella cheese, grated
- Salt and pepper to taste

Brown ground beef with garlic salt and drain. Add tomato soup, tomato sauce, vinegar, oregano, Italian seasoning, salt, pepper, onion, and water. Simmer for 1 hour stirring occasionally. Mix eggs and cottage cheese well. Set aside. Cook lasagna noodles as instructed on package and drain. Layer the following in a 9 x 13 inch dish: meat mixture, egg mixture, mozzarella cheese, and the cooked noodles. Layer as many times as possible (usually 2 to 3 times). End with meat sauce on top and cover with mozzarella cheese. Cover with aluminum foil. Bake in oven at 375 degrees for 35 minutes. Uncover and cook an additional 15 minutes.

Sonya Hendley

Chicken Macaroni Casserole

- 2 cans cream of chicken soup
- 2 cups sharp Cheddar cheese, grated
- 2 cups dry macaroni, cooked
- 1 medium jar pimentos
- 1 small onion, finely diced
- 2 cups chicken, cooked and chopped
- 1 heaping tablespoon Duke's mayonnaise

Mix all ingredients. Bake in buttered casserole for 30 minutes at 350 degrees.

In Memory of Mrs. Noirena Sinclair

Spaghetti Meat Dish

- 2 tablespoons shortening
- 1 medium onion, chopped
- 1 medium green pepper, chopped
- 1 clove garlic, chopped
- 2 pounds ground beef
- 1 (16 ounce) can tomatoes
- ½ cup stuffed green olives, diced
- 1 teaspoon seasoned salt
- ½ teaspoon salt
- 1 cup cheese, grated
- 2 tablespoons Worcestershire sauce
- 1 (4 ounce) can mushrooms
- 1 (10¾ ounce) can tomato soup
- ½ pound cooked spaghetti

Sauté onions, pepper, and garlic in shortening. Add beef and cook 30 minutes or until done. Add tomatoes, olives, salts, and cheese. Cook covered over slow fire 30 minutes. Add Worcestershire sauce, mushrooms, and soup. Mix well with cooked spaghetti, put in covered dish, and leave in refrigerator for 2 days. When ready to serve, heat again.

Jenny Lott

Cindy's Spaghetti Casserole

- 2 pounds ground beef, browned and drained
- 1 small box spaghetti, cooked
- 2 medium size jars Prego sauce
- 8 ounces sour cream
- 8 ounces cream cheese
- 8 ounces cottage cheese
- 10 ounces mozzarella cheese, shredded
- 10 ounces Cheddar cheese, grated

Using one jar of Prego sauce, mix together first 2 items and pour into 9 x 13 pan (bottom layer). Mix together sour cream, cottage cheese, and cream cheese. Spread over spaghetti layer. Next, layer a jar of Prego sauce. Bake 15 to 20 minutes at 350 degrees. Add grated cheeses and put back in oven long enough to melt.

Jean Bowlin

Baked Ziti

- 1½ pounds ground beef
- 1 teaspoon garlic salt
- 1 (8 ounce) package ziti, cooked and drained
- 1 (28 ounce) jar spaghetti sauce
- 2 cups mozzarella cheese, shredded
- 1 small package of ricotta cheese (optional)

Season the ground beef with the garlic salt, add more if desired. Brown the ground beef in a skillet, stirring until crumbly; drain well. Add the ziti and spaghetti sauce and mix well. Add ¼ to ½ cup mozzarella and all ricotta cheese. Mix well. Spoon into a greased 9 x 13 baking dish. Top with the remaining mozzarella cheese. Bake covered with foil at 350 degrees for 30 minutes.

Meghan Lewis

Crockpot Chicken and Spinach Lasagna

- 2 large chicken breasts
- 2 cans cream of chicken soup
- 1 (8 ounce) carton sour cream
- 1 box frozen spinach, chopped (may only use half)
- ½ cup Parmesan cheese, shredded
- 1-2 cups mozzarella cheese, shredded and divided
- 1 cup milk
- ⅓ cup onion, chopped
- ½ teaspoon salt
- ¼ teaspoon pepper
- 9 lasagna noodles, uncooked

Season chicken, cook, and chop into bite-size pieces. (I season with garlic salt, Tony Chachere's , and some Morton Nature's Seasons.) Chop onion. Thaw, drain, and squeeze dry spinach, or cook it in microwave, drain, and squeeze dry. Mix all ingredients together except noodles and some of mozzarella cheese to add on top. Coat bottom of crockpot with cooking spray. Layer a small amount of mixture on bottom of crockpot. Next, layer ⅓ of noodles and more mixture. Repeat this sequence two more times. Top with mozzarella cheese. Cook in crockpot for 1 hour on high, 4-5 hours on low.

Amanda Morgan

Chicken and Spinach Alfredo Lasagna

- **1 (8 ounce) package no-boil lasagna noodles**
- **2 cups half-and-half**
- **1 cup milk**
- **2 cans condensed cream of mushroom soup**
- **1 cup Parmesan cheese, grated**
- **¼ cup butter (½ stick)**
- **1 tablespoon olive oil**
- **½ large onion, diced**
- **Salt, garlic salt, and pepper to taste**
- **4 garlic cloves, minced**
- **5 mushrooms, sliced**
- **1 roasted chicken or 4 large boneless breasts, boiled, deboned, and chopped**
- **1 cup ricotta cheese**
- **1 bunch fresh spinach, washed and dried**
- **3 cups mozzarella cheese, shredded**

Preheat oven to 350 degrees. In a saucepan over low heat, mix together half-and-half, milk, cream of mushroom soup, Parmesan cheese, and butter. Simmer, stirring frequently until well blended. Add a pinch of garlic salt and pepper to taste. Heat the olive oil in a skillet over medium heat. Sauté the onion and garlic in olive oil until tender, and then add mushrooms. Mix in the chicken and cook until heated thoroughly. Season with salt and pepper. Lightly coat the bottom of a 9 x 13 inch baking dish with enough cream sauce mixture. Layer the bottom of the dish with lasagna noodles, ½ of the ricotta cheese, ½ of the spinach, ½ of the chicken mixture, and 1 cup mozzarella cheese. Top with ½ of the cream sauce mixture and repeat the layers. Place the remaining noodles on the top and spread with remaining sauce. Bake 1 hour in 350 degrees oven or until brown and bubbly. Top with mozzarella cheese and Parmesan and continue baking until cheese is melted and lightly browned.

Terri & Steve Bailey

Chicken Spinach Pasta

- **1 cup onion, chopped**
- **1 tablespoon olive oil**
- **3 cups cooked chicken, chopped**
- **8 ounces rigatoni pasta, cooked and drained**
- **1 can Italian tomatoes, diced**
- **1 (8 ounce) container chive and onion cream cheese, softened**
- **10 ounces frozen spinach, thawed, chopped, and drained**
- **½ teaspoon salt**
- **½ teaspoon pepper**
- **2 cups mozzarella cheese, shredded**

Preheat oven to 375 degrees. Put oil in the bottom of a 9 x 13 pan. Add onion and bake for 15 minutes. Remove from oven. Lower oven temperature to 350 degrees. In a large bowl, combine chicken, pasta, tomatoes, spinach, cream cheese, salt, and pepper. Add cooked onions. Pour mixture into pan and bake covered at 350 degrees for 30 minutes. Uncover and top with cheese. Bake uncovered for 10 to 15 minutes. Enjoy!

Jessica Barber

Pasta Salad

- **1 box pasta, cooked**
- **4 boneless chicken breasts**
- **1 cucumber, sliced round**
- **1 large tomato, cut in small pieces**
- **1 bunch green onions, chopped**
- **1 green bell pepper, chopped**

Boil or bake chicken breasts until done. Cut into bite-size pieces. Mix chicken and pasta, and then add other ingredients. Pour dressing over and mix. I normally use colored pasta.

Dressing:

- **1 (8 ounce) Italian dressing**
- **2 cups mayonnaise**
- **Sugar to taste**

Mary Thacker

Pasta Salad

- 1 (16 ounce) package macaroni noodles
- 4 eggs
- 1 cup mayonnaise
- ½ cup sour cream
- 1 teaspoon salt (or to taste)
- ¼ teaspoon ground black pepper (or to taste)
- ¼ teaspoon ground mustard
- 2 tablespoons sweet pickle juice
- 2 tablespoons celery seed
- 1 cup celery, chopped
- ½ cup red onion, chopped
- ½ cup pimento-stuffed green olives
- ¼ cup sweet chopped pickles
- 2 carrots, grated
- 1 green bell pepper, chopped

Cook pasta in a large pot of boiling water until al dente. Drain and rinse with cold water. Set aside. Place eggs in a saucepan and fill with enough cold water to cover by about 1 inch. Bring water to a boil. Cover, remove from heat, and let eggs stand in hot water for 20 minutes. Immediately remove eggs and cool in an ice water bath. When cool enough to handle, peel and chop eggs. In a medium bowl, mix together mayonnaise, sour cream, dry mustard, sweet pickle juice, and celery seed. Season with salt and black pepper. In a large bowl, combine drained pasta, celery, onion, olives, sweet pickles, carrots, green pepper, and chopped eggs. Stir in dressing and mix well. Refrigerate before serving.

Lynn Graham

Hint: To properly cook pasta, bring 4 quarts of water to a full boil. Add 2 tablespoons salt and drop in 1 pound of pasta. If desired, 1 teaspoon of olive oil may be added to the water to help keep the noodles from sticking together.

Spinach-Noodle Chicken Casserole

- **1 (3 to 4 pound) chicken, boiled, boned, and cut in pieces**
- **4 to 6 ounces cooked spinach noodles, prepared in 4 cups chicken stock**
- **1 stick margarine**
- **1 cup bell pepper, chopped**
- **1 cup celery, chopped**
- **1 cup onion, chopped**
- **½ pound Velveeta cheese**
- **1 (6 ounce) can mushrooms**
- **1 can cream of mushroom soup**
- **6 ounces olives or pimentos**
- **1 can water chestnuts, sliced**

Sauté in margarine the chopped peppers, celery, and onion. Stir in Velveeta cheese. Add mushrooms, mushroom soup, olives or pimentos, and sliced water chestnuts. Toss with the drained noodles, chicken, and other ingredients. May be served immediately, refrigerated, or frozen. If frozen, thaw completely and bake at 350 degrees for 45 minutes or until bubbly. I sometimes sprinkle grated cheese on top.

In Memory of Mrs. Nell Harris

Bow Tie Pasta Salad

- **1 box farfalle bow tie pasta**
- **1 cup mayonnaise**
- **2 tablespoons red wine vinegar**
- **¾ cup sugar (or to taste)**
- **1 can condensed milk**
- **2 medium green bell peppers, diced**
- **5 or 6 baby carrots, diced**

Cook pasta according to directions on box; drain and cool. Mix together mayonnaise, red wine vinegar, and sugar. Add to pasta. Mix condensed milk, bell pepper, and carrots together and add to pasta. Stir until all ingredients are evenly mixed. Keep in refrigerator.

Alice Ward

Greek Pasta Salad

- 12 ounces penne pasta
- 2 cups grape tomatoes, halved
- 1 cucumber, sliced
- 4 green onions, sliced
- ⅓ cup pitted Kalamata olives, halved
- ½ cup lemon juice
- ½ cup olive oil
- 2 tablespoons fresh basil
- 2 tablespoons fresh oregano
- 4 cloves garlic, minced
- ¼ teaspoon salt
- ¼ teaspoon black pepper
- 1 cup feta cheese, crumbled

Cook pasta according to package directions. Drain in colander and rinse with cold water. In large bowl, toss together the cooked pasta, tomatoes, cucumbers, green onions, and olives. In small bowl, mix together olive oil, lemon juice, basil, oregano, garlic, salt, and pepper. Drizzle over pasta. Cover and chill. Toss with feta cheese before serving.

Benita Lott

Pasta Salad

- 4 cups rotini pasta, uncooked
- 1 medium zucchini, sliced
- 2 carrots, scraped and sliced
- ½ sweet red pepper, cut into thin strips
- 1 cup broccoli florets
- 1 (6 ounce) can ripe olives, sliced
- 1 (8 ounce) bottle Italian salad dressing

Cook rotini according to package directions; drain. Rinse with cold water and drain. Combine cooked pasta with remaining ingredients in a large bowl, tossing well to coat pasta and vegetables. Serve salad immediately or chill for later. I have added cherry tomatoes.

Betty Dees

Vegetable Pasta Salad

- 1 (1 pound) box bowtie pasta (mini farfalle)
- ½ cup red bell pepper, chopped
- ½ cup yellow bell pepper, chopped
- ½ cup orange bell pepper, chopped
- ½ cup green onion, sliced
- 1 pound fresh asparagus (You may substitute grape tomatoes or other vegetable, if preferred.)
- 1 (16 ounce) bottle Italian-style salad dressing
- ½ cup Parmesan cheese, freshly grated

Cook pasta in large pot of boiling water until al dente. Rinse under cold water and drain. Cut tender ends of asparagus into 1½ to 2 inch pieces, cook one minute in boiling water; cool in ice water; drain. Mix peppers, onion, and asparagus together in large bowl. Add the cooled pasta and mix together. Pour the dressing over mixture, add the Parmesan cheese, and mix well. Chill before serving. Add more Parmesan cheese when serving, if desired.

Mary Lou Gillespie

Avocado Pasta Sauce

- 2 medium tomatoes
- 1 avocado
- 2-3 tablespoons olive oil
- 1 teaspoon fresh basil, chopped
- ¼ teaspoon garlic, minced
- Salt and pepper to taste
- Parmesan cheese, grated

Peel and dice tomatoes and avocado. Add other ingredients and mix. Add sauce to any cooked pasta and top with Parmesan cheese.

Lynn Schofield

Vegetables and Casseroles

"I am the gate; whoever enters through Me will be saved.
They will come in and go out, and find pasture."

John 10:9
(NIV)

Before the building of the Family Ministry Center, this old iron gate served as a courtyard entrance off Cleveland Street.

Vegetables and Casseroles

Asparagus Spaghetti Casserole

- 1 (8 ounce) package spaghetti
- 1½ cups asparagus, cooked
- 2 tablespoons margarine
- 2 tablespoons flour
- 1 cup milk
- 3 drops Tabasco sauce
- ½ teaspoon salt
- ½ cup Cheddar cheese, grated
- ¼ cup breadcrumbs
- Pepper to taste

Cook spaghetti until almost tender. Drain asparagus, reserving liquid. Melt margarine in saucepan; stir in flour. Add asparagus liquid and milk, stirring until it thickens. Remove from heat and add seasonings and cheese. Stir until smooth. Put ½ spaghetti in greased pan, add asparagus, and pour ½ sauce on top. Add rest of spaghetti and sauce. Sprinkle breadcrumbs on top. Bake at 350 degrees for 20 minutes.

Clara Benoist

Oven-Roasted Asparagus

- 1 bunch fresh asparagus
- 1 tablespoon olive oil
- Lemon juice
- 1 tablespoon walnuts, chopped
- Sea salt
- Black pepper

Preheat oven to 425 degrees. Cut tough stem ends off asparagus (about 1 inch of bottom). Place asparagus on cookie sheet and drizzle with olive oil. Sprinkle with a few drops of lemon juice. Toss with hands or spatula until asparagus is covered with oil. Sprinkle with sea salt and coarse-ground black pepper. Roast in center of oven for 10 minutes. May need to turn once. Asparagus should be a deep, brilliant green, not overcooked. Sprinkle with finely chopped walnuts after removing from oven.

Becky Miller

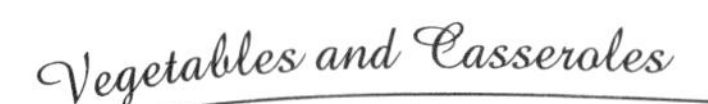

Chilled Marinated Asparagus

- ⅔ cup brown sugar, packed
- ⅔ cup cider vinegar
- ⅔ cup soy sauce
- ⅔ cup vegetable oil
- 4 teaspoons lemon juice
- 1 teaspoon garlic powder
- 2 pounds fresh asparagus, trimmed
- 1 cup pecans, chopped and toasted

In a saucepan, combine the brown sugar, vinegar, soy sauce, oil, lemon juice, and garlic powder. Bring to a boil. Reduce heat; simmer for 5 minutes. Refrigerate until cool. Cook asparagus in microwave. Place asparagus in a large resealable plastic bag; add marinade. Seal bag and turn to coat; refrigerate overnight. Drain and put on platter with garnish and sprinkle with pecans.

Terry Cook

Crockpot Cowboy Beans

- 1 pound ground chuck
- 1 onion, chopped
- 1 bell pepper, chopped
- 1 can lima beans
- 1 can pinto beans
- 1 can pork and beans
- 1 can Great Northern beans
- 1 can chili or kidney beans
- 1 cup ketchup
- ½ cup Worcestershire sauce
- ½ cup brown sugar

Brown ground chuck with onion and bell pepper. Combine in crockpot with remaining ingredients. Cook on high for 1 hour and then on low for 2 hours.

Glennis Coleman
Wife of Rev. Ray Coleman
Smyrna Baptist Association

Barbecued Beans

- 1 pound ground chuck, browned and drained
- 6 strips bacon, cooked and crumbled
- 3 (16 ounce) cans baked beans (Bush's Original is best)
- ½ cup catsup
- ¼ cup mustard
- ¼ cup Worcestershire sauce
- ½ cup brown sugar
- 1 medium onion, chopped
- 1 medium green bell pepper, chopped
- 3 strips bacon, raw

Mix all ingredients together except 3 strips of raw bacon. Pour into a 9 x13 casserole dish and top with raw bacon. Bake at 350 degrees to 375 degrees in a preheated oven for 30 to 45 minutes or until bubbly and hot.

Margaret Lankford

Broccoli Casserole

- 1 small bunch fresh broccoli heads
- 1 can cream of mushroom soup
- 2 cups cooked rice
- 1 medium onion
- ½ stick margarine
- 1 small jar Cheese Whiz

Brown onion in margarine. Boil broccoli heads until tender in water, about 5 minutes. Mix all ingredients together. Bake at 350 degrees about 25 minutes. Serves six to eight people.

In Memory of Mrs. Virginia Norris

Broccoli Casserole

2 packages broccoli, chopped
1 can mushroom soup
1 cup Cheddar cheese, grated
½ cup mayonnaise
2 eggs, beaten
Ritz crackers
Butter

Cook broccoli for 5 minutes and drain. Mix all ingredients together, including cooked broccoli, and top with butter and Ritz crackers. Bake at 350 degrees for 30 minutes.

Jeanne Soar

Broccoli Cottage Bake

1 (16 ounce) container cottage cheese
1 (10 ounce) package frozen broccoli, thawed, chopped, and drained
¾ cup sharp Cheddar cheese, shredded
1 (7 ounce) jar roasted red peppers, well drained and chopped
4 eggs, beaten
3 tablespoons Parmesan cheese
3 tablespoons plain dry breadcrumbs

Heat oven to 350 degrees. Mix all ingredients until well blended. Pour into 9-inch pie plate sprayed with cooking spray. Bake 45 minutes or until center is set. Let stand 10 minutes before cutting into slices to serve.

Note: This recipe doubles and freezes well. Can be made using all low-fat dairy products.

Andrea Bassett

Broccoli and Rice Casserole

- 2 cups cooked rice
- 1 box frozen broccoli, chopped
- ½ cup onion, chopped
- ½ stick butter or margarine
- 1 (8 ounce) Cheese Whiz or Velveeta
- 1 can cream of mushroom soup
- ½ cup water

Cook rice and broccoli according to package directions and set aside. Sauté onion in butter; add cheese, soup, and water. Simmer until well blended. Fold in rice and broccoli. Pour into buttered or sprayed baking dish and bake at 325 degrees for 40 to 45 minutes.

Wylene Coffee

Cabbage Parmesan

- ¼ cup slivered almonds
- 1 medium head of green cabbage
- ¼ cup butter or margarine (I use olive oil.)
- 1 garlic clove, minced
- 1 teaspoon Italian herb seasoning
- ⅓ cup Parmesan cheese, grated
- Salt and pepper to taste

Brown almonds in a medium skillet, stirring occasionally to prevent burning. Remove and set aside. Cut cabbage into ½ inch slices and discard core. Separate cabbage into strips and layer in skillet with butter, garlic, seasoning, salt, and pepper. Cook over medium-high heat until tender, stirring frequently. Garnish with Parmesan cheese and toasted almonds.

Joy Perren

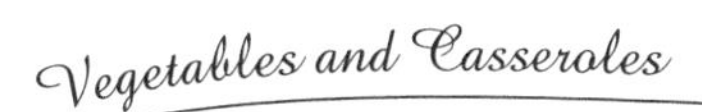

Marinated Carrots

- 2 pounds carrots
- 1 onion, cut into rings
- 1 green bell pepper, cut into rings
- 1 teaspoon Worcestershire sauce
- 1 cup sugar
- 1 teaspoon mustard
- ½ cup salad oil
- ¾ cup vinegar

Dice and boil carrots in salt water until tender; drain and cool. Layer carrots, bell pepper, and onion. Mix remaining ingredients and pour over carrots. Refrigerate overnight.

Judy Drury

Carrot Soufflé

- 1½ pounds of carrots, freshly cooked
- ¾ cup butter, melted
- 1½ teaspoons baking powder
- 1½ cups sugar
- ¼ cup plain flour
- ¼ teaspoon cinnamon
- ¼ teaspoon nutmeg
- 3 large eggs

Peel and slice carrots. Cook in boiling water until tender; drain and blend until smooth. Blend in remaining ingredients and place in a well-greased casserole dish 350 degree oven for about 1 hour. (I usually double this recipe.)

Joy Paulk

Corn Casserole

- 1 can whole kernel corn
- 1 can cream corn (yellow, sweet)
- 1 stick butter
- 2 eggs, beaten
- ½ to 1 tablespoon minced onion or onion flakes (I use 1 teaspoon onion powder.)
- 1 box Jiffy cornbread mix
- ½ cup water
- Salt and pepper to taste

Melt butter and set aside. Mix beaten eggs, water, and onion. Drain a little water out of whole kernel corn. Put both cans of corn in dish. Pour melted butter over corn. Pour egg mixture over corn. Add Jiffy mix and mix with fork. Bake at 350 degrees in a 8 x 8 or 9 x 9 dish for 50 to 60 minutes. A 9 x 11 or 9 x 13 dish bakes for 35-45 minutes. Check with toothpick in middle of casserole to see if done.

Kelly Lastinger

Corn Soufflé

- 3 packages frozen Stouffer's corn soufflé
- 1 package frozen corn
- 1 (4 ounce) package cream cheese
- 4 tablespoons butter
- 3 eggs
- Salt and pepper to taste

Thaw frozen items and mix all of the ingredients. In a soufflé dish, bake for 1 hour at 350 degrees until brown on top and bubbly.

In Memory of Judy Evans

Corn Pudding

- 1 large can cream-style corn
- 1 can white shoepeg corn
- 2 eggs, beaten
- 1 stick butter
- 1 (8½ ounce) box Jiffy corn muffin mix
- 1 (8 ounce) sour cream

Mix all ingredients together well. Put in a 9 x 12 buttered casserole dish and bake at 350 degrees for about 45 minutes or until firm in the middle.

Pam Lewis

Cranberry Casserole

- 3 cups unpeeled apples, chopped
- 1 pound raw cranberries
- 1¼ cups sugar
- 1½ cups quick-cooking oats, uncooked
- ½ cup flour
- ⅓ cup pecans, chopped
- ½ cup butter, melted

Combine apples, cranberries, and sugar. Put in oblong casserole dish. Top with mixture of remaining ingredients. Bake 350 degrees for 1 hour. Can be used as a casserole with meat or topped with whipped cream and used as a dessert.

Note: This was one of two cranberry recipes that were staples at Christmas dinner.

In Memory of Mrs. Ouida Preston

Scalloped Eggplant

- 1 large eggplant
- 3 eggs, beaten
- ½ cup milk
- 1 tablespoon flour
- 1 large onion, grated
- ¾ pound sharp Cheddar cheese, grated
- 4 tablespoons butter or margarine
- 9 to 10 saltine crackers, crushed
- Salt and pepper to taste

Wash eggplant and peel (save peelings). Cut eggplant into large bite-size pieces. Place eggplant into saucepan with enough water to steam, and lay peels on top. Cook until tender (about 5 minutes). Remove and discard the peels, and drain the eggplant. Combine milk, flour, and eggs, and add mixture to drained eggplant. Stir in crackers, salt, pepper, onion, and cheese. Pour mixture into a buttered casserole. Sprinkle cheese over top. Bake at 325 degrees for 40 or 45 minutes or until brown.

Ginny Lockwood

Green Beans with Garlic

- 3 pounds green beans, trimmed
- 3 large garlic cloves, thinly sliced
- 2 tablespoons olive oil
- 1 teaspoon salt
- ½ teaspoon pepper, freshly ground

Cook beans in boiling salted water 5 minutes or just until tender; drain well. In a Dutch oven over medium heat, cook ½ of garlic in 1 tablespoon of hot oil for 1 minute or until golden. Add half of beans and sprinkle with ½ teaspoon salt and ¼ teaspoon pepper. Cook, stirring constantly for 3 minutes. Transfer to a serving dish. Repeat procedure with remaining garlic, oil, beans, salt, and pepper.

Sara Allen

Pineapple Casserole

- 2½ cups crushed pineapple, undrained
- ½ cup sugar
- 2 rounded tablespoons flour
- ¼ teaspoon salt
- ½ cup sharp cheese, shredded
- 4 slices bread (crust removed), buttered on both sides and diced

Layer pineapple in casserole dish. Mix sugar, flour, and salt and sprinkle over pineapple. Layer cheese over this mixture. Sprinkle bread over top. Bake uncovered at 350 degrees for 30 minutes.

In Memory of Mrs. Lois Meeks

Pineapple Casserole

- 1 cup sugar
- 6 tablespoons all-purpose flour
- 2 cups sharp Cheddar cheese, grated
- 2 (20 ounce) cans pineapple chunks, drained
- 6 tablespoons pineapple juice (reserved from pineapple chunks)
- 1 cup cracker crumbs (Ritz)
- 8 tablespoons butter (1 stick), melted
- Extra butter for greasing

Preheat the oven to 350 degrees. Grease a medium-size casserole dish with butter. In a large bowl, stir together the sugar and flour. Gradually stir in the cheese. Add the drained pineapple chunks and stir until the ingredients are well combined. Pour the mixture into the prepared casserole dish. In another bowl, combine the cracker crumbs, melted butter, and reserved pineapple juice. Stir with a rubber spatula until evenly blended. Spread the crumb mixture on top of pineapple mixture. Bake for 25 to 30 minutes or until golden brown.

Jenny Lott

Curried Fruit

- ¾ stick butter
- 1 cup brown sugar, firmly packed
- 1 teaspoon curry powder
- 1 (20 ounce) can of peach slices
- 1 (20 ounce) can pear halves
- 1 (20 ounce) can pineapple slices
- 1 (15 ounce) jar sliced apple rings
- 1 jar of maraschino cherries

Combine butter, sugar, and curry powder. Bring to a boil. Drain fruit. Arrange in 2-quart baking dish and pour hot sauce over it. Bake in oven at 350 degrees about 20 minutes until fruit is bubbly. Serve hot! Very good with duck, ham, or pork.

Marian Brawner Mizell

Cheesy Hash Brown Potato Casserole

- 2 pounds frozen hash browns, defrosted
- ½ cup butter, melted
- 1 teaspoon salt
- ¼ teaspoon pepper
- 1 cup milk
- 1 cup cream cheese or sour cream
- 2 cups sharp cheese (Colby or Cheddar)

Mix above ingredients and put in a 9 x 13 pan sprayed with cooking spray.

Topping:

- 2 cups corn flakes or Ritz crackers, crushed
- ½ cup butter, melted

Melt butter and add corn flakes; mix. Sprinkle over top of potato casserole and bake at 350 degrees for about 45 minutes.

Lynn Meeks

Potato Casserole

- 5 pound bag red skin potatoes
- 1 package ranch dressing mix
- 1 bottle bacon bits
- 1 cup buttermilk
- 1 stick butter
- 4 cups sharp Cheddar cheese, shredded
- 1 (8 ounce) sour cream
- Garlic salt and pepper to taste

Wash potatoes, quarter, and boil until tender. Do not peel! Drain potatoes and add all the ingredients except for 2 cups of cheese. Use a hand mixer and mix but leave lumpy. Pour into a buttered casserole dish, top with the remaining cheese, and bake in 350 degree oven for 30 minutes.

Tonia Guthrie

Vincent's Gratin Dauphinois

(Scalloped Potatoes)

- 1 clove garlic
- 1 cup heavy cream
- 2 teaspoons white pepper
- 4 medium baking potatoes, thinly sliced crossways
- 2 teaspoons salt
- ½ cup Gruyere cheese

Crush garlic and spread in bottom of 8 x 8 pan. Layer the potatoes with cream in pan and season with salt and pepper. Bake for 40 minutes at 375 degrees or until gratin is golden on top. Sprinkle with cheese and brown top.

Allison Brice

Scalloped Potatoes

- 2 pounds potatoes, peeled and thinly sliced
- 3 cups whipping cream
- ¼ cup fresh flat-leaf parsley, chopped
- 2 garlic cloves, chopped
- 1½ teaspoons salt
- ¼ teaspoon freshly ground pepper
- ½ cup Parmesan cheese, grated

Preheat oven to 400 degrees. Layer potatoes in a 9 x 13 inch or 3-quart baking dish. Stir together cream and next 4 ingredients in a large bowl. Pour cream mixture over potatoes. Bake at 400 degrees for 30 minutes. Sprinkle with cheese. Bake 15 to 20 minutes or until bubbly and golden brown.

Eleanor Sammons

Herbed Potatoes

- ¼ cup margarine, melted
- 1 package onion soup mix
- 2 teaspoons rosemary
- 2 teaspoons dill seed
- 3 large potatoes, sliced

Mix all together and bake covered at 350 degrees for 1 hour.

Jeanne Soar

Sweet Potato Soufflé

- 3 cups of sweet potatoes (about 5 large ones)
- ½ cup milk
- ⅓ cup margarine
- 1 cup sugar
- 2 eggs
- 1 teaspoon vanilla
- 10 marshmallows

Boil sweet potatoes until done. Peel and place in mixing bowl. Add 10 marshmallows to make creamy while hot. Mix remaining ingredients and pour into baking dish. Top with additional marshmallows or topping.

Topping:

- ½ cup light brown sugar
- ¼ cup margarine, melted
- ½ cup pecans, chopped
- ¼ cup self-rising flour

Melt margarine. Mix remaining ingredients. Crumble over potato mixture. Bake at 375 degrees for 25 minutes.

June Waldron

Sweet Potato Soufflé

- 3 cups sweet potatoes, cooked and mashed
- 1 cup sugar
- 3 eggs, lightly beaten
- ½ cup milk
- ½ stick butter
- 1 tablespoon vanilla

Topping:

- ½ stick butter
- 1 cup brown sugar
- ½ cup self-rising flour
- 1 cup pecans, chopped

Combine all ingredients except topping. Put in buttered baking dish. Mix topping with hands. Spread on sweet potatoes. Bake at 350 degrees until topping is light brown, about 15 or 20 minutes.

Judy Drury and Grandmother Amy Meeks

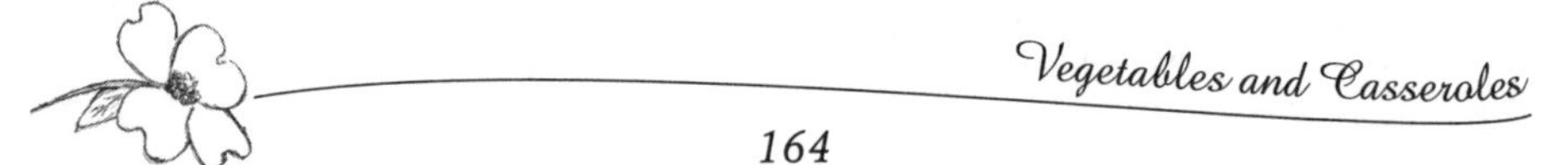

Honey-Roasted Sweet Potatoes

- 2 pounds sweet potatoes, peeled and sliced in 1-inch pieces
- 2 tablespoons olive oil
- 2 tablespoons honey
- 1½ teaspoons fresh lemon juice
- ¼ teaspoon salt

Preheat oven to 350 degrees. Place sweet potatoes in a 9 x 13 inch baking dish. In a small bowl, mix olive oil, honey, lemon juice, and salt. Pour mixture over potatoes and toss to coat. Bake for 1 hour or until tender, stirring occasionally. So good!

Dot McKinnon

Spinach Delight

- 2 eggs whites
- 1 (20 ounce) frozen spinach, thawed and chopped
- ¼ cup water
- 1 onion, diced
- 4 garlic cloves, pressed
- 1 chicken bouillon cube, crumbled
- ¾ cup Cheddar cheese, grated
- 2 tablespoons flour
- ¼ teaspoon pepper
- 2 whole eggs, plus yolks from eggs above
- 1½ cups low-fat sour cream
- 1 cup breadcrumbs

Preheat oven to 350 degrees. Beat egg whites until stiff; set aside. Squeeze water out of spinach. Combine ¼ cup water, onions, garlic, and bouillon cube in nonstick pan over medium heat. Simmer until onions are tender. Add cheese and stir until melted. Sprinkle flour and pepper over mixture and stir. Transfer mixture into large mixing bowl. Stir in spinach, eggs, and sour cream; mix well. Fold in egg whites (you may have to rebeat them before adding). Sprinkle half breadcrumbs in the bottom of an 8 x 8 baking pan. Pour in spinach mixture gently over breadcrumbs; sprinkle with remaining breadcrumbs. Bake 40 to 50 minutes or until center is firm.

Suzanna Bassett

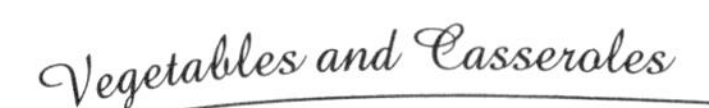

Layered Vegetable Bake

1 (6 ounce) package stuffing mix for chicken
5 eggs, divided
1½ cups Cheddar and Monterey Jack cheeses, shredded and divided
1 onion, chopped
1 (10 ounce) package frozen spinach, thawed, chopped, and drained
½ cup red pepper strips
2 tomatoes, sliced

Preheat oven to 400 degrees. Prepare stuffing as directed on package. Add 1 egg and mix well. Press into bottom of greased 9-inch square baking dish; sprinkle with ¾ cup cheese. Cook and stir onions in medium nonstick skillet sprayed with cooking spray 5 minutes or until tender. Remove from heat; stir in spinach. Spoon over cheese layer in baking dish; top with peppers. Cover with layers of remaining cheese and spinach mixture. Beat remaining eggs; pour over ingredients in baking dish. Top with tomatoes. Bake 35 to 40 minutes or until center is set.

Alena Bassett

Squash Casserole

3 cups cooked squash (about 2 large bags frozen)
1 egg, beaten
½ cup mayonnaise
1 tablespoon sugar
1 cup Cheddar cheese, grated and divided
1½ cups Ritz cracker crumbs, divided
½ stick margarine
Dash of cayenne pepper to taste
Salt and pepper to taste

Put well-drained, hot squash in a large mixing bowl. Add egg, mayonnaise, margarine, sugar, half of cheese, and half of cracker crumbs. Mix well. Put in buttered casserole dish and top with rest of crushed cracker crumbs and remaining cheese. Bake for 25 minutes at 350 degrees.

June Waldron

Squash Casserole

- 3 cups cooked squash, mashed
- 2 eggs, beaten
- 1 cup onion, chopped
- 2 cups Ritz cracker crumbs
- 1 cup evaporated milk
- ¾ stick of butter
- 1 cup sharp Cheddar cheese, grated
- Salt and pepper to taste

Beat eggs and add all other ingredients. Butter casserole dish. Bake 40 minutes at 375 degrees.

Gloria Cloud

Best-Ever Squash Casserole

- 1 pound yellow squash, diced
- 1 large onion, diced (preferably Vidalia)
- 3 to 4 slices bacon, fried and crumbled
- 1 (8 ounce) carton sour cream
- 1 cup Cheddar cheese, shredded
- 8 to 10 Ritz crackers

Butter a large casserole dish. Preheat oven to 350 degrees. In a large frying pan, cook bacon. Remove bacon, crumble, and save for later. In bacon grease, add onion and squash. Cook over low heat until tender. In a buttered casserole dish, combine cooked squash, onions, crumbled bacon, sour cream, and cheese. Sprinkle with crushed crackers. Bake about 25 to 30 minutes.

Joy Perren

Southern Tomato Pie

- 1 frozen deep pie crust
- 1 cup mayonnaise (light or regular)
- 1 cup Cheddar cheese, shredded
- 1 cup mozzarella cheese, shredded
- ¼ teaspoon black pepper
- 1 small or ½ large onion, sliced
- 1⅓ pounds ripe Roma or 3 regular tomatoes, sliced and drained on paper towel
- Olive oil

Prick the sides and bottom of crust with a fork. Place in 350 degree oven for 10 to 12 minutes. Meantime, in a bowl stir together mayonnaise and 1 cup Cheddar cheese. Sprinkle the bottom of the partially cooked crust with 1 cup mozzarella cheese. Sauté onions in olive oil (do not brown). Put onions on top of mozzarella cheese. Put ½ of drained tomato slices over mozzarella cheese and sautéed onions. (You may put some seasoning on tomatoes.) Add ½ of mayonnaise mixture and layer remaining tomato slices. Add remaining mayonnaise mixture, and sprinkle top with extra cheese. Bake at 350 degrees for 35 to 40 minutes. Remove to rack and cool at least 10 minutes before cutting into wedges. I bake the pie on a cookie sheet to be safe. Helps when taking it out of oven!

Charlotte Bacon

"A generous person will be blessed,
for he shares his food with the poor."

Proverbs 22:9
(HCSB)

Tomato Casserole

- 2 cans flaky biscuits
- 1 (8 ounce) sour cream
- 1 cup Cheddar cheese, grated
- 1 cup mayonnaise
- 5 (or more) tomatoes, thinly sliced
- 1 green bell pepper, chopped (optional)
- 1 onion or more, chopped
- Lawry's seasoned salt
- Paprika, pepper, parsley flakes and dill weed
- Butter, melted

Preheat oven to 350 degrees. Spray a 9 x 13 inch pan. Press out biscuits in bottom of the pan. Brush biscuits with melted butter. Sprinkle with parsley flakes. Place a layer of sliced tomatoes over the biscuits. Sprinkle the tomatoes with the seasoned salt. Next, add a layer of the chopped bell pepper and onions. Repeat this two more times - tomatoes, seasoned salt, bell pepper, and onion. Combine the sour cream, mayonnaise, pepper, and a pinch of dill weed. Spread this over the top of the final layer. Sprinkle cheese on top. Bake at 350 degrees for 45 minutes.

Note: You may substitute 1 large package of refrigerated crescent rolls for the biscuits. Follow the same steps as with the biscuits.

Sherri M. Jenkins

Cabbage Casserole

- 1 small head cabbage, diced
- 1 small onion, diced
- 2 cups sharp Cheddar cheese, shredded
- 1 stack Townhouse crackers, crushed
- 1 stick margarine or butter
- 1 can cream of chicken soup
- ½ cup mayonnaise
- Salt and pepper to taste

Dice cabbage and layer in casserole dish. Place onion on top. Melt ½ stick margarine and pour over top. Toss together. Sprinkle with salt and pepper. Mix cream of chicken and mayonnaise and spread over top. Mix crushed crackers, cheese, and remaining melted margarine. Crumble over top of casserole. Cover with tin foil and bake at 350 degrees for 35 to 45 minutes.

Rhonda Saeed
Administrative Secretary

Tomato Pie

Crust:

- 2¼ cups biscuit mix
- ½ cup milk
- ½ teaspoon dried thyme

Filling:

- 1 onion, thinly sliced
- 6 ripe tomatoes, peeled and sliced
- 1 teaspoon sugar
- 2 tablespoons basil, freshly chopped
- 2 tablespoons chives, freshly chopped
- 2 cups mayonnaise
- 1 teaspoon fresh lemon juice
- 6 ounces sharp Cheddar cheese, grated
- Salt and pepper

Preheat oven to 375 degrees. To make the crust, place the biscuit mix and thyme in a large bowl. Quickly stir in the milk with a fork until just blended. Press dough into a greased 10-inch pie pan. Arrange the onion on top of the crust. Layer the tomatoes, sugar, salt, pepper, and herbs on top. In a medium bowl, mix mayonnaise, lemon juice, and cheese. Spread over tomatoes and bake until golden and bubbly on top, about 30-40 minutes. Serve hot or at room temperature.

Jenny Lott

Veg-All Casserole

- 2 cans of Veg-All, drained
- 1 cup mayonnaise
- 1 cup sharp Cheddar cheese, grated
- 1 cup celery, chopped
- ½ onion, chopped
- 1 can cream of celery soup, undiluted
- ½ stick margarine
- Ritz crackers

Mix all ingredients except Ritz crackers and ½ stick of melted margarine. Pour into a large casserole and cover with foil. Bake at 325 degrees for 30 minutes; remove foil. Combine crackers and margarine and sprinkle on top of casserole. Bake 10 more minutes.

Judy Drury

Marinated Vegetables

- 1 can shoepeg corn
- 1 can French-style green beans
- 1 can Le Sueur sweet peas
- ½ ounce jar diced pimentos
- ½ cup celery, chopped
- ½ cup green peppers, chopped

Pour all vegetables in colander to drain; set aside. In a saucepan combine:

- 6 tablespoons sugar
- ½ tablespoon pepper
- 1 teaspoon salt
- ½ cup vegetable oil
- ¾ cup white vinegar

Stir all ingredients over medium heat. Cool liquid and pour over vegetables. Keep refrigerated.

Emma Lou C. Aughinbaugh

Dressing

- 2 eggs
- 1 teaspoon salt added to eggs
- 2 sticks melted Oleo
- 1 pint or 2 cups milk
- 4 or 5 pieces toasted bread
- 2½ cups corn meal
- 1 large chopped onion
- 4 teaspoons baking powder
- Pepper if desired
- Turkey broth

Beat eggs. Add salt, milk, toasted bread crumbled; add onion, meal and just before putting in oven, add baking powder. Mix well. Cook at 350 degrees until done. About 1 hour. Serve with turkey broth.

Note: This is an original recipe that was found several generations after the death of Mrs. Coffee. The terminology is original to the recipe. Mr. A. F. Coffee was one of the first original Deacons of First Baptist Church.

In Memory of Mrs. A. F. (Lena) Coffee
WMU President 1920-1922

Old-Fashioned Dressing and Gravy

Egg Bread:

- **3 eggs**
- **2 cups buttermilk**
- **2 cups self-rising "Hot Rise" meal**
- **½ teaspoon soda**
- **2 teaspoons baking powder**
- **2 sticks butter, melted**
- **½ teaspoon salt**
- **1 teaspoon sugar**

Beat eggs; add buttermilk. Mix soda, baking powder, salt, and sugar with meal and beat into egg mixture. Add melted butter. Mix well. Take 1 to 1½ cups of batter and set aside for gravy. Pour into greased pan. Cook at 350 degrees until browned.

Dressing:

- **1 loaf bread**
- **2 medium onions, chopped**
- **1 can cream of celery**
- **4 eggs, boiled and chopped**
- **½ teaspoon pepper**
- **1 cup butter, melted**
- **1 can cream of mushroom soup**
- **1 can cream of chicken soup**
- **Turkey or chicken broth**

Make dressing while the egg bread is hot. Crumble bread loaf. Soften with turkey broth or chicken broth. If not enough turkey broth, use chicken broth or chicken bouillon cubes. Add eggs, melted butter, black pepper, onions, and soups. If too thin, add more bread. Bake at 350 degrees until brown and toothpick comes out clean from the middle. For oyster dressing, add 2 small cans of oysters and use juice instead of broth to soften the bread.

Gravy:

- **1 cup of dressing**
- **6 boiled eggs, chopped**
- **1 can cream of mushroom soup**
- **1 can cream of chicken soup**
- **4 pieces skinless chicken (short thighs, necks and backs)**

Boil chicken; pull off bone and cut up into small bite-size pieces. Save broth from turkey or chicken. Pour off fat. (You can refrigerate and take off fat.) Mix all ingredients together into a pot on the stove. Simmer on low, stirring occasionally to make sure it will not scorch on the bottom. To thicken, add cornstarch. To thin, add more broth (chicken broth).

Lynn Meeks

Crockpot Mac and Cheese

1 (8 ounce) package cooked elbow macaroni
1 large can evaporated milk
½ cup milk
1 teaspoon salt
2 cups sharp Cheddar cheese, grated
1 cup medium Cheddar cheese, grated
1 stick oleo (margarine)
2 eggs, beaten

Mix all ingredients together saving the eggs for last. Pour into crockpot and top with added cheese. Cook on low 3-3½ hours.

In Memory of Mrs. Vera Turner

Macaroni and Cheese Deluxe

1 (8 ounce) package elbow macaroni
2 cups small curd cream-style cottage cheese
1 cup sour cream
1 egg, slightly beaten
¾ teaspoon salt
8 ounces sharp Cheddar cheese, shredded
Paprika
Dash pepper

Cook macaroni according to package directions; drain well. Combine cottage cheese, sour cream, egg, salt, and pepper. Add shredded cheese, mixing well. Add macaroni. Pour into a greased 9 x 9 x 2 baking dish. Sprinkle with paprika. Bake at 350 degrees for 45 minutes.

Paula Thomas

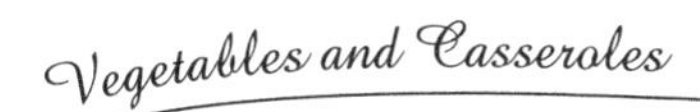

Rice Casserole

- ½ stick of margarine or butter
- 2 onions, chopped
- 1½ cups rice, uncooked
- 2 cans beef consommé
- 1 large can mushrooms and juice (bits and pieces)
- 1 teaspoon curry powder

Melt margarine in frying pan over medium heat. Add chopped onions and rice. Cook and stir 10 minutes (until rice starts to pop). Add consommé, mushrooms with juice, and curry powder. Stir and put in buttered casserole dish. Let stand 3-4 hours. Bake in covered casserole at 350 degrees for 1½ hours.

In Memory of Mrs. Ferne Roadcap

Brown Rice

- 1 cup regular rice, uncooked (long grain rice)
- ½ package dry onion soup mix
- 1 can mushrooms, drained (optional)
- 2 cans beef consommé
- ½ cup butter

Put all ingredients in casserole dish; stir and cover. Bake for one hour at 350 degrees.

Bro. Shep Johnson
Senior Pastor

Red Beans and Rice

- 1 can red kidney beans, washed
- 1 can red kidney beans in sauce (do not wash)
- 2 cans Ro-Tel tomatoes with chiles (mild)
- 1 red onion, chopped
- 1 package sausage, sliced (Polish Kielbasa)
- ½ teaspoon black pepper
- ½ teaspoon salt
- ¼ teaspoon Tony Chachere's Spice N' Herb seasoning

Stir-fry onions and sausage (add extra-virgin olive oil, if needed). Add remaining ingredients. Slowly cook for 1½ hours. Serve over cooked rice.

Hattie Harkleroad

Entrées

**"…If anyone wishes to come after Me, he must deny himself,
And take up his cross daily and follow Me."**

Luke 9:23
(NASB)

Entrées

Ann's Fried Chicken

1½ - 2 pounds boneless chicken breasts
½ cup self-rising flour
½ teaspoon sea salt
1 teaspoon dry mustard
½ teaspoon paprika
½ teaspoon pepper
⅓ cup half-and-half
Canola oil

Wash chicken and pat dry. Place chicken in large bowl. Pour ⅓ cup of half-and-half over chicken and mix well. Set aside. Mix flour, salt, dry mustard, paprika, and pepper. Heat oil (¼ inch) in large skillet. Drain half-and-half from chicken and coat each piece with flour mixture. Cook chicken in oil over medium heat 12 to 15 minutes. Reduce heat, cover tightly, and simmer 25 to 30 minutes or until tender. Turn chicken one time. Remove cover for last 5 minutes to crisp chicken.

Ann Freeman

Down-Home Chicken

½ cup flour
1 teaspoon salt
½ teaspoon pepper
1 broiler/fryer chicken, cut up
¼ cup cooking oil, or more if needed (coconut oil works great)
Hot cooked rice

Sauce:

⅔ cup lemon juice
⅔ cup ketchup
⅔ cup cane syrup
¼ cup Worcestershire sauce
¼ teaspoon ground cloves
Salt and pepper

In a Ziploc bag, combine flour, salt, and pepper. Shake chicken a few pieces at a time in the bag to coat. Meanwhile, heat oil in skillet. Brown chicken pieces on all sides. In a bowl, combine sauce ingredients and pour over chicken. Bring to a boil, reduce heat, and simmer for 35 to 40 minutes until chicken juices run clear. Serve over cooked rice.

Cassandra Collins

Chicken Artichoke Bake

- 4 boneless chicken breasts (skin on optional)
- 1 egg
- ½ cup milk
- 2 cups cornflakes, crushed
- 1 cup fresh mushrooms, sliced
- 1 (15 ounce) can artichoke hearts, rinsed and drained
- ½ cup canned chicken broth
- ½ cup evaporated milk
- 1 can cream of chicken soup
- Salt and pepper to taste

Beat 1 egg and ½ cup milk. Dip chicken in egg/milk mixture. Season with salt and pepper and coat with crushed cornflakes. Place in greased baking dish. Place mushrooms and artichokes in baking dish with chicken breasts. Mix together chicken broth, chicken soup, and evaporated milk. Pour over chicken and cover with foil. Preheat oven to 350 degrees. Bake for 30 minutes. Remove foil and cook for an additional 15 minutes. Optional: Serve over rice or pasta.

JoAnne Lewis

Bacon - Wrapped Chicken

- 6 - 8 boneless chicken breasts
- 1 (16 ounce) sour cream
- 1 (4.5 ounce) package dried beef
- 1 large can cream of mushroom soup
- Bacon

Layer bottom of pan with dried beef. Wrap chicken with bacon and place on top of dried beef. Mix sour cream and soup and pour over chicken. Bake at 350 degrees for 1 hour. Serve over yellow rice.

Norma Lynn Hand

Marinated Baked Chicken Breasts

Marinade:

2 cups sour cream
½ cup lemon juice
4 teaspoons Worcestershire sauce
2 teaspoons celery salt
2 teaspoons paprika
½ teaspoon garlic salt
1 teaspoon pepper

Chicken:

12 chicken breasts or 24 tenderloins
1½ cups Ritz crackers, crushed
1½ cups saltine crackers, crushed
1 cup butter or margarine

Combine marinade ingredients. Place chicken in marinade; cover. Let stand in refrigerator overnight. Remove chicken from marinade and roll in combined cracker crumbs. Arrange in shallow dish. Melt butter and spoon over chicken. Bake at 300 degrees for 1 hour 45 minutes or at 350 degrees for 1 hour.

Teresa Holliday
Wife of Bro. B. J. Holliday
Minister of Music

Italian Chicken

4 chicken breasts
1 package Italian seasoning mix
¼ cup water
1 can cream of chicken soup
1 (8 ounce) package cream cheese
1 small can mushrooms

Combine Italian seasoning mix with water. Cut chicken breasts in strips, pour mixture over chicken, and cook for 3 to 4 hours in slow cooker. Mix cream of chicken soup and cream cheese and pour over chicken. Add mushrooms and cook for 1 hour more. Serve over spinach noodles or rice.

Marvelyne Fletcher

Chicken Strata

First Layer:

- **3 slices white loaf bread, trimmed and cut in squares**
- **2 cups chicken, cooked and chopped**
- **1 small jar pimentos**
- **¼ cup green pepper, chopped**
- **½ cup celery, finely chopped**
- **½ cup onions, finely chopped**
- **½ cup mayonnaise**

Put bread squares in 9 x 12 baking dish. Mix chicken, pimentos, green pepper, celery, onions, and mayonnaise; pour this mixture over bread in casserole dish.

Second Layer:

- **3 slices white loaf bread, trimmed and cut in squares**
- **2 eggs**
- **1½ cups milk**
- **1 can cream of mushroom soup**
- **Grated cheese**

Put 3 more slices of bread pieces on top of first layer. Mix eggs and milk and beat slightly. Pour over bread. Spread cream of mushroom soup over this. Top with grated cheese. Bake at 325 degrees for 50 minutes. Serve with steamed broccoli for a complete meal.

In Memory of Mrs. Lou Ann Walker

Poppy Seed Chicken

- **3 pounds boneless chicken breasts, cooked and cubed**
- **2 cans cream of chicken soup**
- **1 (8 ounce) sour cream**
- **1 sleeve Ritz crackers, crushed**
- **3 - 4 tablespoons poppy seeds**
- **1½ sticks butter, melted**

Place chicken in buttered casserole dish. Mix sour cream, soup, and poppy seeds. Pour over chicken. Mix crackers and butter, and sprinkle over the top of casserole. Bake on 350 degrees for 30 to 40 minutes.

Kristy Weems

Oven-Barbecued Chicken

- 1 (3 pound) fryer, cut into serving pieces
- 3 tablespoons butter
- 1 large onion, finely chopped
- 1 cup water
- ⅔ cup ketchup
- ½ teaspoon salt
- ⅛ teaspoon black pepper
- 1 teaspoon vinegar
- 3 teaspoons brown sugar
- 1 tablespoon prepared mustard
- 2 tablespoons Worcestershire sauce
- ½ cup sweet pickle juice
- Flour

Flour chicken as for frying. Roast for 30 minutes in a preheated 350 degree oven. Melt butter in a frying pan; add onion and brown lightly. Add water and remaining ingredients. Bring to a boil and simmer for 5 minutes. Pour sauce over chicken and continue roasting for 30 minutes longer.

Sue Bordeaux

Chicken Pie

- 1 whole chicken, cut up and cooked
- 1 can cream of chicken soup
- 1½ cups chicken broth
- 1 small onion, finely chopped and sautéed in 1 tablespoon margarine
- 3 eggs, hard cooked and finely chopped

Filling:

Cover and cook chicken in water until tender. Remove chicken and reserve broth. Remove chicken from bones and line bottom of a greased casserole dish. Mix the 1½ cups reserved chicken broth, cream of chicken soup, onions, and cooked eggs. Pour over chicken. Top with crust.

Crust:

- 1 cup self-rising flour
- 1 stick butter
- 1 cup milk

Mix and pour over chicken. Bake at 350 degrees until browned.

Virginia Hendrix

Turkey Pot Pie

- ½ cup mayonnaise or salad dressing
- 2 tablespoons all-purpose flour
- 1 cup milk
- 1½ cups turkey, cooked and chopped
- 1 (10 ounce) package frozen mixed vegetables, thawed and drained
- 1 teaspoon chicken-flavored bouillon granules
- ⅛ teaspoon pepper
- 1 (4 ounce) package refrigerated crescent rolls

Melt mayonnaise in a heavy saucepan over low heat; add flour, stirring until smooth. Cook for 1 minute, stirring constantly. Gradually add milk. Cook over medium heat, stirring constantly until mixture is thickened and bubbly. Stir in turkey and next 3 ingredients. Cook over medium heat until thoroughly heated. Spoon into a 9-inch quiche dish or pie plate. Unroll crescent rolls and place rectangular pieces side by side on a lightly floured surface, firmly pressing perforations to seal. Roll dough into a 10-inch square. Cut into 1-inch strips and arrange in a lattice design over turkey mixture. Bake at 370 degrees for 15 to 20 minutes or until golden brown. Let stand 10 minutes before serving.

Note: This is a great way to use leftover turkey during the holidays – and good too!

Donya Gillespie

Easy Chicken Pie

- 3 cups chicken, cooked and chopped
- 1 can cream of celery soup
- 1½ soup cans chicken broth (homemade or canned)

Crust:

- 1 cup self-rising flour
- 1 cup milk
- 1 stick butter, melted

Spray casserole dish with cooking spray. Place chicken in casserole and pour combined soup and broth over the chicken. (Soup and broth MUST be stirred together or the crust will not form on top.) Combine crust ingredients and pour over chicken mixture. Bake at 350 degrees for about 1 hour or until pie is bubbly and crust is browned. (Double the recipe for a 9 x 13 casserole).

Deidre Taft

Cheese Cache Chicken

- 2 whole chicken breasts, skinned, deboned and halved
- 2 strips Monterey Jack cheese
- 2 eggs
- ¼ teaspoon sage
- 1 teaspoon grated Parmesan cheese
- ¼ teaspoon salt
- ¼ teaspoon pepper
- 1 tablespoon parsley, minced
- Flour
- Clarified butter

Cut pocket in each chicken breast. Place a strip of cheese with ⅛ teaspoon of sage in each pocket and chill for 1 hour. Beat together eggs, salt, pepper, Parmesan cheese, and parsley. Dredge breasts in flour and dip in egg mixture. Sauté in clarified butter until golden brown on both sides. (May refrigerate at this point and bake later.) Transfer to baking dish and bake in a 375 degree preheated oven for about 8-10 minutes or until done.

Lynn Schofield

Chicken Licken

- 1 (8 ounce) cream cheese
- 3 tablespoons butter, melted
- 2 cups chicken, cooked and cubed
- ½ teaspoon salt
- ½ teaspoon pepper
- 3 tablespoons milk
- 3 tablespoons onion
- 1 (8 ounce) package crescent rolls
- ¼ cup butter, melted

Preheat oven to 350 degrees. Blend cream cheese and 3 tablespoons butter until smooth. Add all other ingredients except the ¼ cup butter and crescent rolls. On a large lightly greased flat pan, separate rolls into 4 squares and seal the line in each square. Place desired amount of chicken mixture in the middle of each square and seal all edges. Put butter over the rolls. Bake 15 to 20 minutes.

Note: Try as a crescent ring! I like to serve fresh steamed broccoli with this dish.

Cynthia Deal

Chicken with White Sauce

- 1 (8 ounce) sour cream
- 1 can cream of mushroom soup
- ½ cup white cooking sherry
- 4 to 6 chicken breasts
- Paprika

Place chicken breasts in baking dish. Combine sour cream, cream of mushroom soup, and cooking sherry; pour over chicken. Sprinkle with paprika. Cover dish with foil and bake at 350 degrees for at least 1 hour. Serve with white rice.

Faye Ray

Chicken Packets

- 2 tablespoons olive oil
- 4 chicken breast halves, skinned and deboned, cut into 1-inch pieces
- 1 cup onion, chopped
- ½ cup green bell pepper, chopped
- ½ cup sour cream
- ½ (10¾ ounce) can cream of mushroom soup, undiluted
- ½ teaspoon garlic salt
- ¼ teaspoon pepper
- 3 (8 ounce) cans refrigerated crescent dinner rolls
- 1 (4 ounce) cup mozzarella cheese, shredded

Garnish: fresh parsley sprigs

Pour oil into a medium skillet and place over medium-high heat until hot. Add chicken, onion, and bell pepper; cook, stirring constantly, 5 minutes or until chicken is tender. Drain. Combine chicken mixture, sour cream, and next 3 ingredients, stirring well. Unroll crescent rolls and separate into 12 rectangles; press perforations to seal. Spoon 2 tablespoons chicken mixture in center of each rectangle and sprinkle evenly with cheese. Bring corners of rectangles together and twist, pinching seams to seal. Place on lightly greased baking sheets. Bake chicken packets at 350 degrees for 20 minutes or until golden brown. Garnish, if desired.

Nell Sturgis

Hint: If you have time, marinate chicken pieces in buttermilk overnight. It will tenderize the chicken and improve the flavor.

Awesome Chicken and Broccoli Casserole

- 3 cups broccoli florets, cooked and drained
- 4 cups roasted chicken breasts, cut into small bite-size pieces (To save time, buy a pre-cooked rotisserie chicken.)
- ½ teaspoon celery salt
- 1 cup onion, finely chopped
- 1 egg, beaten
- 1 can cream of chicken soup
- 1 can cream of mushroom with roasted garlic soup
- 1 cup mayonnaise
- ½ cup sour cream
- 2 cups pepper jack cheese, grated

Topping:

- 1 stick butter, melted
- 1 (6 ounce) box or bag of chicken flavored stuffing mix
- ½ cup Parmesan cheese, grated

Preheat oven to 400 degrees. In a large mixing bowl, combine all ingredients except topping ingredients and mix well. Pour mixture into 9 x 12 x 1½ inch (2 quart) glass baking dish. Bake for 35 minutes. Combine melted butter, stuffing mix, and grated Parmesan cheese. Mix well. Remove casserole from oven and evenly spread stuffing mix on top of the casserole. Return to oven and bake an additional 10 minutes or until browned on top.

Janet Pridgen

"For the Lord God is a sun and shield; The Lord gives grace and glory; No good thing does He withold from those who walk uprightly."

Paslm 84:11
(NASB)

Chicken and Rice Casserole

- 3 cups or more chicken, cooked and diced
- 1 package Uncle Ben's long grain and wild rice, cooked
- 1 can cream of celery soup
- 1 jar chopped pimento
- 1 medium onion, chopped
- 1 can French-style green beans, drained
- 1 cup mayonnaise
- 1 can water chestnuts, sliced
- Salt and pepper to taste

Mix all ingredients and pour into 3-quart casserole dish. Bake 350 degrees for 25 to 30 minutes.

Dale Collins

Chicken Casserole

- ½ stick butter
- ½ cup onion
- 1 can cream of chicken soup
- 1 can cream of mushroom soup
- ¾ cup evaporated milk
- Salt and pepper to taste

Cook onions in butter until tender. Add soups, milk, salt, and pepper. Cook until thickened.

- 1 fryer, cooked and cut up
- 2 cups cooked rice
- 1 small jar pimentos
- Cheese

Add these to first mixture and sprinkle with cheese. Bake in a 9 x 13 casserole dish at 350 degrees for 30 minutes.

In Memory of Mrs. Doris Worrell

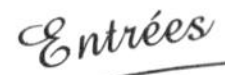

Chicken Casserole

- ½ box (2 sleeves) Ritz crackers
- 4 chicken breasts, cooked and cut up
- 1 cup sour cream
- 1 can cream of chicken soup
- 1 can cream of mushroom soup
- ½ cup butter or margarine, melted

Crush 1 sleeve of Ritz crackers and layer in bottom of 9 x 13 inch casserole dish. Dot with butter. Layer cooked, cut-up chicken over crumbs. Mix together sour cream, chicken soup, and mushroom soup. Layer over chicken. Crush remaining sleeve of Ritz crackers and layer over soup mixture. Pour ½ cup of melted butter or margarine on top. Bake at 350 degrees for 45 to 60 minutes.

Deidre Taft

Chicken Supreme

- 1 large hen, cooked
- 1 can cream of mushroom soup
- 2 large onions, grated
- 1 small jar pimentos strips
- 1 small carton sour cream
- Worcestershire sauce to taste
- 1 cup chicken broth
- 1 package egg noodles
- ¼ cup butter, melted
- Crushed corn flakes
- Slivered almonds
- Salt and pepper to taste
- Salad dressing or mayonnaise

Remove chicken from bones. Cut in bite-size pieces and place in large bowl. Add soup, onions, pimentos, Worcestershire sauce, seasonings, and enough salad dressing to moisten and mix well. Add sour cream and broth and mix well. Cook noodles according to package directions, drain, and stir into chicken mixture. Pour into a greased casserole. Cover with corn flake crumbs. Add almonds and drizzle with butter. Bake at 375 degrees until brown.

Frances Neugent

Tandoori Chicken

(An Indian Dish)

- **4 chicken quarters**
- **6 ounces yogurt (natural, plain, low-fat)**
- **⅓ teaspoon cardamom powder**
- **⅓ teaspoon cinnamon powder**
- **⅓ teaspoon cloves powder**
- **½ teaspoon cumin powder**
- **⅓ teaspoon black pepper powder**
- **1 teaspoon ginger paste**
- **1 teaspoon garlic paste**
- **1½ teaspoons chili powder**
- **¼ teaspoon turmeric**
- **1 teaspoon coriander powder**
- **1 tablespoon lemon juice**
- **1 teaspoon salt**
- **2 tablespoons cooking oil (canola or corn)**
- **Few drops red food coloring**
- **Garnish: Mixed salad leaves, lime wedges, and 1 tomato, sliced**

Remove the skin and pat dry the chicken quarters. Make 2 slits on the chicken pieces, place in a dish, and set aside. Mix together the yogurt and rest of the ingredients to form a thin paste. Cover the chicken quarters with the mixed spice paste and marinate for 3 hours. Preheat the oven to 475 degrees. Bake for 25 to 30 minutes or until the chicken is cooked thoroughly and browned on top. Remove from the oven and transfer onto a serving dish and garnish with salad leaves, lime, and tomato. You can also put it on a BBQ grill. Delicious!

Seema Furtado

"Blessed are those who hunger and thirst for righteousness, for they will be filled."

Matthew 5:6
(NIV)

Teriyaki Stir-Fry

½ cup Kikkoman teriyaki marinade and sauce
2 tablespoons sugar
1½ pounds chicken breasts (boneless and skinless, cut into ½ inch thick slices, crosswise)
2 teaspoons cornstarch
2 tablespoons vegetable oil
2 tablespoons sesame oil
Hot cooked rice
Steamed vegetables

Combine teriyaki sauce and sugar in measuring cup, stirring until sugar dissolves. Remove 3 tablespoons of mixture and pour over chicken in large plastic food storage bag. Press air out of bag and close top securely. Turn bag over several times to coat pieces well. Marinate 15 minutes. Meanwhile, add enough water to remaining teriyaki sauce mixture to measure ⅔ cup; blend in cornstarch. Heat oils in large skillet or wok. Add chicken and sauté 5 minutes. Add teriyaki sauce mixture. Cook, stirring about 1 minute or until sauce boils and thickens slightly. Spoon chicken and sauce over rice in large individual serving bowls. Serve vegetables on top of rice or on the side.

Note: This recipe is quick and feeds a large number of people. Fried egg rolls are great to serve with this dish.

Suzanne Harper

Hint: Stir-frying is a versatile, quick-cooking method used with meat, poultry, and seafood. One of the advantages of stir-frying is that much of the slicing and chopping can be done in advance. Cook your rice while you stir-fry, and it will be done at the same time.

Chicken Tortilla Bake

- ½ cup Miracle Whip
- ½ cup flour
- 3 cups milk
- 8 ounces Cheddar cheese, shredded and divided
- 1½ pounds cooked chicken breasts (boneless and skinless), cut into bite-size pieces
- ½ cup chunky salsa, chosen level of heat
- ½ cup fresh parsley, chopped
- 16 flour tortillas (6 inch)

Preheat oven to 375 degrees. Whisk Miracle Whip and flour in medium saucepan until well blended. Gradually stir in milk. Bring to boil on medium heat, stirring constantly; cook and stir until thickened. Add 1 cup cheese and cook until melted, stirring constantly. Reserve 1 cup sauce. Stir chicken, salsa, and parsley into remaining sauce. Spoon ⅓ cup down center of each tortilla. Roll up. Place 8 roll-ups, seam side down, in each of (2) 9 x 13 inch baking dishes sprayed with cooking spray. Top with reserved sauce and remaining cheese. Place remaining 8 roll-ups in a pan for freezing. Bake 25 minutes or until heated thoroughly.

Note: This recipe is designed to make two meals—one for immediate use and one for freezer.

Andrea Bassett

Sweet and Sour Sauce

- 1 can whole cranberry sauce
- 1 large onion, chopped
- ½ cup brown sugar
- 2 tablespoons vinegar
- ¼ cup soy sauce
- 1 cup chili sauce
- 2 tablespoons mustard
- 1 teaspoon hot sauce

Cook onion in olive oil until tender, add remaining ingredients, and heat thoroughly. Serve over pork.

Mary Thacker

Chicken Enchiladas

Rotisserie chicken, finely chopped
- **½ small onion, chopped and sautéed**
- **3 tablespoons Parmesan cheese, grated**
- **1 cup Monterey Jack cheese, shredded**
- **1 (4 ounce) can green chilies**
- **1 (13 ounce) can tomatillos, drained or 1¾ cup drained canned tomatoes**
- **¼ cup cilantro leaves**
- **¾ cup whipping cream**
- **1 egg**
- **8 thick, corn tortillas or 8 small flour tortillas**
- **1 cup Cheddar or Monterey Jack cheese, shredded**

Salt to taste

Guacamole, sour cream, shredded lettuce, black olives

Combine chicken, onion, Parmesan cheese, and 1 cup shredded Monterey Jack cheese. Taste and add salt, if needed. Set aside. In blender or food processor, combine green chilies, tomatillos or tomatoes, cilantro, whipping cream, and egg. Blend until smooth. Add salt to taste. Set aside. Preheat oven to 350 degrees. To soften tortillas, microwave them for 5-10 seconds. Divide chicken mixture evenly between 8 tortillas. Press the mixture to make it compact and roll tightly. Place seam side down into greased 7½ x 12 baking dish. Pour chile-cream mixture over enchiladas. Bake for 15-20 minutes. Take out and sprinkle evenly with 1 cup shredded Cheddar or Monterey Jack cheese and put back into oven 5 minutes or until cheese melts. Serve with guacamole, sour cream, shredded lettuce, and black olives.

Allison Brice

"For I was hungry, and you gave Me something to eat; I was thirsty, and you gave Me something to drink; I was a stranger, and you invited Me in."

Matthew 25:35
(NASB)

Chicken and Three-Cheese French Bread Pizzas

- ½ cup butter or margarine, softened
- ⅓ cup Parmesan cheese, freshly grated
- ¼ teaspoon dried Italian seasoning
- 1 (10 ounce) can white chicken, drained and flaked
- ¼ cup red bell pepper, chopped
- ½ cup Cheddar cheese, shredded
- 1 clove garlic, pressed
- 1 (16 ounce) loaf sliced French bread
- 1 cup mozzarella cheese, shredded
- ¼ cup green onions, chopped

Combine butter, Parmesan cheese, Cheddar cheese, garlic, and dried Italian seasoning in a small bowl; spread evenly over bread slices. Top with chicken and sprinkle with mozzarella cheese, bell pepper, and green onions. Bake at 350 degrees for 10 minutes or until cheese melts.

Note: 1½ cooked and chopped chicken breasts may be substituted.

Sherry Patterson

Tangy Chicken

- 1 chicken, cut up
- 2 teaspoons salt
- ¼ cup butter, melted
- ¼ cup lemon juice
- ¼ cup vinegar
- 1 teaspoon onion salt
- ½ teaspoon pepper

Mix all ingredients except chicken. Dip chicken into sauce and place skin side up in baking dish. Pour remaining sauce over it. Bake at 350 degrees for one hour.

In Memory of Mrs. Ruth Greer

Prime Rib Roast

Tell the butcher how many you're feeding, and he'll know what size roast you'll need. Unless you're buying the entire loin of ribs, ask for the first ribs. Ask the butcher to cut off the bones and tie them back on. The roast is a lot easier to carve this way.

If you'd like to age the roast before cooking, remove the wrapping and place in a pan in the refrigerator, uncovered, for two days. After aging, the roast may have a bit of crust on it, but that's okay. Place the roast on a roasting rack (like the broiler pan that usually comes with your oven). Baste it with canola oil and then coat the top heavily with coarse salt and coarse black pepper and just a dash of garlic salt. Do not cover the roast.

Bake at 325 degrees. Allow 25 minutes per pound for rare; 30 minutes per pound for medium. Anything beyond that ruins the roast! Use a meat thermometer to determine when it is done to your liking—130 degrees is rare; 150 degrees is medium. Caution: You will need to remove from oven 10 degrees before it reaches the desired temperature because it will continue cooking after it is removed.

Once you've removed the roast, leave it in the pan and wrap in aluminum foil for at least 15 minutes before carving. This allows the juices to redistribute throughout the roast and not seep out when you carve.

Cathalene Taylor

House Seasoning

1 cup salt
¼ cup black pepper
¼ cup garlic powder

Mix ingredients together and store in an airtight container for up to six months. Makes a great gift!

Meghan Lewis

Debra Stevens' Rump Roast

1 rump roast (4 to 5 pounds)
3 to 4 large onions
2 tablespoons Worcestershire sauce
Olive oil
Kosher salt
2 tablespoons soy sauce
2 tablespoons red wine vinegar (or balsamic)

Peel onions, slice into rings, and place in bottom of Dutch oven to form thick layer. Pat roast dry with paper towel and place fat side up on top of onions. Brush olive oil over roast and sprinkle generously with kosher salt. Mix together Worcestershire sauce, soy sauce, and vinegar and slowly drizzle over roast. Bring to a boil on stovetop, turn to simmer, and cover. Bake for 3 to 4 hours or until done. Let rest. Cut fat layer off before slicing.

Note: This recipe makes its own gravy. I have tried different cuts of beef but a rump roast tastes best. If desired, you may also allow roast to cool and use an electric knife for uniform slices. Submerge sliced roast back into gravy and keep warm in oven or on stovetop.

Mollie Morgan

Steak Marinade

2 cups soy sauce or teriyaki sauce
1 cup light brown sugar
4 tablespoons ground ginger
4 tablespoons garlic powder
4 tablespoons meat tenderizer
4 tablespoons oil
4 tablespoons water
2 tablespoons black pepper

Combine all ingredients. Recipe will marinate 15 to 18 steaks. It can be made and stored.

Brenda Lycett
Wife of Bro. Ed Lycett
Former Minister of Education

Marinated Eye of Round with Horseradish Sauce

1 (4 pound) eye of round roast
1 cup soy sauce
½ cup vegetable oil
4 cloves garlic, crushed

Horseradish Sauce:
1 cup heavy cream
1 cup mayonnaise
Pinch of salt
¼ cup prepared horseradish or to taste

Place the roast in a large Ziploc bag. In a small bowl, combine the soy sauce, oil, and garlic and mix well. Pour the marinade into the bag with the roast, close the bag tightly, and refrigerate for 48 hours, turning the roast several times. When ready to cook the meat, preheat the oven to 350 degrees. Pat the roast dry and bake until a meat thermometer registers medium rare (about 1 hour). Remove the roast from the oven and immediately wrap in foil and refrigerate. (This process stops the meat from continuing to cook.)

To prepare the sauce, place the cream in a medium-size bowl and whip until soft peaks form. Beat in the mayonnaise and salt. Blend in the horseradish by hand. For a lighter sauce, omit the mayonnaise. At serving time, slice the meat very thin and serve on rolls with the horseradish sauce.

Note: The meat may be served on Parker House rolls or any other small rolls.

Mary Lou Gillespie

"But to each of us grace was given according to the measure of Christ's gift."
Ephesians 4:7
(NASB)

Marinated Beef Tenderloin

1 (4 pound) beef tenderloin (prepare meat by removing pearlescent membrane)
1 cup vegetable oil
½ bottle soy sauce
Juice of 2 lemons

Combine oil, soy sauce, and lemon juice. Place meat and marinade in Ziploc bag and refrigerate overnight. Preheat oven to 500 degrees. Place tenderloin on broiler pan and bake for 30 minutes until meat is crusty.

In Memory of Mrs. Dottie Morgan

Buffalo "Trow"

Several hours before cooking, place green pecan wood in a stack 4-foot square by 4-foot high. Let wood burn down until there's a big bed of coals.

10 pieces boneless sirloin beef roast, 2 to 2½ inches thick. Coat meat on both sides with seasoning of choice and let stand for several hours. Place meat in hot coals 30 minutes on each side. Turn with a pitch fork. Remove meat and wipe with a towel to remove some of the ashes.

Heat sauce on a fish cooker outside until a rolling boil is reached. Cut meat into strips across the grain and dip small amounts of meat into sauce and quickly remove. This washes off any remaining ashes.

Sauce:

4 (15 ounce) bottles soy sauce
4 quarts lemon juice
1 (15 ounce) bottle Worcestershire sauce
4 pounds butter

Note: Buffalo "Trows" are done across the South by many churches (as fundraisers) and individuals to entertain friends and family. It's interesting to watch and the meat is delicious!

Mr. Ernest Ricketson

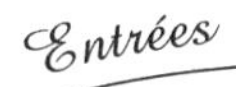

Company Casserole

- 1 (8 ounce) package egg noodles
- 1½ pound ground chuck
- 2 tablespoons margarine
- 1 tablespoon salt
- ½ teaspoon black pepper
- 4 teaspoons garlic salt
- 1 (8 ounce) can tomato sauce
- 1 cup cottage cheese
- 1 cup sour cream
- 4-5 green onions with tops, chopped
- ¾ cup sharp Cheddar cheese, grated

Cook noodles with ½ teaspoon oil added to water. Drain and set aside. Brown meat in margarine. Add salt, pepper, garlic salt, and tomato sauce. Simmer 5 minutes. In separate bowl, combine noodles, cottage cheese, sour cream, and green onions. In a 9 x 13 pan, alternate layers of meat mixture and noodle mixture. Top with grated cheese. Bake in 350 degree oven for 30 minutes or until bubbly hot.

Ruby S. Harper

Mexican Steak and Beans

- 1.5 pounds beef flank steak
- 1 (10 ounce) can tomatoes with green chili peppers, chopped
- 1 medium onion, chopped
- 2 garlic cloves, minced
- 1 tablespoon snipped fresh oregano
- 1 teaspoon dried oregano
- 1 teaspoon chili powder
- 1 teaspoon ground cumin
- ¼ teaspoon salt
- ¼ teaspoon black pepper
- 3 small peppers, cut into strips (green, red, or yellow)
- 1 (15 ounce) can pinto beans, rinsed and drained
- 3 cups hot cooked rice

Place meat in slow cooker. Add together remaining ingredients and pour over meat. Slow cook 7-9 hours. Serve over hot rice topped with queso fresco or feta cheese. Topping optional.

Leigh McKinnon

Mexican Treat

3 cups cooked white rice
2 pounds lean ground beef
1 can tomato paste
1½ cups water
1 envelope taco seasoning
Dash salt
2 cans Cheddar cheese soup
2 ounces Velveeta cheese, cubed
1 can Ro-tel tomatoes, chopped
Doritos
Top with tomatoes, onions, and cheese

Cook meat and drain. Add tomato paste, water, taco seasoning, and salt. Cook on low heat for 20 minutes. In top of double boiler, add Cheddar cheese soup, Velveeta cheese, and tomatoes. Heat until smooth and hot. Arrange in individual serving plates in this order: handful of crushed Doritos, cooked rice, meat sauce, cheese sauce and top with chopped tomatoes, onions, and shredded cheese.

Maudine Wright

Texas Hash

1½ pounds hamburger meat
¼ cup onion, grated
½ cup bell pepper, chopped
1 teaspoon chili powder
1 can tomatoes
1½ cups cooked rice

Brown hamburger and drain. Pour all ingredients into a 9 x 13 inch casserole dish sprayed with cooking spray. Salt to taste. Add ½ to ¾ cup of water. Cover and bake for 30 minutes at 350 degrees.

Sonya Hendley

Doc's Blackened Steak

- **1/3 cup paprika**
- **1 tablespoon each garlic and onion powder**
- **1 teaspoon each white, black, and cayenne pepper**
- **1/2 teaspoon each dried thyme, basil, and oregano**
- **1/4 cup salt**
- **1 1/4 sticks whole butter, cut in pats**
- **2 pounds prime sirloin beef, cut in 1 1/2 to 2 inches thick**
- **1/2 cup vegetable oil**
- **Kosher salt**

Combine all dry ingredients for rub. Trim fat on sirloin and coat with oil. Cover steak with seasoning rub on all sides and massage into meat. Heat a skillet outside on cooker until very, very hot (red hot) and add 2 to 3 pats of butter. Immediately place steak in pan and sear for 4 to 5 minutes on each side. Place steak on a hot grill to complete cooking. Let steak rest for 5 to 10 minutes before serving. Slice steak across the grain and serve with steak gravy or Creole mustard.

Creole Mustard Sauce:

- **1 cup Creole mustard**
- **2 tablespoons mayonnaise**
- **1 tablespoon Worcestershire sauce**
- **1 teaspoon black pepper, freshly ground**

Mix together ingredients and chill. Keep refrigerated.

Note: This recipe is a family favorite and was introduced to us by my late father-in-law, Dr. Donald Gillis. He was a master chef and had a knack for cooking up the best dishes and barbecue ever.

Pam Gillis

Meat Loaf

2 eggs
⅔ cup milk
3 slices bread
1 onion, chopped
¼ cup bell pepper, chopped
½ cup cheese, shredded
1½ pounds ground beef
2 teaspoons salt
¼ teaspoon pepper
½ cup catsup
¼ cup brown sugar
1 tablespoon prepared mustard

Mix together eggs, milk, bread, onion, bell pepper, cheese, salt, and black pepper; pour over ground beef. Mix well; pack in loaf pan. Bake for 30 minutes. Combine catsup, brown sugar, and mustard. Spread over top of meat loaf and continue to bake for 30 minute. Bake in 350 degree oven.

Mirt Dockery

Patty Melts

1 stick butter
1 whole large onion, halved and sliced
1 to 1½ pounds ground beef
Salt and pepper to taste
5 dashes Worcestershire sauce
8 slices Swiss cheese
8 slices rye bread

In a medium skillet, melt 2 tablespoons of butter over medium-low heat. Add onions and cook slowly, 20 to 25 minutes, stirring occasionally until brown and soft. In a medium bowl, mix beef, salt, pepper, and Worcestershire. Form into 4 patties. Melt 2 tablespoons butter in a separate skillet over medium heat. Cook patties on both sides until done in the middle. Assemble melts this way: slice of bread, slice of cheese, hamburger patty, ¼ of cooked onions, another slice of cheese, another slice of bread. On a clean griddle or skillet, melt 2 tablespoons butter and grill sandwiches over medium heat until golden brown. Flip and cook other side until brown and cheese is melted. Slice in half and serve immediately!

Kellie Lingenfelter

Porcupine Meatballs

- 1 pound ground beef
- 1 can tomato soup
- 1 cup water
- 2 tablespoons shortening
- 1 teaspoon salt
- ¼ cup onion, minced
- 1 egg, beaten
- ¼ cup uncooked rice

Mix ¼ cup tomato soup with ground beef, rice, egg, onion, and salt. Shape into balls. In a skillet, brown balls in shortening. Mix remaining soup and water and cover meatballs. Simmer 40 minutes or until rice is tender.

Note: I usually shape into balls, cover with the soup mixture, and put in the oven at 350 degrees for about an hour or so. This can be made the night before and cooked the next day.

Linda Raybon

Marilyn's Hot Tamale Pie

- 1½ pounds ground beef
- 1 onion, chopped
- ½ cup green pepper, chopped
- 1 package chili seasoning mix (hot or mild)
- 1 teaspoon salt
- 1 (1 pound) can tomatoes
- 1½ cups whole kernel corn
- 1 (3¼ ounce) can black olives, drained
- 1 cup self-rising yellow cornmeal
- 2½ cups cold water
- ¼ cup diced pimentos, drained
- 1 cup sharp Cheddar cheese, shredded

Brown beef, onion, and pepper in skillet and drain. Add next 3 ingredients and simmer 5 minutes. Stir in corn and olives. In small saucepan combine cornmeal and water. Cook, stirring until thick (add pinch of salt if needed during cooking). Stir in pimentos. Line greased shallow pan or 2-quart baking dish with a part of the cornmeal mixture. Pour in beef mixture and make a border of remaining cornmeal mixture around the edge of baking dish. Bake at 350 degrees for 40 minutes. Sprinkle cheese over top and bake an additional 5 minutes.

Carol Sawyer

Crockpot Cola Ham

- 1 (3 to 4 pound) precooked ham
- ½ cup light brown sugar
- 1 teaspoon dry mustard
- 1 teaspoon horseradish
- ¼ cup Coca-Cola (not diet)

Mix mustard, horseradish, and brown sugar together. Mix in a small amount of Coca-Cola to form a paste and rub all over ham. Place ham in crockpot and pour remaining Coca-Cola over ham. Cook on high for 1 hour and reduce to low and cook for 6 to 7 hours.

Lynn Schofield

Cornbread Pie

- 1 pound ground beef
- 1 medium onion, chopped
- ½ green pepper, chopped
- 1 teaspoon salt
- 1 tablespoon chili powder
- 1 cup fresh corn or canned whole kernel corn, drained
- 1 can tomato soup
- ½ stick butter or Oleo
- 2 cups water
- ½ teaspoon black pepper

Sauté onion and green pepper in skillet in butter. Remove and sauté the beef until gray-looking. Combine the two mixtures and add soup, water, corn, and seasonings. Pour into a buttered oblong casserole dish. Cover with the following topping.

Topping:

- ¾ cup cornmeal
- ½ teaspoon salt
- 1½ teaspoons baking powder
- ½ cup milk
- 1 tablespoon flour
- 1 tablespoon sugar
- 1 egg, beaten
- 1 tablespoon butter, melted

Sift dry ingredients together and add beaten egg. Add milk and melted butter. Cover meat mixture with topping. Bake at 325 degrees for about 1 hour or until top is golden brown.

Laura Mell Pope

Slow Cooker Pork Chops and Field Peas

- 1 (16 ounce) package frozen field peas with snaps, thawed
- 1½ teaspoons dry mustard
- 1 teaspoon salt
- ½ teaspoon garlic powder
- 6 bone-in chops (1 inch thick)
- ½ cup all-purpose flour
- 2 tablespoons vegetable oil
- 1 large sweet onion, sliced
- 1 (10½ ounce) can condensed chicken broth

Place peas in a lightly greased 6-quart slow cooker. Combine dry mustard, salt, and garlic powder; sprinkle over pork chops. Dredge pork in flour. In a large nonstick skillet over medium-high heat, heat oil. In batches cook pork for 3 to 4 minutes on each side until browned. Transfer pork to slow cooker. Reserve drippings in skillet. Sauté onion in hot drippings over medium-high heat 6 to 7 minutes or until tender. Add chicken broth and cook 2 minutes, stirring to loosen particles from bottom of skillet. Spoon onion mixture over pork in slow cooker. Cover and cook on low 6 hours. We love it served with hot rice.

Dot McKinnon

Jezebel Sauce

- 1 cup apple jelly
- 1 cup pineapple preserves
- 1 (6-ounce) jar prepared mustard
- 1 (5-ounce) jar prepared horseradish
- ¼ teaspoon pepper

Beat apple jelly in a mixing bowl at medium speed with an electric mixer until smooth. Add preserves and remaining ingredients. Beat at medium speed until blended. Cover and chill. Good served with pork tenderloin. Drain horseradish well by pressing between layers of paper towels.

Mary Lou Gillespie

Sweet and Spicy Pork Chops

- 2 pork chops, butterflied (¼ inch thick)
- ¼ cup peanut oil
- 2 cloves garlic, minced
- ¼ cup cooking sherry
- ¼ cup soy sauce
- 2 tablespoons brown sugar
- ½ tablespoon red pepper, crushed
- ¼ pound vermicelli or thin spaghetti, cooked and drained
- 1 teaspoon toasted sesame seeds for garnish

Pound pork chops to ⅛ inch thickness. Brown in oil with garlic over medium heat. Pour off drippings. Combine cooking sherry, soy sauce, brown sugar, and red pepper and pour over chops. Cover tightly and cook slowly 20 minutes or until chops are tender. Place chops over cooked vermicelli, pour sauce over, and sprinkle with toasted sesame seeds to serve.

Note: Bone-in ham steaks can be substituted for pork chops.

Mollie Morgan

Pork Chop Dinner

- 2 (½ inch thick) loin pork chops
- 1 tablespoon vegetable oil
- ¼ cup onion, diced
- ¼ cup green peppers, diced
- ½ cup regular rice, uncooked
- Salt and pepper to taste
- 1½ cups canned tomatoes, chopped
- 1 teaspoon salt
- ½ teaspoon sugar
- ½ teaspoon prepared mustard

Sprinkle pork chops with salt and pepper; brown on both sides in hot oil. Remove chops and drain on paper towels. Reserve drippings in skillet. Add onion and green pepper to skillet; sauté until tender. Stir in rice, tomatoes, salt, sugar, and mustard. Add pork chops. Bring to boil. Reduce heat; cover and simmer about 30 minutes or until rice is tender and pork chops are done. (I put mine in baking dish and bake in oven for about 40 minutes.)

Audrey Wilkerson

Pork Chops for the Slow Cooker

- 6 boneless pork chops
- ¼ cup ketchup
- ¼ cup brown sugar
- 2 cloves garlic, crushed
- 1 teaspoon ground ginger
- ½ cup soy sauce
- Salt and pepper to taste

Place pork chops in a slow cooker. Combine remaining ingredients and pour over pork chops. Cook on low setting for 5-6 hours, until internal temperature of pork has reached 160 degrees.

Note: Serve this with mashed potatoes and pour the gravy on top. It is easy and delicious!

Suzanne Harper

Pork Loin with Red Plum Sauce

- 1 (5 to 8 pound) pork loin
- 2 tablespoons butter
- ¾ cup onion, chopped
- 1 cup red plum preserves
- ½ cup brown sugar, packed
- Garlic salt
- Onion salt
- ⅔ cup water
- 2 tablespoons lemon juice
- ⅓ cup chili sauce
- ¼ cup soy sauce
- 2 teaspoons prepared mustard
- 3 drops Tabasco

Preheat oven to 325 degrees. Sprinkle pork generously with garlic and onion salts; place fat side up in roasting pan. Roast in 325 degree oven for 25 minutes per pound. You may prefer to place roast on rack and add water to roasting pan. Melt butter in saucepan, add onion, and cook until tender. Add remaining ingredients, simmer 15 minutes. Pour fat off pork; pour about half the sauce over meat. Bake about 20 to 30 minutes longer, basting often. Serve extra sauce on side.

Bro. Shep Johnson
Senior Pastor

Pork Tenderloin

- 1 pork tenderloin
- 1 package bacon
- 1 tablespoon garlic powder
- 1 teaspoon season salt
- 1 teaspoon basil
- ½ teaspoon oregano
- 1 teaspoon pepper
- Extra-virgin olive oil

Combine seasonings and completely rub pork tenderloin. Wrap bacon (5 to 6 pieces) around pork tenderloin. Coat with olive oil and bake at 375 degrees for 1 hour.

Karrie LaRiccia

Pork Loin Dijonnaise with Peach Sauce

- ¼ cup Dijon mustard
- ¼ cup mayonnaise
- 1 (2 pound) boneless center-cut pork loin roast
- 2 cups Italian-seasoned breadcrumbs
- 1 tablespoon butter or margarine
- 1 small onion, diced
- 2 garlic cloves, minced
- 3 cups peach-flavored white grape juice
- 1 tablespoon chicken bouillon, granules
- 1 (6 ounce) can peach slices, undrained and diced

Combine mustard and mayonnaise; brush over roast. Coat roast with breadcrumbs and place roast on a rack in a roasting pan. Bake at 400 degrees for 20 minutes; reduce heat to 325 degrees and bake 1½ hours or until meat thermometer inserted into thickest portion registers 160 degrees. Slice roast and keep warm. Melt butter in a heavy saucepan. Add onion and garlic and sauté until tender. Stir in grape juice, bouillon granules, and peach slices; bring to a boil. Cook 10 minutes or until mixture is reduced by two-thirds, stirring occasionally. Serve with pork.

Betty Dees

Sausage-Wild Rice Casserole

- 1 (6 ounce) package long grain and wild rice mix
- 1 pound bulk sausage
- 1 (10 ounce) can cream of mushroom soup
- 1 cup fresh mushrooms, chopped
- ½ cup onion, chopped
- ½ cup green pepper, chopped
- ½ cup sharp Cheddar cheese, shredded
- ½ cup chicken broth
- ¼ cup celery, finely chopped
- 1 tablespoon dried parsley flakes
- 1 teaspoon coarsely ground black pepper

Cook rice per directions; set aside. Brown sausage, stirring to crumble; drain well. Combine cooked rice, sausage, and remaining ingredients in a large bowl and mix well. Put in baking dish and bake for 1 hour at 350 degrees.

Mary Thacker

Dirty Rice with Smoked Sausage

- 2 cups long grain white rice
- 5 cups chicken stock, divided
- 2 tablespoons vegetable oil
- 1 pound smoked pork sausage, sliced
- 1 clove garlic, minced
- 1 large onion, chopped
- 1 stalk celery, chopped
- 1 medium green bell pepper, chopped
- ¼ teaspoon cayenne pepper
- ¼ cup fresh parsley leaves, chopped
- Kosher salt and freshly ground black pepper

In a medium saucepan, combine the rice and 4 cups of chicken stock. Bring to a boil, reduce the heat, and simmer until all the stock is absorbed into the rice, about 20 minutes. Heat the oil in a heavy sauté pan over medium-high heat and brown the sausage. Once browned, add the garlic, onion, celery, and bell pepper. Cook until softened, about 5 minutes. Add 1 cup chicken stock and cayenne. Add the cooked rice and parsley and stir thoroughly. Season with salt and pepper. (Add more chicken broth as needed.)

Dwayne Gillis

Sausage and Peppers with Parmesan Cheese Grits

- 1 (19 ounce) package of sweet Italian sausage
- 3 bell peppers, cut into strips (red, green, or yellow)
- 1 large sweet onion, cut in half and thinly sliced
- 2 garlic cloves, minced
- 1 to 2 teaspoons Italian seasoning
- 1 teaspoon salt
- ½ teaspoon garlic powder
- ½ teaspoon pepper
- Parmesan Cheese Grits
- Garnish: shredded Parmesan cheese

Remove sausage casings. Cook sausage and next 7 ingredients in a large skillet over medium-high heat, stirring until sausage crumbles and is no longer pink and vegetables are tender. Serve over Parmesan Cheese Grits. Garnish if desired. Serves 4.

Parmesan Cheese Grits:

- 1 cup grits
- 4 cups water
- ¾ teaspoon salt
- 1 tablespoon butter or margarine
- 1 (5 ounce) package Parmesan cheese, shredded

Cook grits according to package directions, using 4 cups water. Stir in salt, butter, and Parmesan cheese. Good on a cold winter night!

Cheryl Skipper

Spaghetti Sauce

- 5 pounds ground beef, cooked and drained
- 2 packages dry spaghetti sauce mix
- 1 gallon spaghetti sauce
- 1 heaping spoon dried parsley
- 1 heaping spoon dried onion
- 1 heaping spoon dried garlic
- 8 ounces mushroom pieces
- 10 bay leaves

Brown beef and drain. Mix all ingredients together and simmer until done.

Note: This recipe was made ahead of time, frozen, and served on the 2013 Youth Snow Ski Trip to feed hungry skiers.

Carolyn Ricketson

Quesadillas

- 2 (4 ounce) cans green chilies, drained
- 2 cups Cheddar cheese, shredded
- ½ teaspoon coriander
- ½ tablespoon butter
- Flour tortillas
- Taco sauce

Mix chilies, cheese, and coriander. Melt ½ tablespoon butter in nonstick skillet on low heat. Place tortilla flat on skillet. Spread ¼ cup chili mixture over half of tortilla. When cheese melts, fold tortilla in half. Cook until golden brown and crispy on both sides. Serve warm with taco sauce. Repeat with remaining tortillas.

In Memory of Mr. David Slowik

Taco Pie

- ½ cup water
- 1 can crescent rolls
- 1 (6 ounce) can tomato sauce
- 1 package taco seasoning mix
- 1½ pounds hamburger meat
- 1 pint sour cream
- 1 pound sharp Cheddar or Colby cheese
- Taco chips

Grease a 9 x 13 pan. Lay crescent rolls down and press to cover bottom of dish. Brown meat; drain. Add taco seasoning, tomato sauce, and water. Simmer awhile. Crush chips and put ½ of the bag on top of crescent rolls. Place hamburger meat on top of chips. Cover with sour cream and cheese. Top with other half of crushed chips. Bake at 350 degrees for 30 minutes.

Dale Collins

Taco Casserole

- 1½ pounds ground beef
- 1 medium onion, chopped
- 1 package taco seasoning
- 2 cans refried beans
- 1 (8 ounce) taco sauce
- 12 ounces Cheddar cheese, grated
- Sour cream
- Tortilla chips

Brown ground beef and onion. Add taco seasoning and water as directed on package. Simmer 15 to 20 minutes. In a 2-quart casserole, layer beans, beef and onion mixture, taco sauce, and cheese. Bake at 350 degrees for 30 minutes. Top with sour cream and eat on tortilla chips.

Betsy Hodges

Sour Cream Enchiladas

- 1½ pounds ground beef
- 1 tablespoon garlic powder
- 2 tablespoons Worcestershire sauce
- ½ teaspoon ground cumin
- ½ small can green chilies, chopped
- 1 large onion, chopped
- 2 tablespoons Picante sauce
- 3 tablespoons chili powder
- 4 drops Tabasco sauce
- 1 package flour tortillas (12)
- 2 cups Cheddar cheese, grated

Brown the meat in large skillet; drain any fat. Add next 8 ingredients. Simmer until onions are transparent. Grease bottom of 9 x 13 inch pan. On each tortilla place 2 tablespoons meat mixture, sprinkle some grated cheese, and roll. Place in pan with open side down. After all tortillas are placed in pan, pour the sour cream sauce over them. Sprinkle with remaining cheese. Bake 25 minutes at 325 degrees or until bubbly and lightly toasted on top.

Sour Cream Sauce:

- 4 tablespoons self-rising flour
- ¼ pound margarine
- 2 cups milk
- ¼ pound Velveeta cheese
- 1 pint sour cream
- ½ small can green chilies, chopped

Melt margarine and add flour. Slowly add milk, stirring until smooth. Add Velveeta in chunks to the sauce and simmer until melted. Add sour cream and chilies.

Sue Bordeaux

Smothered Quail and Rice Pilaf

6 quail
3 slices bacon
1 stick butter
2 tablespoons cooking sherry
2 tablespoons cornstarch
Salt and pepper
Flour

Clean quail, split down back, and draw (cut fowl open and remove entrails). Dust lightly with flour. In heavy skillet, fry bacon until crisp. Drain bacon and save. Add butter to drippings and sauté quail until golden brown. Remove quail and make gravy, using cornstarch to thicken. Add sherry, crumbled bacon, salt, and pepper to taste. Place quail in gravy and simmer at least 30 minutes. Serve with Rice Pilaf.

Rice Pilaf:

2 tablespoons butter
1 onion, finely chopped
2 garlic cloves, minced
1 bay leaf
1 cup rice, uncooked
1 teaspoon salt
1½ cups chicken broth
1½ cups water

Melt butter in heavy saucepan. Add onion, garlic, and bay leaf. Cook gently 5 minutes. Add rice, salt, chicken broth, and water. Stir to blend. Bring to a boil. Cover, lower flame, and simmer for 5 minutes; remove bay leaf. Bake uncovered in a 1-quart casserole at 375 degrees for 30 minutes. Place quail on large platter and surround with rice to serve.

In Memory of Mrs. Dottie Morgan

Grinders

4 hoagie rolls
½ pound Virginia baked ham, sliced
8 very thin slices hard salami
1 jar sliced mild banana peppers
¼ head shredded lettuce
1-2 tomatoes, sliced
1-2 onions, thinly sliced
6 thin slices of provolone cheese
Mayonnaise
Oregano
Red wine vinegar

Cut hoagie rolls, spread with mayonnaise, and sprinkle with oregano. Layer ham, salami, provolone, tomatoes, onion, and pepper rings on sandwich. Add lettuce and sprinkle with red wine vinegar. Wrap in foil. Oven bake at 400 degrees for approximately 10 minutes.

Sandy Borland Cason

Pizza Burgers

1 pound hamburger meat, browned
1 can Hunt's tomato sauce
1 cup Cheddar cheese, diced
½ cup olives, chopped
Garlic salt
Salt and pepper
Hotdog rolls

Combine all ingredients and place in hotdog rolls. Wrap in foil and bake at 350-400 degrees for 30 minutes.

Clara Benoist

Seafood

"…Follow Me, and I will make you fishers of men."
Matthew 4:19
(NASB)

Glorifying…Growing…Going
Missions to Haiti

Seafood

Crab Cakes

- 1 cup unseasoned breadcrumbs, divided
- 1 egg, beaten
- 3 tablespoons mayonnaise
- 1 tablespoon lemon juice
- 1 tablespoon fresh parsley, chopped
- 1 teaspoon whole grain mustard
- ½ teaspoon salt
- ¼ teaspoon pepper
- ¼ teaspoon cayenne pepper
- 1 pound lump crabmeat
- ¼ cup vegetable oil

In a medium bowl, combine ½ cup breadcrumbs, egg, mayonnaise, lemon juice, parsley, mustard, salt, pepper, and cayenne pepper. Gently fold in crabmeat. For each crab cake, shape ⅓ cup crabmeat mixture to form ½ inch thick patty. In a shallow dish, place remaining ½ cup breadcrumbs. Coat crab cakes with breadcrumbs. Cover and refrigerate at least 2 hours or overnight. Heat vegetable oil in a large skillet. Cook crab cakes over medium-high heat for 4 minutes or until lightly brown. Carefully flip crab cakes and cook an additional 4 minutes. Drain on paper towel.

Pam Gillis

Crabmeat Casserole

- 1 (12 ounce) can crabmeat
- 1 package Pepperidge Farm stuffing mix
- 2 cans cream of mushroom soup
- 2 stalks celery, chopped
- 1 onion, chopped
- 1 green bell pepper, finely chopped
- ¼ cup Duke's mayonnaise
- ¼ cup Worcestershire sauce
- Butter or margarine

Sauté celery, onion, and bell pepper in butter or margarine. Mix crabmeat, stuffing, and soup. Blend mayonnaise and Worcestershire sauce. Mix all ingredients together and place in a buttered casserole dish; top with crushed chips of choice. Bake for 30 minutes at 325 degrees.

In Memory of Mrs. Noirena Sinclair

Quick and Easy Salmon Patties

- 1 large can pink salmon
- 1 egg
- ½ cup self-rising flour
- 2 tablespoons onion, chopped
- ½ cup self-rising meal
- ¼ teaspoon salt
- ¼ teaspoon black pepper

Combine all ingredients and mix well. Form into small patties. Fry in hot shortening until brown, about 5 minutes.

In Memory of Mrs. Catherine Taylor

Crab Casserole

- 1 cup half-and-half
- 2 eggs
- 1 can cream of mushroom soup
- 1 teaspoon salt
- 1 teaspoon pepper
- 1 teaspoon hot sauce
- 1 teaspoon Worcestershire sauce
- 1 medium onion, chopped
- 1 medium bell pepper, chopped
- 1 cup breadcrumbs (or crushed Waverly Wafers)
- 2 pounds fresh canned crabmeat (found in refrigerator section)

Mix together first 9 ingredients. Fold in breadcrumbs and crab to mixture. Pour in greased baking dish and bake at 350 degrees for 1 hour or until top is brown.

JoAnne Lewis

Cedar-Planked Salmon

Dressing:

- 2 tablespoons fresh lime juice
- 2 tablespoons rice vinegar
- 2 tablespoons Dijon mustard
- 2 tablespoons honey
- 2 tablespoons fresh chives, minced
- 1 teaspoon kosher salt
- ½ teaspoon granulated garlic or garlic powder
- ½ teaspoon black pepper, freshly ground
- ¼ teaspoon ground cayenne pepper
- ¼ cup extra-virgin olive oil

Salmon

- 1 large salmon fillet, with skin
- ½ teaspoon kosher salt
- ¼ teaspoon black pepper, freshly ground
- 1 untreated cedar plank (submerged in water for at least 1 hour)

In a blender, combine the dressing ingredients except the oil. Mix until well blended. With the blender still running, slowly pour in oil to make a smooth dressing. Season the fresh side of the salmon with salt and pepper. Pour about half of the dressing over the salmon and use a brush to coat evenly. Remove the plank from the water and immediately place over direct heat on grill until the edges start to smoke and char, 3 to 10 minutes. If plank begins to flame, douse with water. Move plank to indirect heat. Place salmon on the plank, skin side down. Grill until the salmon is just slightly pink in the center and brown on the edges, 20 to 25 minutes. Be careful not to overcook. Serve with the remaining dressing.

Pam Gillis

Baked Salmon

- 2 cloves garlic, minced
- 6 tablespoons light olive oil
- 1 teaspoon dried basil
- 1 teaspoon salt
- 1 teaspoon ground black pepper
- 1 tablespoon lemon juice
- 1 tablespoon fresh parsley, chopped
- 2 (6 ounce) salmon fillets

Preheat oven to 375 degrees. In a medium-size glass bowl, prepare marinade by mixing garlic, light olive oil, basil, salt, pepper, lemon juice, and parsley. Place salmon fillets in a medium glass baking dish and cover with the marinade. Marinate in the refrigerator for about one hour, turning occasionally. Place fillets in aluminum foil, cover with marinade, and seal. Place sealed salmon in the glass dish and bake for 35-45 minutes, until easily flaked with a fork.

Peggy Hurd
Family Ministry Center Director

Seafood Batter

- 1¼ cups plain flour
- 1 tablespoon baking powder
- 1 teaspoon garlic powder
- 1 egg
- 1 teaspoon sugar
- 1 teaspoon salt
- 1 teaspoon paprika
- 1 cup milk

Mix all ingredients. Coat seafood in batter and fry.

Betty Mullis

Emmeline and Hessie's Shrimp and Green Noodles

- ½ (8 ounce) package spinach noodles
- 2 pounds shrimp, peeled and deveined
- ½ cup clarified butter
- 1 can cream of mushroom soup
- 1 cup sour cream
- 1 cup mayonnaise
- ½ teaspoon Dijon style mustard
- 1 tablespoon chives, chopped
- 4 tablespoons cooking sherry
- ½ cup sharp Cheddar cheese, grated

Cook noodles as directed on package. Line a casserole dish with noodles and make into a nest. In large frying pan, sauté the shrimp in ½ cup clarified butter until pink and tender, about 5 minutes. Cover noodles with shrimp. Combine soup, sour cream, mayonnaise, and chives; add mustard and cooking sherry. Pour sauce over shrimp and sprinkle Cheddar cheese over all. Bake at 350 degrees for 30 minutes until cheese has melted and is bubbly.

Note: This recipe is from the former Emmeline & Hessie's Restaurant on St. Simons Island and is a legendary favorite of many.

Mollie Morgan

Oyster Stew

- 1 pint standard oysters
- Salt and pepper
- 1 stick butter
- 1 gallon whole milk

In a large pot, melt butter, add oysters with juice, and cook until oyster edges begin to curl. Add other ingredients. Cook over medium heat until hot. Be careful not to boil or scorch. Serve with saltines, oyster crackers, and your favorite hot sauce.

Dawn Burch Moore

Shrimp Creole

- ⅔ cup onions
- ½ cup green pepper, finely chopped
- ½ cup celery, chopped
- 2 tablespoons butter
- 2 bay leaves
- 2 cloves garlic, minced
- 1 (8 ounce) can tomato sauce
- 1 (28 ounce) can tomatoes
- 1½ pounds fresh shrimp, peeled and deveined
- 1 teaspoon salt
- ½ teaspoon pepper
- ½ teaspoon oregano
- Cooked rice

Sauté onions, green pepper, garlic, and celery in butter. Add tomatoes, tomato sauce, and seasonings. Simmer about 40 minutes. Add shrimp and cook about 3 more minutes. Serve over cooked rice.

Note: Chicken and pork chops are delicious when baked in this sauce at 350 degrees for 1 hour.

Angie O'Steen

Shrimp Etouffee

- 2 medium onions, chopped
- 1 cup celery, chopped
- 1 small green pepper, chopped
- 1 stick oleo or butter
- 2-3 sprigs parsley, finely chopped
- ½ can cream of celery soup
- ½ can cream of mushroom soup
- 1 bunch green onions, finely chopped
- 1 pound raw shrimp
- Salt and pepper to taste

Put onion, celery, and green pepper in blender for 5 seconds on chop (very fine). Cook in oleo/butter until soft. Add shrimp and cook until almost done. Add soups, green onion, and parsley. Cook about 25 minutes over low heat. Season to taste with salt and pepper. Serve over rice. Serves 4.

Ann Sheppard

Shrimp Scampi

- 2 pounds fresh jumbo shrimp
- ¼ teaspoon salt
- ¼ cup olive oil
- ⅛ teaspoon ground pepper
- 3 cloves garlic, minced
- 2 tablespoons parsley, chopped
- ¼ cup butter, melted
- 2 tablespoons lemon juice

Shell and devein shrimp, leaving fantail on. Split each shrimp lengthwise. Combine all remaining ingredients. Mix well. Dip shrimp in mixture. Place in shallow pan in single layer. Pour remaining sauce over shrimp. Broil a few inches from heat for 6 to 8 minutes. Watch carefully.

Betsy Hodges

Steve's Shrimp Etouffee

- 2-2½ pounds raw shrimp, peeled
- ¼ cup butter
- 3 tablespoons flour
- 2 tablespoons garlic, minced
- 1 tablespoon dill weed
- ¼ cup green pepper, chopped
- ¾ cup celery, chopped
- 2 tablespoons green onions, chopped (optional)
- 1 cup onion, chopped
- ½ cup water
- ½ teaspoon salt
- ½ teaspoon cayenne pepper
- 1 tablespoon lemon juice

Melt butter in a large frying pan. Blend in flour. Add garlic, dill weed, green onion, green pepper, celery, and onion. Cover and cook 8 minutes or until tender. Add water and stir. Add salt, cayenne pepper, and lemon juice. Push vegetables to side of pan. Add raw shrimp and spoon vegetables over shrimp. Cover and cook over low heat until shrimp are pink and tender. Serve over rice.

Steve Bailey

Curried Shrimp and Rice

1 pound boiled shrimp, peeled and deveined
1 cup cooked white rice
1 cup celery, chopped
1 cup green bell pepper, chopped
1 small onion, chopped
Add curry powder to taste
Mayonnaise

Mix all ingredients together with desired amount of mayonnaise and curry to taste. You will want the mixture to be smooth. Keep refrigerated.

Karen Barlow

Crab Soup

2 tablespoons butter
2 tablespoons flour
1 pint milk
Salt and pepper
1 can Carnation milk
1 cup water
2 cups white lump crabmeat
4 tablespoons cooking sherry

Melt butter in top of double boiler. Blend in flour. Add milk gradually, stirring constantly. Add Carnation milk and water. As mixture begins to thicken, add salt, pepper, and crabmeat. When soup is at desired consistency, remove from heat, add cooking sherry, and stir well. Serve with garnish of hard-boiled egg yolks, finely crumbled, if desired.

Ginny Lockwood

Garlic Shrimp Casserole

- 2 pounds medium-size fresh shrimp, unpeeled
- 1 tablespoon Creole seasoning (I like Tony Chachere's, and I usually add a little extra.)
- 2 tablespoons bacon drippings
- 3 tablespoons all-purpose flour
- 1 tablespoon vegetable oil
- ⅓ cup onion, finely chopped
- ⅓ cup green bell pepper, finely chopped
- ⅓ cup celery, finely chopped
- 2 garlic cloves, minced
- 1 teaspoon dried thyme
- 1 teaspoon dried oregano
- ¾ teaspoon salt
- ½ teaspoon pepper
- 4 green onions, chopped
- ½ cup chicken broth or water
- 2 cups whipping cream
- 1 pound uncooked spaghetti, broken in half and cooked according to package directions (I sometimes substitute linguini for the spaghetti.)
- 1 cup Parmesan cheese, freshly grated

Garnish: additional chopped green onions

Peel and devein shrimp. Combine shrimp and Creole seasoning in a medium bowl, set aside. Cook bacon drippings, flour, and oil in a large skillet over medium heat, whisking constantly, 20 to 25 minutes or until roux is the dark brown color of pecan shells. Add ⅓ cup onion and next 3 ingredients; cook 5 minute or until tender. Add thyme and next 3 ingredients; cook 1 minute, stirring constantly. Add shrimp and 4 green onions, cook over medium-high heat 3 minutes or until shrimp are almost done. Transfer to a large bowl. Add broth to skillet, scraping bottom of skillet to loosen browned bits. Add whipping cream. Bring to a boil over medium-high heat; reduce heat, and simmer 6 minutes. Add to shrimp. Stir in cooked pasta; toss well to combine. Pour into a lightly greased 9 × 13 inch baking dish. Sprinkle with Parmesan cheese. Bake, uncovered, at 350 degrees for 20 minutes or until thoroughly heated. Garnish, if desired.

Mary Lou Gillespie

Shrimp and Crab Casserole

- **1 medium green pepper, chopped**
- **1 medium onion, chopped**
- **1 cup celery, chopped**
- **1 (16½ ounce) package frozen crabmeat**
- **1½ pounds shrimp, boiled (cut shrimp in half if long)**
- **½ teaspoon salt**
- **½ teaspoon pepper**
- **1 teaspoon Worcestershire sauce**
- **1 cup Kraft mayonnaise**
- **1 cup breadcrumbs, buttered**

Mix all ingredients together. Bake in a 9 x 13 sprayed casserole dish at 300 degrees for 20-30 minutes. Serves eight. Easily doubled for a 10 x 15 inch casserole.

In Memory of Mrs. Lois Meeks

Savannah Georgia Shrimp and Grits

- **1 cup stone-ground grits**
- **½ stick butter**
- **2 cups Cheddar cheese, shredded**
- **1 pound uncooked shrimp, rinsed, peeled and deveined, and roughly chopped**
- **6 slices bacon, cooked and chopped (save drippings)**
- **4 teaspoons fresh lemon juice**
- **2 tablespoons fresh parsley, chopped**
- **1 cup green onions, thinly sliced (white and green parts)**
- **1 large clove garlic, minced**
- **Salt and pepper to taste**

Cook grits with salt and pepper until creamy as directed on package. Remove from heat and stir in the butter and cheese. Keep covered until ready to serve. In the grease the bacon was fried, sauté shrimp over medium heat for about 3 minutes. Don't overcook! Immediately add lemon juice, parsley, green onions, and garlic. Remove from heat. Pour grits into serving bowls and pour shrimp mixture over grits. Garnish with crumbled bacon.

Angie O'Steen

Saucy Shrimp Casserole

- ¼ cup butter
- ¼ cup flour
- 2 cups milk
- ½ teaspoon Worcestershire
- 8 ounces extra sharp Cheddar cheese, shredded
- 6 eggs, hard-cooked and sliced
- 1 pound shrimp, cooked and peeled
- 1 teaspoon salt
- Couple shakes of Tabasco sauce

Melt butter. Stir in flour until smooth. Add milk and seasonings and cook until it looks like a sauce. Add cheese and stir until melted and smooth. Remove from heat. Alternate layers of egg, shrimp, and sauce in 1½ quart casserole. Sprinkle with paprika, if desired, for color. Bake at 350 degrees for 25-30 minutes until hot and bubbly. Serve with plain white rice.

Note: I cook my shrimp according to directions on Old Bay seasoning container and then peel. I usually double recipe. You can use any size shrimp, but I think it's worth the extra money to get the jumbo.

Debbie Fender

Shrimp-Rice Casserole

(Quick and Easy)

- 1 package frozen salad shrimp (add more if needed)
- 3 to 4 green onions, chopped
- ½ stick butter, melted
- 1 can cream of mushroom soup, undiluted
- 4 cups cooked rice

Sauté onions and shrimp in butter. Add rice and soup to onions and shrimp. Mix well and serve.

Note: Add a salad and bread and you have a quick meal. This can easily be changed to serve more people or adjusted for heartier appetites.

Sherri M. Jenkins

Seafood Casserole

- 1 pound shrimp, cooked and ready to eat
- 1 teaspoon butter
- 1 pound crabmeat, cooked
- 1 cup onion, finely chopped
- 1 cup celery, finely chopped
- 1 can cream of mushroom soup
- 1 can Carnation evaporated milk
- 1 cup mayonnaise
- 2 tablespoons self-rising flour
- 1 can water chestnuts, sliced
- 1 to 1½ cups potato chips, crushed
- Red pepper

Saute onion and celery in a teaspoon of butter; set aside. Mix soup, milk, mayonnaise, and flour well. Add onion, celery, and water chestnuts to mixture. Add shrimp and crabmeat and mix well. Pour into a greased Pyrex dish, at least an 8 x 12 or larger. Bake at 350 degrees for 30 to 40 minutes. The last 5 minutes of baking, top with crushed potato chips and sprinkle with red pepper.

In Memory of Mrs. Catherine Taylor

Seafood Casserole

- 1 can shrimp, drained
- 1 can crabmeat, drained
- 1 can celery soup
- 2 (2 ounce) jars diced pimentos
- 2 tablespoons butter
- 2 cups green onions, cooked
- 1 (8 ounce) cream cheese
- ½ cup milk
- 1 cup cooked rice
- 1 cup celery, chopped and cooked
- Ritz crackers, crushed

Combine ingredients. Top with crushed crackers. Bake at 350 degrees for 20 minutes.

Elaine Norris Maley

Seafood Casserole

- 1 small can crabmeat
- 2 cans small shrimp
- 1 cup mayonnaise
- 3 cups cooked rice
- 1 can cream of mushroom soup
- 1 cup milk
- 1 small can mushroom pieces
- 1 tablespoon lemon juice
- 1 whole bell pepper, diced
- 1 cup celery, diced
- ½ cup onion, diced
- 1½ teaspoons black pepper
- Salt to taste

Sauté celery, bell pepper, onion, salt, and pepper. Butter a 2- to 3-quart casserole dish. Combine all other ingredients and pour into casserole. Bake uncovered at 350 degrees for 45 to 60 minutes.

Note: I have used fresh and imitation crab and frozen shrimp. You could use 3 cups chicken instead of seafood. I also have used boil-in-bag rice. This recipe works well as a cold salad.

Peggy Hurd
Family Ministry Center Director

Seafood Quiche

- 2 regular size unbaked pie shells
- 1 cup half-and-half
- 3 eggs, beaten
- 1 cup mozzarella cheese and New York Cheddar, blended
- 2 green onions, chopped into small pieces
- 1 can crabmeat
- 12 large raw shrimp, peeled and deveined, diced into small pieces

Mix all ingredients. Pour into pie shells and bake 350 degrees for 30 minutes.

Alena Connell
Wife of Rev. William Connell
Former Pastor, First Baptist Church

Broiled Tilapia Parmesan

- ½ cup Parmesan cheese
- ¼ cup butter, softened
- 3 tablespoons mayonnaise
- 2 tablespoons fresh lemon juice
- ¼ teaspoon dried basil
- ¼ teaspoon ground black pepper
- ⅛ teaspoon onion powder
- ⅛ teaspoon celery salt
- 2 pounds tilapia fillets

Preheat your oven's broiler. Grease a broiling pan or line pan with aluminum foil. In a small bowl, mix together the Parmesan cheese, butter, mayonnaise, and lemon juice. Season with dried basil, pepper, onion powder, and celery salt. Mix well and set aside. Arrange fillets in a single layer on the prepared pan. Broil a few inches from the heat for 2 to 3 minutes. Flip the fillets over and broil for a couple more minutes. Remove the fillets from the oven and cover them with the Parmesan cheese mixture on the top side. Broil for 2 more minutes or until the topping is browned and fish flakes easily with a fork. Be careful not to overcook the fish.

Rhonda Saeed
Administrative Secretary

Baked Fish

- 2 to 3 pounds fish fillets (grouper or red snapper is best)
- 2 tomatoes, sliced
- 2 onions, sliced
- Monterey Jack cheese, sliced
- Parmesan cheese, freshly grated
- Salt and pepper to taste

Preheat oven to 425 degrees. Spray large baking dish with cooking spray. Place fish fillets on baking dish. Sprinkle salt and pepper to taste. Bake for approximately 2 to 3 minutes (depending on thickness of fillet). Place sliced onions on fillets and bake for 2 to 3 minutes. Place sliced tomatoes on fillets and bake for approximately 2 to 3 minutes. Add sliced cheese and bake for approximately 2 minutes. Add grated cheese and serve.

Note: There are several steps to this recipe, but it's very, very easy. So delicious!!

Maudine Wright

Pecan Crusted Trout

- 4 (6 to 8 ounce) large trout fillets
- 1 tablespoon fresh lemon juice
- ½ cup seasoned breadcrumbs, divided
- 1 cup Georgia pecans, toasted
- Salt and pepper to taste
- 2 teaspoons dried rosemary
- ⅓ cup all-purpose flour
- 1 egg, beaten with 2 to 3 teaspoons water
- 2 tablespoons vegetable oil, divided
- 2 tablespoons butter, divided

Season trout fillets with salt, pepper, and lemon juice. Let stand at room temperature for 10 to 15 minutes. Combine 2 tablespoons of breadcrumbs with pecans in blender or food processor and grind finely. Combine with remaining breadcrumbs and rosemary. Transfer to a plate. Dredge fillets in flour and shake off excess. Dip in egg wash. Press fillets skin side up in crumb mixture. In a large skillet, heat 1 tablespoon each of oil and butter over medium-high heat. Place 2 fillets skin side up in skillet and cook until golden brown, about 3 minutes. Using a spatula, turn fillets and cook until opaque in center, about 3 more minutes. Transfer to plate. Repeat with remaining butter, oil, and fillets.

Maudine Wright

Baked Shrimp

- 5 pounds medium shrimp
- 1 (16 ounce) bottle Italian salad dressing
- 2 sticks butter, melted
- Juice of 5 lemons, optional

Mix butter, salad dressing, and lemon juice. Pour over raw shrimp in roasting pan. Cover tightly with foil and bake for 45 minutes at 350 degrees. Stir after 20 minutes. Do not overcook.

Trina Wilkerson

Tuna Fish Casserole

- 1 (8 ounce) package egg noodles
- 1 tablespoon butter
- ¼ cup onion, chopped
- ¼ cup green bell pepper, chopped
- 2 (7 ounce) cans light tuna
- 1 tomato or 1 can of tomatoes, diced
- 1 (4 ounce) can mushrooms
- 1 tablespoon lemon juice
- ¼ teaspoon each of salt and pepper
- ½ cup mayonnaise
- ⅓ cup milk
- ½ cup cheese

Boil noodles as directed on package. Sauté onion in butter over low heat and add other ingredients. Simmer. Pour noodles and sauce together and bake in a large casserole dish at 400 degrees for 20 minutes.

Marvelyne Fletcher

New England Clam Chowder

- 4 (6.5 ounce) cans minced clams
- 6 tablespoons butter or margarine, divided
- 3 cups milk
- ¼ teaspoon pepper
- 3 medium potatoes (2 pounds)
- 1 small onion, diced
- ½ teaspoon salt

Drain clams, reserving clam juice. Peel potatoes and cut into ½-inch cubes. Melt 2 tablespoons butter over medium heat in a Dutch oven; add diced onion and sauté until tender. Add clam juice and potatoes; bring to a boil over medium-high heat. Reduce heat and simmer, stirring occasionally, 10 minutes or until potatoes are tender. Remove 1 cup potatoes with a slotted spoon; mash and return to Dutch oven. Stir in clams, remaining 4 tablespoons butter, milk, salt, and pepper. Cook, stirring occasionally until thoroughly heated.

Bro. Shep Johnson
Senior Pastor

Shrimp Pasta with Creole Cream Sauce

- 1½ pounds medium shrimp, unpeeled
- 2 teaspoons Creole seasoning
- 12 ounces penne pasta
- 2 tablespoons butter
- 4 green onions, sliced
- 2 garlic cloves, minced
- 1½ cups whipping cream
- 1 teaspoon hot sauce
- ¼ cup fresh parsley, chopped
- ½ cup Parmesan cheese, grated

Peel and devein shrimp; toss with Creole seasoning. Set aside. Cook pasta; drain and keep warm. Melt butter in a large skillet over medium heat. Add shrimp; cook until pink, about 5 minutes. Remove shrimp, add green onions and garlic. Sauté about 2-3 minutes. Reduce heat to medium. Stir in cream and hot sauce; bring to a boil. Reduce heat and simmer 8-10 minutes, stirring constantly. Sauce will begin to thicken. Stir in shrimp and parsley. Toss with pasta and sprinkle with cheese.

Kim Knight

Zesty Shrimp and Pasta

- ½ pound linguine, uncooked
- ¾ cup zesty Italian dressing, divided
- 2 cups fresh mushrooms, sliced
- 1 small onion, thinly sliced
- 1 (14 ounce) can artichoke hearts, drained and quartered
- 1 pound large shrimp, peeled and deveined
- 1 tablespoon fresh parsley, chopped
- ¼ cup Parmesan cheese, grated

Cook pasta as directed on package, omitting salt. Meanwhile, heat ½ cup dressing in large skillet on medium heat. Stir in mushrooms, onions, and artichokes; cook 3 minutes or until onions are crisp-tender, stirring occasionally. Add shrimp and parsley; stir. Cook 2 minutes or until shrimp are pink and vegetables are tender, stirring occasionally. Drain pasta and return to pot. Add shrimp mixture and remaining dressing; toss lightly. Sprinkle with cheese.

Andrea Bassett

Low Country Boil

- 6 pounds smoked sausage, cut into 2-inch pieces
- 9 pounds shrimp (26 count)
- 36 small red potatoes
- 4 large onions, quartered
- 18 small ears of yellow corn
- 1 (5 ounce) package shrimp boil, or to taste
- 5 gallons of water

Using an outside cooker, place 5 gallons of water in a 10-gallon pot. Add the shrimp boil package and bring to a boil. Add the sausage and cook for 10 minutes. Add potatoes, onions, and corn and boil for 15 minutes. (It is best to place potatoes in a mesh cooking bag.) Check potatoes for tenderness. At this point, turn off heat and add shrimp. After about 10 minutes, drain all liquid from pot and spread cooked food over large brown paper bags. Serve with melted butter and cocktail sauce. Serves 18.

Note: Butter, crab, cabbage, or rutabagas may be added. A removable drain basket makes the process easier. The larger the shrimp the better.

Rule of Thumb: For preparation per person use 2 small red potatoes, 1 ear of corn, ⅓ pound sausage, and ½ pound shrimp.

Gil Morgan

Cocktail Sauce

- 1 gallon ketchup
- 1 cup vinegar
- 1 cup lemon juice
- 2 cups mustard
- 2 tablespoons Worcestershire sauce
- 3 tablespoons Heinz 57 sauce
- 10 ounces horseradish

Mix all ingredients together in a two-gallon stockpot. Stir until mixture is smooth and creamy. Keep in refrigerator. Yield: about 1½ gallons.

Alice Ward

Cakes and Frostings

"But He said to me, 'My grace is sufficient for you, for My power is made perfect in weakness.'"

2 Corinthians 12:9

(NIV)

Cakes and Frostings

Cream Cheese Pound Cake

3 sticks butter, softened
3 cups cake flour
3 cups sugar
6 eggs, separated
½ teaspoon salt
1 teaspoon vanilla flavoring
1 teaspoon lemon flavoring (optional)
1 (8 ounce) package cream cheese

Cream butter, cream cheese, and sugar together well. Separate eggs. Add yolks one at a time, beating well after each one. Sift together flour and salt and add gradually to creamed mixture. Add flavorings. Beat egg whites until stiff and fold in cake batter. Bake in tube pan at 300 degrees for 1½ hours.

Gloria Cloud

Cream Cheese Pound Cake

2 sticks butter, softened
1 (8 ounce) package cream cheese
3 cups sugar
1 teaspoon vanilla flavoring
½ cup Crisco shortening
6 eggs
3 cups sifted cake flour

Cream butter and Crisco. Add sugar and cream cheese and beat until light and fluffy. Add flour gradually. Add eggs one at a time, beating after each addition. Add vanilla. Pour into a greased and floured 10-inch tube pan. Bake in a 325 degree oven for 1 hour and 20 minutes or until done.

Myrna Parker

Blueberry Pound Cake

- 1 (8 ounce) package cream cheese, softened
- 3 sticks butter, softened
- 3 cups all-purpose flour
- 1½ teaspoons vanilla
- 6 eggs
- 1 cup blueberries
- 3 cups sugar
- 2 tablespoons flour
- Dash of salt

Cream together softened cream cheese, butter, and sugar. Blend in flour, salt, and vanilla. Add eggs 1 at a time, beating well after each egg. Toss blueberries in flour. Shake off loose flour. Gently fold in blueberries by hand. Pour into well-greased and floured tube cake pan and bake for 1 hour and 20 minutes at 325 degrees.

Sonya Hendley

Mamie's Pound Cake

- 9 eggs
- 1½ cups Crisco shortening
- 3 cups sugar
- 3 cups cake flour
- 1½ teaspoons lemon juice
- 1½ teaspoons vanilla flavoring

Combine sugar and Crisco until creamy. Add eggs one at a time, beating between each egg. Slowly add cake flour, beating well. Add lemon juice and vanilla. Pour into a tube pan and bake at 325 degrees for 1½ hours.

In Memory of Mrs. Mamie Farrar

Mrs. Dottie's Pound Cake

- **1 cup Crisco**
- **1 stick real butter, softened**
- **2 cups sugar**
- **1 tablespoon vanilla flavoring**
- **1 teaspoon lemon juice**
- **1 box 4X powdered sugar**
- **10 large eggs**
- **3 cups self-rising flour (measure and sift 3 times before adding to batter)**

On high speed of mixer beat Crisco, butter, sugar, vanilla, and lemon juice. Add 4X sugar to Crisco mixture and beat on high until blended. Turn mixer to low speed. Alternate adding eggs and sifted flour, ending with flour. Oil and flour a long loaf pan and add batter. Bake at 350 degrees for 1 hour and 10 to 20 minutes. Watch for cake to leave sides of pan.

In Memory of Mrs. Dottie Morgan

Five-Flavor Cake

- **2 sticks butter**
- **½ cup Crisco shortening**
- **3 cups sugar**
- **5 eggs, well beaten**
- **3 cups all-purpose flour**
- **½ teaspoon baking powder**
- **1 cup milk**
- **1 teaspoon coconut extract**
- **1 teaspoon butter extract**
- **1 teaspoon rum extract**
- **1 teaspoon lemon extract**
- **1 teaspoon vanilla extract**

Cream butter, shortening, and sugar until light and fluffy. Add eggs and beat well. Combine flour and baking powder; then add to creamed mixture alternating with milk and flavorings. Spoon mixture into greased 10-inch tube pan. Bake at 325 degrees for 1½ hours.

In Memory of Mrs. Virginia Brown

Chocolate Pound Cake and Chocolate Frosting

- **2 sticks butter, softened to room temperature**
- **½ cup Crisco shortening**
- **3 cups sugar**
- **5 eggs**
- **3 cups sifted all-purpose flour**
- **½ teaspoon baking powder**
- **½ teaspoon salt**
- **4 tablespoons cocoa**
- **1 cup milk**
- **1 tablespoon vanilla**

Cream butter, Crisco, and sugar. Add one egg at a time. Mix in flour, baking powder, salt, and cocoa, alternating with milk as you mix. Add 1 tablespoon of vanilla. Mix until ingredients are well blended. Pour into a 10-inch tube pan. Bake in a 300 degree oven for 80 minutes.

Chocolate Frosting:

- **4 tablespoons butter**
- **6 tablespoons cocoa**
- **1 (16 ounce) box powdered sugar**
- **1 teaspoon vanilla**
- **Black coffee or cream**

Cream butter, cocoa, powdered sugar, and vanilla. Add a small amount of cream or black coffee to make frosting spread easily. (Mama always used coffee.)

Paula Thomas

"...so that being justified by His grace we would be made heirs according to the hope of eternal life."

Titus 3:7
(NASB)

Coconut Pound Cake

- 6 large eggs
- 1 cup Crisco shortening
- ½ cup unsalted butter, softened to room temperature
- 3 cups sugar
- ½ teaspoon almond extract
- ½ teaspoon coconut extract
- 3 cups sifted cake flour
- 1 cup milk
- 2 cups packaged or fresh flaked coconut

Preheat the oven to 300 degrees. Grease and flour a 10-inch tube pan. Separate the eggs. Set the whites aside and allow to come to room temperature. Beat the egg yolks with the Crisco and butter at high speed until well blended. Gradually add the sugar, beating until light and fluffy. Add the extracts and beat at low speed. Beat in the flour (¼ at a time), alternating with the milk (about ⅓ at a time). Begin and end with the flour. Add the coconut and beat on medium speed until well blended. In a clean bowl, beat the egg whites until stiff peaks form. Gently fold the whites into the batter. Pour into the prepared pan. Bake for 2 hours. Cool the cake in the pan on a wire rack for 15 minutes. Remove from the pan and finish cooling on a rack.

Cathalene Taylor

Hint: Use name-brand ingredients. Store brands of sugar are often more finely ground than name brands, yielding more sugar per cup, which can cause a cake to fall. Store brands of butter may contain more liquid fat and flours more hard wheat, making the cake heavy.

Blueberry Cake

- 1½ cups sugar
- ½ cup shortening
- 2 eggs
- 1 teaspoon vanilla
- 4 cups all-purpose flour
- 1 teaspoon salt
- 4 teaspoons baking powder
- 1 cup milk
- 4 cups blueberries

Mix sugar, shortening, eggs, vanilla, salt, baking powder, and milk. Add flour and blueberries. Pour into a tube cake pan.

Topping:

- 1 cup sugar
- ¼ cup shortening
- ¼ cup margarine
- 3 teaspoons cinnamon
- ⅔ cup flour

Mix together and put on top of cake. Bake at 350 degrees for 60-65 minutes.

Connie Bowers

Sour Cream Pound Cake

- 2 sticks butter
- 3 cups sugar
- 6 eggs
- 3 cups all-purpose flour
- 1 cup sour cream
- ½ teaspoon baking soda
- 1 teaspoon vanilla
- ½ teaspoon lemon extract

Preheat oven to 300 degrees. Cream butter and sugar. Add eggs 1 at a time, beating after each addition. (Creaming of butter and sugar and beating well after addition of each egg is important.) Add soda to sour cream. Add flour 1 cup at a time alternately with sour cream mixture. Add flavorings. Bake in a Bundt or tube pan for 1½ hours until done.

Eleanor Sammons

Brown Sugar Pound Cake

- 1 cup butter
- ½ cup solid Crisco
- 1 (1 pound) box and 1 cup light brown sugar
- 5 eggs
- 3½ cups all-purpose flour
- 1 teaspoon baking powder
- 1 cup milk
- 2 teaspoons vanilla

Preheat oven to 325 degrees. Spray angel food cake pan (I use tube pan.) with Baker's Joy. Cream first 4 ingredients together. Beat well. Add baking powder to flour and add alternately with milk to the creamed mixture (making sure last ingredient added is flour). Again, beat well. Stir in the vanilla. Bake for 1 hour and 20 minutes. Let cool in pan for 10 minutes and then invert on rack. Cool completely. Cover well to store.

Carol Sawyer

Chocolate Sour Cream Pound Cake

- 1 cup butter, softened
- 2 cups sugar
- 1 cup light brown sugar, firmly packed
- 6 large eggs
- 2½ cups all-purpose flour
- ¼ teaspoon baking soda
- ½ cup cocoa
- 1 (8 ounce) sour cream
- 2 teaspoons vanilla extract

Beat butter at medium speed with an electric mixer about 2 minutes or until soft and creamy. Gradually add sugars, beating at medium speed 5 to 7 minutes. Add eggs one at a time, beating just until yellow disappears. Combine flour, baking soda, and cocoa; add to creamed mixture, alternating with sour cream, beginning and ending with flour mixture. Mix each addition at lowest speed until just blended. Stir in vanilla. Spoon batter into a greased and floured 10-inch tube pan. Bake at 325 degrees for 1 hour and 20 minutes or until a wooden pick inserted in center comes out clean. Cool in pan on a wire rack 10 to 15 minutes. Remove from pan and cool completely on a wire rack.

Renee Roberson

Chocolate Chip Pound Cake

- 1 box Pillsbury yellow cake mix
- 1 box chocolate instant pudding (smaller box)
- ½ cup sugar
- ¾ cup water
- ¾ cup oil
- 5 eggs
- 1 (8 ounce) sour cream
- 1 teaspoon vanilla
- 8 to 10 ounces semi-sweet chocolate chips

Preheat oven to 350 degrees. Mix all ingredients. Pour into a Bundt or tube pan that has been sprayed with cooking spray. Bake for 1 hour. Enjoy!

Jessica Barber

William's Pound Cake

- ¾ pound butter
- 3 cups all-purpose flour
- 2¼ cups sugar
- 1 teaspoon vanilla flavoring
- 1½ cups eggs
- 2 teaspoons baking powder
- 1 teaspoon lemon flavoring
- 1 teaspoon almond flavoring (optional)
- Pinch of salt

Add baking powder and salt to eggs. Beat until light. Add sugar gradually. Beat well. Cream butter with flour and combine two mixtures. Add flavorings; beat well. Pour into greased and floured tube pan. Bake 1½ hours at 300 degrees.

Note: You may use 1 teaspoon of almond flavoring instead of vanilla or use all 3.

Janice Preston

Celebration Cake

- 1 package Duncan Hines yellow cake mix (dry)
- 1 cup chocolate chips or grated chunks (use food processor)
- 1 cup coconut
- 1 cup sour cream
- 1 cup pecans, chopped
- 1 small package instant vanilla pudding
- ¾ cup Wesson oil
- 3 eggs

Mix all ingredients well and pour into greased and floured tube pan. Bake 1 hour in 350 degree oven.

Debbie Fender

Franklin Nut Cake

- 1 pound butter
- 2 cups sugar
- 6 eggs, beaten
- 1 teaspoon baking powder
- ¼ teaspoon salt
- ½ pound candied cherries, chopped
- ½ pound candied pineapple, chopped
- 1 pound pecans, chopped
- 2 teaspoons vanilla flavoring
- 4 cups all-purpose flour

Cream butter and sugar; add beaten eggs. Sift together 3 cups flour, baking powder, and salt and add to butter and sugar. Mix remaining flour with cherries, pineapple, and nuts and fold into mixture; add vanilla. Bake at 250 degrees for 3 hours.

Winifred Vaughn

Fresh Apple Cake

- 3 large apples, cut in small pieces
- 1 cup pecans, finely chopped
- 1¼ cups vegetable oil
- 2 cups sugar
- 2 eggs, well beaten
- 3 cups all-purpose flour
- 1½ teaspoons baking soda
- 1 teaspoon salt
- 2 teaspoons vanilla flavoring

Add nuts, oil, sugar, and eggs to apples. Add flour, soda, and salt to mixture. Add vanilla. Bake at 325 degrees in a greased and floured Bundt or tube pan for about 1½ hours or until done.

Icing:

- ½ cup evaporated milk
- 1 cup sugar
- ½ stick margarine

Combine evaporated milk, sugar, and margarine. Boil together for 1½ minutes. Cool. Pour over cake.

Ellen Fitzgerald
Grandmother Drury

Myrtice Hill's Fruitcake

- 2 sticks butter
- 2 cups sugar
- 6 eggs, beaten
- 4 cups all-purpose flour
- 1 teaspoon baking powder
- ½ teaspoon salt
- 1 pound red cherries (candied)
- 1 pound pineapple (candied)
- 4 cups pecans, finely chopped
- 1 (15 ounce) box raisins
- 1 cup walnuts, chopped
- 2 teaspoons vanilla flavoring

Cream butter and sugar; add beaten eggs. Add 3 cups of flour with the baking powder and salt. Mix remaining 1 cup flour with fruit and nuts. Add coated fruit to cake batter; add vanilla. Stir. Bake at 250 degrees for 3 hours. Let cool in the pan.

Patsy Herlocker

Mama Thurman's Fruitcake

- 2 jars cherries, regular size
- 1 large package mixed candied fruit
- ½ cup cane syrup
- 1 cup milk
- 1 pound butter
- 8 eggs
- 2 cups sugar
- 3 cups self-rising flour
- 1 cup Brazil nuts, chopped
- 1 cup English walnuts, chopped
- ½ (15 ounce) box raisins
- 2 cups pecans, chopped
- 1 tablespoon pumpkin pie spice
- 1 tablespoon cloves

Beat eggs, sugar, and butter. Add syrup and milk and beat well. Roll fruit and nuts in self-rising flour and add to mixture. Add pumpkin pie spice and cloves. Mix and pour into small loaf pans. Bake at 350 degrees for about 45 minutes. If baked in a tube pan, cook for about 2 hours. Test with toothpick to see if done. This was my mother's recipe.

Eloise Spivey

Hint: Don't fill the pan all the way! The fruitcake will expand while it's cooking. When you're pouring the batter into the pan, don't fill the pan more than half full. That way the cake will have room to rise. Just use more pans or use a bigger pan than you think you need.

Icebox Fruitcake

- **2 large boxes vanilla wafers, crushed**
- **2 (1 pound) packages miniature marshmallows**
- **1 gallon pecans, roasted**
- **1 pound candied cherries, coarsely chopped**
- **1 pound candied pineapple, coarsely chopped**
- **1½ to 2 cans Eagle Brand condensed milk**

Prepare pans by lining with plastic wrap, using enough to fold over cake after packed in pans. Toast nuts to taste. Fold marshmallows over warm nuts and mix well until marshmallows are melted. Add wafers and fruit. Add milk and mix well and pack in prepared pans. Refrigerate overnight. Will keep in refrigerator 3 to 4 weeks. Freezes well. Use aluminum foil loaf pans—5 (2 pound) sizes or 10 (1 pound) sizes. Use a tablespoon to pack it in the corners and all over the pans. Mix with hands if too stiff.

In Memory of Mrs. Tish Overstreet

Sweet Potato Cake

- **¾ cup oil**
- **2½ cups sweet potatoes, cooked and mashed**
- **1½ teaspoons vanilla flavoring**
- **1½ teaspoons rum flavoring**
- **1½ teaspoons cinnamon**
- **1½ teaspoons nutmeg**
- **3 cups sugar**
- **6 eggs**
- **2½ cups self-rising flour**
- **1 cup pecans, chopped**
- **1 cup coconut**

Mix oil, sugar, sweet potatoes, vanilla, and rum flavorings. Add eggs one at a time, mixing after each addition. Combine flour, nutmeg, and cinnamon. Add to sweet potato mixture and mix well. Add coconut and pecans and mix with spoon. Pour into a greased and floured large tube pan. Bake 1½ hours on 300 degrees or until done.

Elouise Kirkland

Hawaiian Pound Cake

- 6 eggs
- 3 cups sugar
- ½ cup Crisco shortening
- ½ cup Crisco oil
- 3 cups all-purpose flour
- ½ teaspoon salt
- 1 tablespoon lemon flavoring
- 1 teaspoon baking powder
- 1 tablespoon vanilla flavoring
- 1 (8 ounce) sour cream
- ½ cup crushed pineapple, drained
- ½ cup maraschino cherries, chopped
- ⅓ cup coconut

Mix together eggs, sugar, shortening, and oil. Add remaining ingredients and mix well. Pour into a greased and floured tube pan. Start in a cold oven at 325 degrees for 1 hour and 15 minutes. Cool.

Cream Cheese Frosting:

- 1 (8 ounce) cream cheese
- 1 box 10X sugar
- ½ stick margarine, softened
- 1 tablespoon vanilla flavoring

Using mixer, blend cream cheese and margarine well. Add sugar and vanilla. Frost cake when cooled.

Patsy Herlocker

Strawberry Cake

- 1 box yellow cake mix
- 1 cup strawberries, crushed
- 4 eggs
- ¾ cup Wesson oil
- 1 package strawberry Jell-O
- 4 teaspoons all-purpose flour

Mix and bake in tube cake pan at 350 degrees about 1 hour.

Filling:

- 1 box 4X powdered sugar
- ¾ stick butter or margarine
- ⅓ cup strawberries

Beat together and spread on cake.

Winifred Vaughn

Ambrosia-Frosted Daisy Cake

- **2¼ cups cake flour or self-rising flour**
- **1¼ cups sugar**
- **½ cup shortening**
- **1 cup milk**
- **2 eggs, unbeaten**
- **1 teaspoon vanilla**

Sift together flour and sugar into a large bowl. Add shortening and ¾ cup milk. Beat 2 minutes on low, and then medium speed. Add remaining milk, eggs, and vanilla. Beat for 2 minutes. Pour into 2 round layer pans, well greased and floured on bottoms only. Bake at 350 degrees for 25 to 35 minutes. Cool.

Fluffy Ambrosia Frosting:

- **¾ cup sugar**
- **¼ cup light corn syrup**
- **2 unbeaten egg whites**
- **¼ teaspoon cream of tartar**
- **¼ teaspoon salt**
- **2 tablespoons water**
- **1 tablespoon orange rind**
- **2 drops orange food coloring**
- **Coconut**

In top of double boiler, combine first 6 ingredients. Cook over rapidly boiling water, beating with electric mixer until mixture stands in peaks. Remove from heat. Continue beating until thick enough to spread. Fold in orange rind and food coloring. Frost cake and cover with coconut.

In Memory of Mrs. Lou Ann Walker

Basic Two-Layer Cake

- 2¼ cups all-purpose White Lily flour
- 3 teaspoons baking powder
- 1 teaspoon salt
- 1½ cups sugar
- ½ cup Crisco
- 1 cup milk
- 2 eggs
- 1 teaspoon vanilla flavoring

Mix together all dry ingredients. Add Crisco and ½ cup milk. Blend with electric mixer for 2 minutes. Add remaining milk, vanilla, and eggs. Blend together well. Pour into 2 greased 9-inch round pans or 1 rectangular pan. Bake at 325-350 degrees for 25 to 30 minutes. Makes a great cake for strawberry or peach shortcake.

Cathy Tatum

Buttermilk Cake and Icing

- 1 cup sugar
- ¾ cup buttermilk
- ¾ teaspoon baking soda
- ¾ cup Crisco shortening
- 2 eggs
- 2 cups sifted cake flour
- 1 teaspoon vanilla

Mix soda and buttermilk. Let mixture rise to make one cup. Cream Crisco and sugar; add eggs. Add buttermilk and soda mixture. Add flour and vanilla. Grease and flour 2 cake pans. Pour mixture into pans. Bake at 335 degrees for 20 minutes. Cool.

Icing:

- 1 (8 ounce) cream cheese, softened
- 1 (16 ounce) box 4X powdered sugar
- 1 tablespoon evaporated or regular milk
- ½ teaspoon almond extract

Combine ingredients and beat until smooth. Spread icing on cake layers.

In Memory of Mrs. Jonell Garrett

Daddy's Butternut Cake

- 1 cup shortening
- 2 cups sugar
- 4 eggs
- 2 tablespoons butternut flavoring
- 1 teaspoon baking powder
- 1 tablespoon vanilla flavoring
- 1 cup milk, divided
- 1 cup self-rising flour
- 2 cups all-purpose flour
- ½ teaspoon salt

Cream shortening and sugar until creamy. Add eggs one at a time, beating after each addition. Add flavorings. Add self-rising flour and ½ cup milk. Sift all-purpose flour with salt and baking powder. Add to batter along with rest of milk. Beat well and pour into 3 greased and floured 8-inch cake pans. Bake at 350 degrees until toothpick comes out clean.

Filling:

- 1 stick butter or margarine, melted slowly
- 3 egg yolks, beaten well
- 1 cup sugar
- 1 large can evaporated milk
- 1 tablespoon vanilla flavoring
- 1 tablespoon butternut flavoring
- 1 cup pecans, chopped
- 2 cups coconut

Combine melted butter and beaten eggs. Add sugar and evaporated milk. Cook over low heat until good and thick. Remove from heat. Add flavorings, pecans, and coconut. Spread on cooled cake.

Note: The original recipe calls for baking this in a tube pan. I have adapted the instructions to make a 3-layer cake. Also, I believe he made extra filling to spread on top and sides of cake. Decorate the top with a few pecan halves.

Glennis Coleman
Wife of Rev. Ray Coleman
Smyrna Baptist Association

Caramel Cake

- 3 cups all-purpose flour
- 3 teaspoons baking powder
- ½ teaspoon salt
- 1 cup butter (2 sticks)
- 2 cups sugar
- 1 teaspoon vanilla
- 4 eggs
- 1 cup milk

Sift together flour, baking powder, and salt. Set aside. Cream butter and sugar and then add vanilla. Add eggs one at a time beating well after each. Add flour mixture alternately with milk, ending with flour. Pour into 3 cake pans and bake at 350 degrees for 25 to 30 minutes.

Caramel Filling:

- ½ cup sugar
- ¼ cup hot water
- 3½ cups sugar
- 1 cup milk
- ¾ stick butter
- 2 tablespoons white Karo syrup

Brown ½ cup sugar in heavy saucepan on medium heat to a deep caramel color. Add hot water, remove from heat, and add rest of sugar, milk, butter, and Karo syrup. Cook almost to a soft-ball stage. Put in mixing bowl and beat until creamy. Spread on cake. If you cook it too long, add a few drops of hot water.

Catherine Moodie

"It is good to give thanks to the Lord and to sing praises to Your name, O Most High; To declare Your lovingkindness in the morning and Your faithfulness by night."

Psalm 92:1-2
(NASB)

Aunt Jean's Carrot Layer Cake

Filling:

- 1 cup sugar
- 2 tablespoons all-purpose flour
- ¼ teaspoon salt
- 1 cup whipping cream
- ½ cup butter or margarine
- 1 cup pecans, chopped
- 1 teaspoon vanilla extract

In a heavy saucepan, combine sugar, flour, and salt. Stir in cream; add butter. Cook and stir over medium heat until the butter is melted; bring to a boil. Reduce heat. Simmer uncovered for 30 minutes, stirring occasionally. Stir in nuts and vanilla. Set aside to cool.

Cake:

- ¼ cup vegetable oil
- 2 cups sugar
- 2 cups all-purpose flour
- 2 teaspoons ground cinnamon
- 2 teaspoons baking powder
- 1 teaspoon baking soda
- 1 teaspoon salt
- 4 eggs
- 4 cups carrots, finely chopped
- 1 cup raisins
- 1 cup pecans, chopped

In a mixing bowl, beat oil and sugar for 1 minute. Combine next five ingredients. Add to the creamed mixture alternately with eggs. Mix well. Stir in carrots, raisins, and nuts. Pour into 3 greased and floured 9-inch round cake pans. Bake at 350 degrees for 35 to 40 minutes or until layers test done. Cool in pans 10 minutes. Remove to wire racks and cool .

Frosting:

- ¾ cup butter or margarine, softened
- 2 (3 ounce) packages cream cheese, softened
- 1 teaspoon vanilla extract
- 3 cups confectioners' sugar

Beat butter, cream cheese, and vanilla until smooth. Gradually beat in sugar. Place cooked filling between layers and frost top and sides of cake with cream cheese frosting. Store in refrigerator.

Kathy Stone

Eunice's Yummy Chocolate Cake

- **2½ cups sugar**
- **1 cup Crisco shortening**
- **1 stick butter**
- **1 teaspoon baking powder**
- **½ teaspoon salt**
- **3 cups all-purpose flour**
- **1 cup milk**
- **5 eggs, room temperature**

Cream Crisco, butter, and sugar. Add eggs one at a time and beat. Mix dry ingredients and add alternately with milk. Bake at 325 degrees for 30 minutes. Makes 3 large layers. Split each layer and ice.

Chocolate Icing:

- **2 cups granulated sugar**
- **10 large marshmallows**
- **¾ cup evaporated milk**
- **1 (6 ounce) package chocolate chips**
- **1 stick margarine**

Mix sugar, milk, and marshmallows. Cook until marshmallows melt, stirring constantly. Remove from heat. Add chocolate chips and margarine. Mix well. Spread icing on cake while warm.

Note: Cake layers may be made ahead of time and frozen; split layers while still partially frozen.

Cindy Williams

Chocolate Layer Cake

- 4 eggs
- 3 cups cake flour
- 2 cups sugar
- 1 cup whole milk
- 2 sticks butter
- 3 teaspoons baking powder
- ½ teaspoon lemon extract
- 1 teaspoon vanilla extract
- Dash salt

Sift flour, salt, and baking powder together; set aside. Cream sugar and butter until well blended. Add eggs one at a time to butter and sugar mixture. Add milk and flour alternating, ending with flour. Add flavorings. Mix well but don't overbeat. Pour into 4 well-greased cake pans. Tap pans on counter to make bubbles come to top. Bake at 325 degrees for 20-25 minutes.

Chocolate Icing:

- 2¼ squares semi-sweet baking chocolate
- 3 cups sugar
- 1½ cups whole milk
- 1½ sticks butter
- 1½ teaspoons vanilla extract

Bring all ingredients except vanilla to a boil in large saucepan and continue cooking until mixture reaches the "soft-ball" stage. Remove from heat and add vanilla. Put pan with mixture in sink of cold water to cool. Beat until it's thick enough to spread on cake layers.

Anna Johnston

Hint: To keep chocolate cakes brown on outside, grease pans and dust with cocoa instead of flour.

German Chocolate Cake

- 2½ cups cake flour, sifted
- 4 eggs, separated
- 1 bar German Chocolate (dissolved in ½ cup hot water)
- ¼ teaspoon salt
- 2 cups sugar
- 1 cup shortening
- 1 cup buttermilk
- 1 teaspoon baking soda
- 1 teaspoon vanilla

Beat egg whites until stiff and set aside. Cream sugar and shortening. Add 1 egg yolk at a time, beating after each addition. Add flour alternately with ½ cup buttermilk. Dissolve soda in remaining buttermilk. Add to mixture. Add the dissolved chocolate, salt, and vanilla. Fold in the beaten egg whites. Bake in 3 layers at 350 degrees for 40 minutes.

Filling:

- 1 large can Pet evaporated milk
- 1 cup sugar
- 1 cup pecans, chopped
- 1 teaspoon vanilla
- 3 egg yolks
- 1 stick butter
- 1 cup coconut

In saucepan combine milk, egg yolks, sugar, and butter. Cook on medium heat until thick. Beat with electric mixer until partly cooled. Add coconut, vanilla, and pecans. Spread on cake.

Pam Gillis

Chocolate Icebox Angel Food Cake

- 2 (16 ounce) cartons heavy whipping cream
- 1 (12 ounce) package semi-sweet or dark chocolate chips
- 2 teaspoons vanilla flavoring
- ¼ cup sugar
- 1 angel food cake mix
- 2 egg yolks
- 2 teaspoons water

Part 1: Bake angel food cake according to box directions and let cool. Slice into 3 layers.

Part 2: Whip until stiff, 2 cartons of heavy whipping cream with sugar and vanilla flavoring.

Part 3: Melt package of large chocolate chips with 1 teaspoon of water (microwave is easier). Beat 2 egg yolks and 1 teaspoon water together and add to chocolate to cool mixture.

Part 4: Fold the melted chips into whipped cream.

Part 5: Place mixture/icing into freezer and watch for thickness (approximately 30 minutes).

Part 6: Spread icing between layers, top, and sides of cake. (When icing layers, insert toothpicks to help hold cake together.)

Part 7: Store in refrigerator. Cake is better made a day before serving.

In Memory of Mrs. Dottie Morgan

Coconut Cake

- 1 Duncan Hines yellow butter cake mix
- 2 (6 ounce) packages frozen coconut
- ¾ cup sugar
- 1 cup sour cream
- 1 (8 ounce) carton Cool Whip

Bake cake in 2 layers according to directions on the box. Let cake cool. Cut into 4 layers. Mix 1¾ packages of coconut, sugar, and sour cream. Set ½ cup of this mixture aside. Spread remaining part of mixture between layers. Mix ½ cup of mixture with Cool Whip. Spread on sides and top. Take ¼ of package of frozen coconut and spread on top. Refrigerate cake until ready to serve. This may be made 2 days before.

Laura Mell Pope

Hummingbird Cake

- 3 cups all-purpose flour
- 2 cups sugar
- 1 teaspoon salt
- 1 teaspoon baking soda
- 1 teaspoon cinnamon
- 1 (8 ounce) can crushed pineapple with juice
- 2 bananas, chopped
- 3 eggs, beaten
- 1½ cups vegetable oil
- 1 teaspoon vanilla
- ½ cup pecans, chopped

Combine dry ingredients in a large bowl. Add eggs and vegetable oil, stirring until dry ingredients are moistened. Do not beat. Stir in vanilla, pineapple, pecans, and bananas. Bake at 350 degrees for 25-30 minutes. Makes 3 layers.

Cream Cheese Icing:

- 1 (8 ounce) cream cheese, softened
- ½ cup butter, softened
- 1 pound box powdered sugar
- 1 teaspoon vanilla extract
- ½ cup nuts, chopped

Beat cream cheese and butter until creamy. Add sugar, vanilla, and nuts. Frost cake.

In Memory of Mrs. Eunice Traynham

Italian Cream Cake

- 1 stick butter, softened
- 2 cups sugar
- ½ cup Crisco
- 5 egg yolks
- 2 cups all-purpose flour
- 1 teaspoon baking soda
- 1 cup buttermilk
- 1 teaspoon vanilla
- 1 package frozen coconut
- 1 cup pecans, chopped
- 5 egg whites, beaten

Cream butter and sugar; add Crisco and beat until smooth. Add egg yolks and beat well. Combine flour and soda and add along with buttermilk. Stir in vanilla, coconut, and nuts. Fold in egg whites. Bake 3 layers at 350 degrees for 25 minutes. Frost when cool with Cream Cheese Frosting.

Cream Cheese Frosting:

- 1 (8 ounce) package cream cheese, softened
- ½ stick butter
- 1 box 4X powdered sugar
- 1 teaspoon vanilla
- Chopped pecans and coconut

Mix cream cheese and butter until smooth. Add sugar and vanilla and beat. Frost cake and sprinkle top and sides with pecans and coconut.

In Memory of Mrs. Virginia Brown

Hint: Always bring butter and eggs to room temperature (at least two hours) before using to bake a cake.

Japanese Fruitcake

- 1 cup butter or margarine
- 2 cups sugar
- 4 eggs
- 1 cup buttermilk
- 1 cup raisins, chopped
- 1 cup nuts, chopped
- 3 cups flour
- ½ teaspoon salt
- 1 teaspoon cinnamon
- 1 teaspoon allspice
- 1 teaspoon cloves
- 1 teaspoon nutmeg
- 1 teaspoon baking soda

Cream butter and sugar together. Add eggs one at a time, beating well after each. Sift dry ingredients together. Alternate adding dry ingredients and buttermilk, ending with dry ingredients. Flour raisins and nuts and add to mixture. Pour into 3 greased and floured layer cake pans and bake in 300 degree oven about 1 hour or until cake leaves sides of pan. Cool on racks.

Filling for Japanese Fruitcake:

- 1 orange (grated rind and juice)
- 2 lemons (grated rind and juice)
- 1½ cups sugar
- 3 tablespoons cornstarch
- 3 egg yolks
- 1 cup water
- 1½ cups 4X powdered sugar
- 1 cup coconut
- 1 cup pecans, chopped
- Few raisins

Combine all ingredients and cook until thick. Cool slightly and spread between layers of cake.

Elizabeth White

Hint: Fruitcakes require time to assemble. The night before baking, chop fruit and nuts and combine dry ingredients.

Japanese Fruitcake

4 eggs
3 cups cake flour
2 cups sugar
1 cup whole milk
2 sticks butter
3 teaspoons baking powder
½ teaspoon lemon flavoring
1 teaspoon vanilla flavoring
Dash salt

Sift flour, salt, and baking powder together. Set aside. Cream sugar and butter until well blended. Add eggs, one at a time to butter and sugar mixture. Add milk and flour alternating, ending with flour. Add flavorings. Mix well but don't overbeat. Pour ½ of batter into 2 well-greased cake pans.

Add to remaining ½ of batter:
1 teaspoon allspice
1 teaspoon cinnamon
½ teaspoon ground cloves
1 cup raisins, dusted with flour

Pour into 2 well-greased cake pans. Tap pans on counter to make bubbles come to top. Bake at 325 degrees for 20-25 minutes.

Icing:
Juice and rind of 2 lemons
1 cup grated coconut (frozen is best)
1 small can crushed pineapple
1 jar maraschino cherries, drained and halved (reserve some for top)
2 cups sugar
1 cup water mixed with 2 heaping tablespoons cornstarch

Mix lemon juice, lemon rind, coconut, sugar, and cornstarch mixture and bring to boil in saucepan. Stir until thickened. Take off heat; add pineapple. Start icing dark layer and add halved cherries. Add light layer and ice alternating dark and light layers. Top with cherries. Refrigerate after cooling.

Anna Johnston

Luscious Pumpkin Cake

1 package (2 layer size) yellow cake mix
1 (15 ounce) can pumpkin, divided
½ cup milk
⅓ cup oil
4 eggs
1½ teaspoons pumpkin pie spice, divided
1 (8 ounce) package Philadelphia cream cheese, softened
1 cup powdered sugar
1 (8 ounce) tub Cool Whip whipped topping, thawed
¼ cup Planters pecans, chopped
Caramel ice cream topping

Heat oven to 350 degrees. Beat cake mix, 1 cup pumpkin, milk, oil, eggs, and 1 teaspoon spice in large bowl with mixer until well blended. Pour into 2 greased and floured 9-inch round pans or small amount of batter in 4 cake pans. Bake until toothpick inserted in center comes out clean. Cool in pans 10 minutes. Remove from pans to wire racks to cool completely. Beat cream cheese in medium bowl with mixer until creamy. Add sugar, remaining pumpkin, and spice; mix well. Gently stir in Cool Whip. If using 2 cake pans, cut cake in half horizontally to make 4 layers. Stack on serving plate, spreading cream cheese filling between layers. Do not frost top layer. Drizzle with caramel topping just before serving. Top with pecans. Refrigerate leftovers.

Terry Cook

"...for the kingdom of God is not eating and drinking, but righteousness and peace and joy in the Holy Spirit."
Romans 14:17
(NASB)

Malinda's Key Lime Cake

- 1 box Duncan Hines lemon supreme cake mix
- 2 small boxes lime Jell-O
- 5 eggs
- 1⅔ cups canola oil
- ¾ cup orange juice

Mix well and pour into 3 greased and floured cake pans. Bake at 350 degrees for 30 minutes.

Icing:

- 12 ounces of cream cheese, softened
- 6 cups 10X powdered sugar
- 1½ sticks butter, softened
- ¾ teaspoon vanilla flavoring

Mix all ingredients until blended well. Spread on cooled layers.

Note: This cake is always popular at family reunions, holiday dinners, or wherever it is served. You will take home an empty cake plate for sure. Thanks to my sister-in-law, Malinda, for sharing her recipe with me!

Rosemary Brown

Pink Lemonade Cake

- 1 white cake mix
- ¾ cup pink lemonade frozen concentrate
- ½ cup water
- 4 egg whites
- ⅓ cup oil
- 3 cups 10X sugar
- 1 stick unsalted butter, softened
- 2 tablespoons pink lemonade concentrate
- Pink coloring to tint

Beat together first 5 ingredients and bake as directed on cake mix box. In a mixer, beat sugar, butter lemonade concentrate, and coloring until smooth. Spread on cool cake.

Patsy Herlocker

Easy Plum Cake

- 2 cups self-rising flour
- 1 cup canola oil
- 2 cups sugar
- 4 eggs
- ½ teaspoon ginger
- 2 (4 ounce) jars plum-with-apple baby food
- 1 cup pecans, chopped
- 1 teaspoon each of cinnamon and cloves

Place all ingredients except nuts in a mixing bowl and beat for several minutes. Stir in nuts. Pour into a greased and floured (9 to 10 cup size) Bundt pan. Bake at 325 degrees for 1 hour. Cool in pan for 10 minutes before removing.

Glaze:

- 2 cups powdered sugar
- Lemon juice or milk to thin

Pour over cake while it is still warm.

In Memory of Mrs. Jeane McNeil

Orange Cake

- 1 box Duncan Hines orange supreme cake mix
- 1 (8 ounce) carton whipping cream
- 1 (8 ounce) carton sour cream
- 1 teaspoon vanilla extract
- Sugar to taste

Bake cake mix according to directions. Whip whipping cream to desired consistency. Fold in sour cream. Add vanilla flavoring and sugar to taste. Frost cake. Keep refrigerated.

Carole Vaughn
Former Children's Ministry Director

Red Velvet Cake

- 1½ cups Wesson oil
- 1½ cups sugar
- 1 cup buttermilk
- 2½ cups self-rising flour
- 1 teaspoon vanilla
- 2 eggs
- 1 teaspoon vinegar
- 1 teaspoon cocoa
- 1 teaspoon baking soda
- 1 bottle red food coloring

Mix sugar and oil. Add eggs one at a time. In another bowl, mix soda and flour. Add to batter alternating with the buttermilk. Add cocoa, vanilla, and vinegar. Mix well, then add food color slowly, mixing well and not splattering. Pour into 3 (8-inch or 9-inch) round pans lined with wax paper and sides greased and floured. Bake at 350 degrees for 25 to 30 minutes. Do not over bake. Let layers cool completely on wire racks before stacking and frosting.

Frosting:

- 1 box 10X confectioners' sugar
- 1 stick margarine, softened
- 1 (8 ounce) cream cheese, softened
- 1 cup pecans, chopped

Mix first three ingredients together and then add nuts.

Cathy Tatum

Red Velvet Cake

- 1 cup Crisco
- 2 eggs
- 1½ cups sugar
- 2 ounces red cake coloring (4 tablespoons)
- 2 tablespoons cocoa
- 2½ cups cake flour
- 1 cup buttermilk
- 1 teaspoon baking soda
- 1 tablespoon vinegar
- 1 tablespoon vanilla
- ½ teaspoon salt

Cream shortening and sugar; add eggs. Mix cocoa and coloring in measuring cup until it makes a paste; add to above. Add vanilla. Pour buttermilk into measuring cup to get out all the coloring. Sift flour and salt and add alternately with buttermilk to batter; beat well. Fold in soda and vinegar. Bake at 300 degrees in 3 (8-inch) pans for about 20 minutes.

Filling:

- 2 sticks butter or margarine, softened
- 1 teaspoon vanilla
- 1 cup granulated sugar
- 2 tablespoons cornstarch
- 1 cup water

Cream butter or margarine well. Add vanilla and sugar and beat until fluffy. Cook 2 tablespoons cornstarch and 1 cup water until thick. Allow this to cool. Add to creamy base. Beat this mixture really well (may take 5 to 10 minutes). It will look like whipped cream. Spread between layers and on cake.

Nell Sturgis

Hint: To make buttermilk, add 1 tablespoon of white vinegar per cup of whole milk.

Granny Lucree's Spice Cake

- 1 box yellow cake mix (add contents as directed on box)
- 2 tablespoons cocoa
- 1 teaspoon allspice
- 1 teaspoon nutmeg
- 1 teaspoon cloves
- 1 stick butter
- 1 cup sugar
- 1 can evaporated milk

Mix together cake mix following directions on box. Add cocoa, allspice, nutmeg, and cloves. Mix well and bake in 3 layers at 325 degrees until done. Bring butter, sugar, and milk to a boil. Stir until sugar is dissolved and mixture thickens. Pour filling on cooled layers. Add nuts as desired.

Note: This cake is a holiday tradition at our house. It will disappear within minutes when we all get together. I always add just a shake or two of ginger to the mix as well.

Karen Barlow

Strawberry Cake

- 1 white cake mix
- 1 small strawberry Jell-O
- ½ cup Wesson oil
- ½ cup water
- ½ cup frozen strawberries, thawed
- 4 eggs

Mix all together and pour into 3 or 4 prepared pans. Bake for 30 minutes at 350 degrees.

Icing:

- 1 stick butter or margarine, softened
- 1 box 4X powdered sugar
- ½ cup frozen strawberries, thawed

Beat margarine, sugar, and strawberries. Spread onto cake layers.

In Memory of Mrs. Jonell Garrett

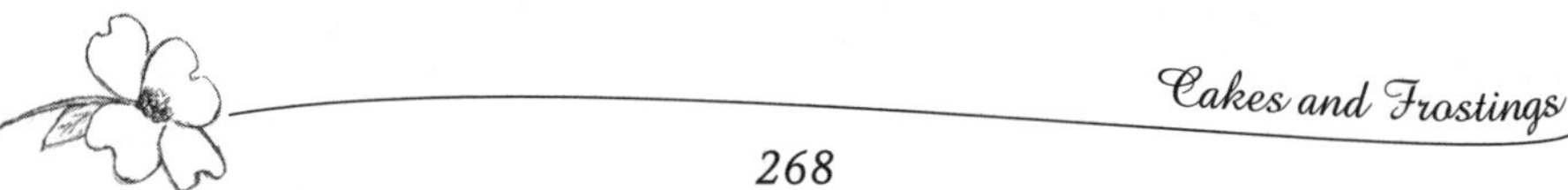

White Chocolate Cake

- 1 cup butter, softened
- 1 teaspoon baking powder
- 2 cups sugar
- 1 teaspoon salt
- 4 egg yolks, beaten
- 1 cup buttermilk
- 1 teaspoon vanilla extract
- 4 egg whites, stiffly beaten
- 4 ounces white chocolate, melted
- 1 cup pecans, chopped
- 2½ cups cake flour
- 1 cup flaked coconut

Preheat the oven to 350 degrees. Cream the butter, sugar, egg yolks, vanilla, and white chocolate in a mixer bowl until light and fluffy. Combine the cake flour, baking powder, and salt in a bowl. Add to the creamed mixture alternately with the buttermilk, mixing well after each addition. Fold in the egg whites. Stir in the pecans and coconut. Pour into 3 greased and floured 8-inch round cake pans. Bake for 30 minutes or until layers test done. Cool on wire racks. Spread White Frosting between layers and over top and side of cake.

White Frosting:

- 1 cup butter, softened
- 2 teaspoons vanilla extract
- 2 pounds confectioners' sugar
- 2 (8 ounce) packages cream cheese, softened
- 2 cups pecans, chopped

Combine the butter, confectioners' sugar, vanilla, and cream cheese in a mixer bowl. Mix well. Stir in pecans and add a little milk if needed to make spreading consistency.

Jenny Lott

White Mountain Cake

- 1 cup butter
- 2 cups sugar
- 8 egg whites, stiffly beaten
- 1 cup milk
- 3 cups cake flour
- 1 tablespoon baking powder
- 1 teaspoon vanilla

Cream butter and sugar. Mix flour and baking powder. Add flour mixture alternately with milk to butter mixture. Add vanilla. Fold in egg whites. Place 3 cups and 3 tablespoons of batter to each pan when equaling batter to bake. Preheat oven to 325 degrees. Bake about 25 minutes.

White Mountain Filling:

- 2 cups sugar
- 8 egg yolks
- 2 sticks butter

Mix and cook in double boiler about 5 minutes.

- 1 cup fresh coconut
- 1 cup raisins
- 1 cup walnuts
- 1 cup pecans
- 1 bottle cherries
- 1 teaspoon vanilla

Chop and add to filling mixture. Spread filling mixture between layers.

Note: Mama Norris would bake this cake and ship to Granddaddy Norris while he was in service overseas during World War II. It kept well.

In Memory of Mrs. Virginia Norris

Hint: Keep the oven door closed until the minimum baking time has elapsed.

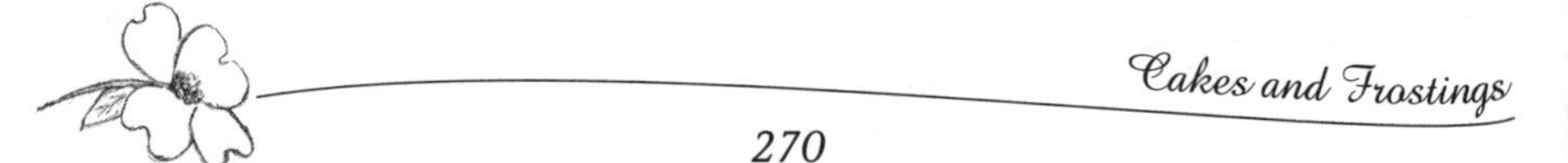

Fresh Apple Cake with Sauce

- 4 cups apples, peeled and sliced
- 2 cups sugar
- 2 cups flour
- 1½ teaspoons baking soda
- 2 teaspoons cinnamon
- 1 teaspoon salt
- 2 eggs
- ¾ cup vegetable oil
- 2 teaspoons vanilla extract
- 1 cup pecans, chopped

In a large bowl, stir together apples and sugar. Add dry ingredients and stir. In another bowl, beat eggs, oil, and vanilla. Stir egg mixture into apples and blend until moist. Stir in pecans. Pour into 9 x 13 greased pan and bake at 350 degrees for 50 minutes.

Sauce:

- 1 cup sugar
- ½ cup butter
- ½ cup heavy cream or evaporated milk

Place all ingredients in saucepan and stir. Bring to a boil over medium heat and cook for 3 minutes. Serve warm. Spoon some sauce on each piece of cake as served.

Dotty Hutchinson

Fresh Apple Cake

- 1¼ cups Wesson oil (1 cup is less oily)
- 3 eggs
- 2 cups sugar
- 1 tablespoon vanilla flavoring
- 3 cups apples, chopped
- 3 cups all-purpose flour
- 1 teaspoon baking soda
- 1 teaspoon salt
- 1 cup pecans, chopped

Beat eggs well and add sugar, oil, and vanilla. Add apples. Sift flour with baking soda and salt. Add pecans to flour, and then add apple batter to flour. Blend well by hand. Bake in a tube or layer pan at 325 degrees starting in a cold oven.

Topping:

- 1 stick oleo (margarine)
- ½ cup evaporated milk
- 2 cups light brown sugar

Combine and bring to a boil. Cool and spread on cake. To thicken, cook longer.

Elaine Mathis

Banana Split Cake

- 3 cups vanilla wafers, crumbled
- 2 sticks margarine
- 2 cups confectioners' sugar
- 2 eggs
- 3-5 bananas, sliced
- 2 cups crushed pineapple, drained
- 1 large Cool Whip
- Pecans
- Cherries

Mix 3 cups crumbled vanilla wafers with 1 stick melted margarine and press into 9 x 13 inch pan. Mix 2 cups confectioners' sugar with 2 eggs and 1 stick margarine. Beat these ingredients for 15 minutes on high; spread over crust. Slice 3 to 5 bananas (depending on size) and put over mixture. Layer 2 cups drained pineapple over bananas. Spread 1 large tub of Cool Whip over bananas and pineapple. Sprinkle pecans and cherries over top, if desired.

Eloise Spivey

Coconut Sheet Cake

- 1 box white cake mix
- 1 can Eagle Brand condensed milk
- 1 can cream of coconut
- 1 container Cool Whip
- Coconut

Prepare cake mix according to directions on box and bake in a sheet pan. Prick holes all over top of cake when warm. Blend together condensed milk and cream of coconut and pour over warm cake. Ice with 1 container of Cool Whip. Sprinkle coconut on top and refrigerate overnight.

In Memory of Mrs. Vera Turner

Earthquake Cake

- 1 cup flaked coconut
- 1 cup pecans, chopped
- 1 (18.25 ounce) package German chocolate cake mix
- 1 (8 ounce) package cream cheese
- 4 cups confectioners' sugar
- ½ cup butter
- 1 teaspoon vanilla extract

Preheat oven to 350 degrees. Lightly grease the bottom and sides of a 9 x 13 inch baking pan. Layer coconut and pecans in the bottom of pan.

Prepare cake mix according to package instructions and pour over pecans and coconut. Combine cream cheese, butter or margarine, vanilla, and confectioners' sugar and beat until smooth. Pour over cake mix. Bake at 350 degrees for 30 minutes. Toothpick will NOT come out clean.

Note: Cake will crack down the middle; that is why it is called an earthquake cake!

Susan Ranson

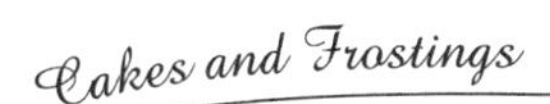

Éclair Cake

- 2 small packages instant French vanilla pudding
- 3 cups milk
- 9 ounces Cool Whip
- 1 box graham crackers

Mix together pudding and milk. Let stand 15 minutes and add Cool Whip. Grease a 9 x 12 inch pan. Place a layer of whole grahams on bottom, then ½ pudding mixture, another layer grahams, rest of the pudding mixture, and top with another layer of graham crackers.

Frosting:

- 1½ cups powdered sugar
- 2 tablespoons light Karo syrup
- 2 tablespoons butter or margarine
- 1 teaspoon vanilla flavoring
- 3 tablespoons milk
- 2 ounces unsweetened chocolate, melted

Mix ingredients until well combined and creamy. Pour over top of graham crackers. Refrigerate overnight.

Beth Nichols

Georgia Cornbread

- 1 cup sugar
- 1 cup brown sugar
- 4 eggs
- 1 cup vegetable oil
- 1½ cups self-rising flour
- 1 teaspoon vanilla flavoring
- Pecans, chopped (whatever amount you like)

Mix together sugar, brown sugar, eggs, and oil. Add flour and vanilla. Add nuts. Pour into greased sheet pan. Bake at 300 degrees until almost done. It will still be soft in center when done.

Charline McElroy

Girdle Buster

- 1 box yellow cake mix
- 1 stick margarine, melted
- 3 eggs
- 1 cup pecans, chopped
- 1 (8 ounce) package cream cheese
- 1 box confectioners' sugar
- ½ bag chocolate chips

Preheat oven to 350 degrees. For the first layer, combine cake mix, melted margarine, 1 egg, and 1 cup of nuts. Mix together and press into a greased 9 x 11 pan.

2nd layer: Mix 2 eggs and cream cheese together, gradually add the entire box of confectioners' sugar. Pour this layer on top of 1st layer. Top with ½ bag of chocolate chips.

Bake at 350 degrees for 45-55 minutes or until top is golden brown.

Jessica Barber

Plaza Park Squares

- 1 box Duncan Hines cake mix (lemon or any flavor)
- 1 egg
- 1 stick margarine

Mix all together by hand and press into a greased 9 x 13 pan.

Topping:

- 1 box 10X sugar
- 3 eggs
- 1 (8 ounce) cream cheese

Mix and spread on top of cake mixture. Bake at 325 degrees for 40 minutes. Cool and cut into squares.

Sue Brantley

Pumpkin Gooey Butter Cake

- 1 (18 ¼ ounce) package yellow cake mix
- 1 egg
- 8 tablespoons butter, melted

Preheat oven to 350 degrees. Combine the cake mix, egg, and butter and mix well with an electric mixer. Pat the mixture into the bottom of a lightly greased 9 x 13 inch baking pan.

Filling:

- 1 (8 ounce) package cream cheese, softened
- 1 (15 ounce) can pumpkin
- 3 eggs
- 1 teaspoon vanilla
- 8 tablespoons butter, melted
- 1 (16 ounce) box powdered sugar
- 1 carton whipping cream, freshly whipped

Filling: In a large bowl, beat the cream cheese and pumpkin until smooth. Add eggs, vanilla, and butter; beat together. Add the powdered sugar and mix well. Spread pumpkin mixture over cake batter and bake for 40 to 50 minutes. Make sure not to over bake as the center should be a little gooey. Serve with fresh whipped cream.

Note: This is a crowd pleaser at Thanksgiving and Christmas…even for those who don't normally like pumpkin dishes!

Liz Grantham

"Therefore, accept one another, just as Christ also accepted us to the glory of God."

Romans 15:7
(NASB)

Lemon Cake

1	box yellow cake mix	¾	cup corn oil
1	(3 ounce) box lemon Jell-O	¾	cup water
4	eggs		

Mix all ingredients together and pour in a sheet cake pan. Bake cake as directed on box.

Icing:

2	cups 4X powdered sugar	3	tablespoons butter, melted
Juice of 1½ lemons			

Mix all ingredients together and pour icing over cake after baked.

Marvelyne Fletcher

Mexican Pineapple Cake

1	(20 ounce) can crushed pineapple, undrained	1	teaspoon baking soda
2	cups all-purpose flour	2	cups sugar
1	cup nuts, chopped	2	eggs

Mix all ingredients by hand. Pour into a 9 x 13 inch baking dish. Bake in a 350 degree oven for 35-40 minutes.

Icing:

1	(8 ounce) cream cheese, softened	1	stick margarine or butter, melted
2	cups confectioners' sugar, sifted	1	teaspoon vanilla

Mix all ingredients and pour over hot cake.

Paula Scott

Pecan Pie Cake

- **1 package (18.25 ounce) plain yellow cake mix**
- **1 stick butter, melted**
- **4 eggs**
- **1½ cups light corn syrup**
- **½ cup dark brown sugar, firmly packed**
- **1 teaspoon vanilla**
- **2 cups pecans, toasted and chopped**

Heat oven to 325 degrees. Place cake mix, melted butter, and 1 egg in a large bowl. Beat on low speed until well combined, about 30 seconds. Measure out ⅔ cup batter; set aside. Spread remaining batter in bottom of ungreased 9 x13 x 2 inch baking dish. Bake in oven for 15 minutes or until top lightly browns and puffs up. Remove from oven and cool for 10 minutes. Leave oven on.

Place reserved ⅔ cup batter, corn syrup, sugar, remaining 3 eggs, and vanilla in large bowl of electric mixer. Beat on low speed for 1 minute. Stop machine; scrape down bowl. Beat on medium speed until well combined, about 1 minute. Fold in pecans. Pour pecan mixture on top of warm cake in baking dish. Gently smooth out evenly over cake. Bake in 325 degree oven for 40 to 50 minutes or until edges are browned but middle is still soft. Remove to wire rack and cool 30 minutes. Slice. Serve with vanilla ice cream, if desired.

Terry Cook

"But He gives a greater grace, therefore it says, 'God is opposed to the proud, But gives grace to the humble'"

James 4:6
(NASB)

Toasted Nut Spice Cake

- **2⅓ cup sifted flour**
- **1 teaspoon baking powder**
- **1 pound package light brown sugar (save one cup for icing)**
- **¾ teaspoon salt**
- **2 tablespoons white sugar**
- **¾ cup Crisco shortening**
- **2 eggs, separated**
- **1¼ cups buttermilk (add 1 teaspoon baking soda in buttermilk)**
- **1 teaspoon cinnamon**
- **1 teaspoon cloves**
- **1 cup nuts, chopped**
- **1 teaspoon vanilla flavoring**

Cream shortening and brown sugar. Add egg yolks. Add dry ingredients and buttermilk alternately. Add vanilla, cinnamon, and cloves to mixture. Mix well. Pour into greased and floured 9 x 13 pan. Beat 2 egg whites and gradually add 1 cup of brown sugar. Beat well. Add 1 cup of chopped nuts. Cover the cake batter with this icing and bake at 350 degrees for 45 minutes.

Rose Williams

Oreo Dirt Cake

- **Kid's sand pail and shovel set or 1 new 8" flower pot**
- **1½-2 pounds Oreo cookies**
- **1 (8 ounce) cream cheese**
- **1 cup powdered sugar**
- **½ stick butter, softened**
- **3½ cups milk**
- **2 small packages instant vanilla pudding**
- **12 ounces Cool Whip**

Cream together cream cheese, powdered sugar, and softened butter. Mix 3½ cups milk and instant pudding for 2 minutes and add Cool Whip. Add liquid mixture to creamed mixture. Place Oreo cookies in large Ziploc bag and crush to desired "dirt" texture with a rolling pin. Put 1½ inches of cookie crumbs on the bottom of the sand pail or flower pot (lined with aluminum foil) and layer the pudding mixture and crumbs. End with pudding mixture. Refrigerate for 2 hours. Just before serving, add 1 more inch of cookie crumbs and decorate with gummy worms.

Kim Knight

Pineapple Upside-Down Cake

- ½ cup butter or margarine
- 1 cup light brown sugar, firmly packed
- 3 (8 ounce) cans pineapple slices, undrained
- 11 maraschino cherries, halved

Batter:

- 1 cup flour
- 1 teaspoon baking powder
- ½ teaspoon salt
- 2 eggs
- 1 cup sugar
- ½ cup milk
- 1 tablespoon butter or margarine

Preheat oven to 350 degrees. Melt butter in 10-inch cast iron skillet over low heat. Sprinkle light brown sugar in skillet. Remove from heat. Drain pineapple. Cut pineapple slices in half, reserving one whole slice. Place whole slice in center of skillet. Arrange 10 pieces, spoke-fashion, around whole slice in center of skillet. Place a cherry half between each piece of pineapple; place a cherry half in center of whole slice. Arrange remaining pineapple pieces, cut side up, around sides of skillet. Sift flour, baking powder, and salt several times. Beat eggs until thick. Add sugar one tablespoon at the time, beating hard. Stir flour into egg/sugar mixture just enough to mix. Heat milk and butter to warm and mix into batter. Pour over pineapple and bake 40 to 50 minutes. Cool 5 minutes and then turn upside down into serving plate. Serve with whipped cream.

Ruby S. Harper

Tiramisu Cupcakes

- 1 box white cake mix
- ¾ cup sour cream
- 2 egg whites
- ¾ cup buttermilk
- 1 egg
- 2 teaspoons vanilla extract
- ⅓ cup oil
- ¼ cup strong coffee

Preheat oven to 350 degrees and line pan with cupcake liners. Sift cake mix into a small bowl and set aside. In a large bowl, gently whisk egg whites, egg, oil, buttermilk, sour cream, and vanilla. Stir cake mix into wet ingredients. Using half of the batter, fill cupcake liners about ⅓ full. With the remaining cake batter, add the strong coffee and mix. (You may need to add 1 or 2 tablespoons of flour to thicken the batter.) Scoop the coffee cake batter over the regular batter so each cupcake liner is filled about ¾. (One layer of vanilla cake and a top layer of coffee cake.) Bake for 16-20 minutes or until an inserted knife comes out clean.

Filling:

- 8 ounces mascarpone cheese
- 1 tablespoon strong coffee
- ½ cup powdered sugar

Combine all ingredients in a small bowl using a spoon.

Whipped Topping:

- 8 ounces cream cheese, softened
- 1 teaspoon vanilla extract
- 1 cup powdered sugar
- 1 pint heavy whipping cream

Using a whisk attachment on your stand mixer, beat cream cheese and powdered sugar until smooth. Add vanilla. Slowly add in heavy cream and beat until stiff peaks form. To assemble, cut a cone-shaped piece of cake out of the top of each cupcake (make sure cakes are cooled). Generously spoon in your filling. Pipe your whipped topping over the hole with the filling and top with chocolate shavings and cocoa powder.

Note: You can substitute Cool Whip for heavy whipping cream.

Lynn Graham

Milky Way Chocolate Icing

3 Milky Way bars (large size)
2 cups sugar
1 cup Carnation milk
1 stick margarine
2 tablespoons cocoa powder

Mix together the sugar, milk, margarine, and cocoa. Boil to the soft-ball stage and take from stove. Break Milky Way bars and add them to the hot mixture. Beat the icing until spreading consistency. This will ice a three or four layer cake.

Paula Thomas

My Mom's Chocolate Icing

4 squares Bakers unsweetened chocolate squares
1 (16 ounce) powdered sugar
½ cup butter (1 stick)
2 teaspoons vanilla flavoring
⅓ cup milk

Microwave chocolate squares 1½ minutes or until melted. Add sugar, butter, and vanilla and start mixing. Add milk until right consistency. Most of the time I double this and use leftover for icing cookies.

Faye Ray

Caramel Icing

2½ cups white sugar
1 pint heavy whipping cream

Slowly boil 2 cups sugar with heavy whipping cream. Brown ½ cup sugar in heavy skillet (caramelize). Remove sugar and cream from heat and slowly add the caramelized sugar. (This may boil over if not removed from heat.) Continue cooking slowly to a soft-ball stage. Cool. Spread onto cake layers.

In Memory of Mrs. Noirena G. Sinclair

Aunt Bea's Chocolate Icing for 14-Layer Cake

- 1 stick butter
- 1 cup sugar
- 1 box semi-sweet chocolate
- 1 can evaporated milk
- 1 tablespoon light Karo syrup
- 1 teaspoon vanilla flavoring

Melt butter and chocolate. Add sugar and milk and bring to a boil. Then add syrup and lower to a medium heat until a rolling boil is reached. Add vanilla flavoring and stir. Stir often so it won't stick.

Faye Ray

Seven-Minute Frosting

- 3 unbeaten egg whites
- 2¾ cups sugar
- 3 teaspoons light corn syrup
- ⅓ teaspoon cream of tartar
- ⅓ cup plus 2 tablespoons cold water
- 1 teaspoon vanilla flavoring
- Dash of salt

Place all ingredients except vanilla in top of double boiler. Do not overheat. Beat with electric mixer over hot boiling water for one minute. Beat constantly until stiff peaks form (about 7 minutes). Don't overcook. Remove from heat and add vanilla. Beat until fluffy consistency. Frost top and sides of 3 (9-inch) cake layers.

Emma Lou C. Aughinbaugh

A Woman of Noble Character

An excellent wife, who can find?
For her worth is far above jewels.
The heart of her husband trusts in her,
And he will have no lack of gain.
She does him good and not evil
All the days of her life.
She looks for wool and flax
And works with her hands in delight.
She is like merchant ships;
She brings her food from afar.
She rises also while it is still night and gives food to her household
And portions to her maidens.
She considers a field and buys it;
From her earnings she plants a vineyard.
She girds herself with strength
And makes her arms strong.
She senses that her gain is good;
Her lamp does not go out at night.
She stretches out her hands to the distaff,
And her hands grasp the spindle.
She extends her hand to the poor,
And she stretches out her hands to the needy.
She is not afraid of the snow for her household,
For all her household are clothed with scarlet.
She makes coverings for herself;
Her clothing is fine linen and purple.
Her husband is known in the gates,
When he sits among the elders of the land.
She makes linen garments and sells them,
And supplies belts to the tradesmen.
Strength and dignity are her clothing,
And she smiles at the future.
She opens her mouth in wisdom,
And the teaching of kindness is on her tongue.
She looks well to the ways of her household,
And does not eat the bread of idleness.
Her children rise up and bless her;
Her husband also, and he praises her, saying:
"Many daughters have done nobly,
But you excel them all."
Charm is deceitful and beauty is vain,
But a woman who fears the LORD, She shall be praised.
Give her the product of her hands,
And let her works praise her in the gates.

Proverbs 31:10-31
(NASB)

Cookies, Candies, and Bars

"Train up a child in the way he should go,
Even when he is old he will not depart from it."

Proverbs 22:6
(NASB)

Cookies, Candies, and Bars

Inside-Out Carrot Cake Cookies

- 1⅛ cups all-purpose flour
- 1 teaspoon cinnamon
- ½ teaspoon baking soda
- ½ teaspoon salt
- 1 stick unsalted butter, softened
- ⅓ cup plus 2 tablespoons packed light brown sugar
- ⅓ cup plus 2 tablespoons granulated sugar
- 1 large egg
- ½ teaspoon vanilla
- 1 cup carrots, coarsely grated
- 1 scant cup walnuts, chopped
- ½ cup raisins
- 1 (8 ounce) package cream cheese
- ¼ cup honey

Put oven racks in upper and lower sections of oven and preheat oven to 375 degrees. Butter 2 baking sheets. Whisk together flour, cinnamon, baking soda, and salt in a bowl. Beat together butter, sugars, egg, and vanilla in a bowl with an electric mixer at medium speed until pale and fluffy, about 2 minutes. On low speed, mix in carrots, nuts, and raisins. Add flour mixture and beat until combined. Drop 1½ tablespoons batter per cookie 2 inches apart on baking sheets. Bake for 12 to 16 minutes until cookies are lightly browned and springy to the touch, switching positions of the sheets halfway through baking. Leave cookies on baking sheets 1 minute and then transfer cookies to racks to cool completely. While cookies are baking, blend cream cheese and honey in a food processor until smooth. Sandwich a generous tablespoon of cream cheese filling between two flat sides of cookies.

Note: I put confectioners' sugar with honey and cream cheese to make the filling sweeter. Also, I double the recipe and make smaller cookies since you're using two cookies together.

Lynn Graham

Chocolate Chip Cookies

- ⅓ cup shortening
- ⅓ cup butter
- ½ cup sugar
- ½ cup brown sugar
- 1 egg
- 1 teaspoon vanilla

Mix the above together. Add the following ingredients to butter mixture:

- ½ teaspoon salt
- 1½ cups flour
- ½ teaspoon baking soda
- ½ cup nuts, chopped
- 6 ounces semi-sweet chocolate chips

Bake at 375 degrees for 8 to 10 minutes. Recipe doubles easily.

Renee Roberson

Chocolate Chip Oatmeal Cookies

- 2 cups all-purpose flour
- 1 teaspoon baking soda
- ½ teaspoon baking powder
- 1 teaspoon salt
- 1 cup old-fashioned rolled oats
- 2 sticks unsalted butter, softened
- 1¼ cups light brown sugar, firmly packed
- ¼ cup granulated sugar
- 2 large eggs
- 1 teaspoon vanilla
- 2 cups semi-sweet chocolate chips

Preheat oven to 350 degrees. In a bowl, whisk together flour, baking soda, baking powder, salt, and oats. In another bowl with an electric mixer, cream butter and sugars until light and fluffy. Beat in eggs, 1 at a time, beating well after each addition. Beat in vanilla. Beat in flour mixture and stir in chocolate chips. Drop by rounded tablespoons 2 inches apart onto buttered baking sheets. Bake cookies in batches in middle of oven for 12 to 15 minutes or until golden. Cool cookies on racks. Cookies keep in airtight containers for 5 days.

Lynn Graham

Chocolate Oatmeal Cookies

- 3 cups minute oatmeal
- 1 teaspoon vanilla
- 1 cup pecans, chopped
- 2 cups sugar
- ½ cup cocoa
- ½ cup milk
- 1 stick butter

In a bowl mix, oatmeal, vanilla, and nuts. In saucepan on stove, combine sugar, cocoa, milk, and butter. Bring to a boil and boil 2-4 minutes, stirring constantly. Pour melted chocolate mixture over oatmeal mixture. Work quickly and drop by tablespoon onto wax paper. Let cool and harden.

Note: I started baking before I started school. This was one of the first things I learned to make because I love chocolate. Thanks, Mom, for letting me in the kitchen, make a mess, and learn from you.

Cathy Tatum

German Butter Cookies

- 2 sticks butter
- ⅓ cup sugar
- ¼ cup whole milk
- 1 teaspoon vanilla
- 3¼ cups of plain flour
- ½ cup of apple jelly
- ½ cup nuts, chopped

Mix butter, sugar, and milk together well. Add flour one cup at a time. Then add 1 teaspoon of vanilla. Roll into balls. Put on greased 9 x 13 inch pan. Make indention in middle of balls and add mixture of apple jelly and nuts. Bake at 325 - 350 degrees until light golden brown. Watch carefully.

Nancy Roadcap

Gram's Icebox Cookies

- 1 cup brown sugar
- 1 cup sugar
- 1 cup shortening
- 3 cups flour
- 1 teaspoon soda
- 1 teaspoon salt
- 1 teaspoon cinnamon
- 1 cup pecans, chopped
- 2 eggs

Mix together all ingredients, adding flour and nuts last. Shape into a log and place in refrigerator for several hours. Slice cookies about ¼ inch. Bake at 425 degrees for 5-6 minutes.

Connie Bowers

Fruitcake Cookies

- 1 pound red cherries
- 1 pound pineapple
- 7 cups pecans
- 1 cup butter
- 1 cup brown sugar
- 3 cups self-rising flour
- 1 cup milk
- 3 eggs

Chop fruits and pecans. Mix sugar with butter. Add eggs and milk with 2¾ cups of flour. Mix ¼ cup flour with fruit and add to other mixture. Mix well. Drop by teaspoon and bake in 300 degree oven for about 20 minutes.

In Memory of Mrs. Thelma Underwood

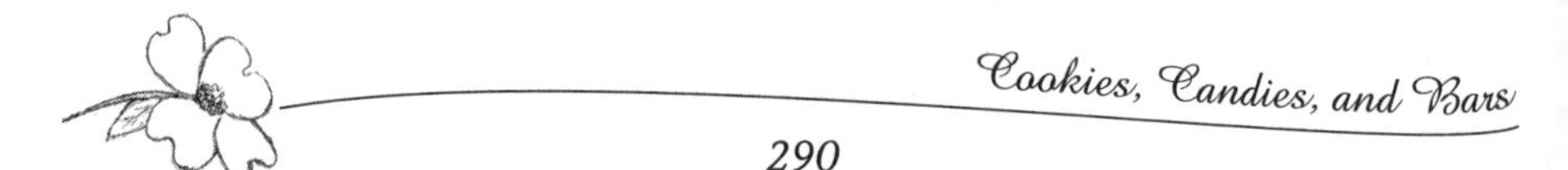

Christmas Fruitcake Cookies

- 1 cup brown sugar
- 1 cup oleo (margarine)
- 3 eggs, well beaten
- 1 cup plain flour
- 1 teaspoon baking soda
- 1 teaspoon cinnamon
- 1 teaspoon cloves
- 1 teaspoon nutmeg
- ½ cup milk
- ½ pound cherries
- ½ pound pineapple
- 1 package dates
- 7 cups pecans, chopped
- ¾ box raisins

Cream margarine and sugar; add eggs one at a time. Combine flour, soda, cinnamon, cloves, nutmeg, and milk. Chop fruit and pecans and toss with a little flour. Mix into dough. Drop from spoon on greased pan. Bake 250 degrees for 20-30 minutes. Makes many cookies. Good and chewy!

June Waldron

Fruitcake Cookies

- 1 box Duncan Hines moist deluxe butter recipe cake mix
- 4 ounces each red and green cherries, chopped into little pieces
- 4 cups pecans, chopped
- ½ teaspoon cinnamon
- 1 teaspoon vanilla flavoring
- ¾ cup cooking oil

Mix all ingredients together adding oil a little at a time. Divide batter into small amounts, spoon dough onto cookie sheet, and bake at 375 degrees for 14 minutes (depending on oven).

Jackie Wilson

Christmas Cookies

- 1½ pounds dates
- ½ pound candied cherries
- ½ pound pineapples
- 1 pound pecans
- 1 cup butter
- 1½ cups sugar
- 2½ cups flour
- 2 eggs
- 1 teaspoon salt
- 1 teaspoon soda
- 1 teaspoon cinnamon

Chop fruit and nuts. Mix and set aside. Mix flour, salt, soda, and cinnamon; set aside. Cream butter and sugar. Add eggs and beat well. Add part of the dry ingredients to the fruit and nuts; mix well. Add remaining dry ingredients to the creamed mixture until all is well blended. Fold in chopped fruit and nuts. Drop by teaspoon onto lightly greased (Butter Pam) cookie sheet. Bake at 350 degrees for 10-15 minutes.

Gloria Cloud

Lady Fingers

- 1½ sticks butter, room temperature
- 7 tablespoons powdered sugar
- 2 cups flour, sifted
- ¾ teaspoon salt
- ¼ to ½ teaspoon ice cold water
- 2½ teaspoons vanilla
- 1 cup pecans, chopped medium to fine
- More powdered sugar for coating cookies

Cream butter and sugar; add flour, salt, cold water, and vanilla. Stir in nuts. Batter will be stiff. Roll into finger-sized pieces. Place on lightly greased or sprayed cookie sheet and bake at 350 degrees for 15 minutes. DO NOT BROWN. Remove from oven when lightly golden. Cool slightly and roll in powdered sugar. Store in airtight container with waxed paper between the layers of cookies.

Allison Cowart

Lady Fingers

- ¼ pound butter
- 4 tablespoons powdered sugar
- 1 teaspoon vanilla flavoring
- 1 tablespoon water
- 2 cups flour
- 1 cup nuts, chopped
- Powdered sugar

Cream butter, work in sugar, add the rest of the ingredients, and mix well. Roll in shape of finger. You will need some water to add from time to time so the dough will stick together. Bake in a preheated oven at 350 degrees until light brown, about 15 minutes. Cool for 5 minutes and roll in powdered sugar.

Elizabeth White

Awesome Oatmeal Cookies

- 1 cup shortening
- 1 cup brown sugar
- 1 cup sugar
- 2 eggs
- 1 teaspoon vanilla
- 1½ cups flour
- 1 teaspoon salt
- 1 teaspoon soda
- 3 cups oatmeal
- 1 cup raisins

Mix all ingredients together, adding flour, oatmeal, and raisins last. Bake 375 degrees for 5-7 minutes.

Connie Bowers

"Let your speech always be with grace, as though seasoned with salt, so that you will know how you should respond to each person."

Colossians 4:6
(NASB)

Lace Cookies

- 2 cups old-fashioned oats
- 1 tablespoon flour
- 2 sticks butter, melted (very hot)
- 2 cups white sugar
- 2 eggs, beaten
- 1 teaspoon salt
- 1 teaspoon vanilla

Put oats, sugar, flour, and salt into large bowl. Pour very hot butter over mixture. Stir until sugar melts. Add beaten eggs and vanilla. Cover cookie sheets with foil. Drop ½ teaspoon 2 inches apart. Bake at 325 degrees for approximately 10 minutes until light golden brown. Cookies peel off foil easily when cool. Store in airtight container. Yield 6 dozen.

In Memory of Mrs. Annabelle Waters

Ranger Cookies

- 2 sticks margarine
- 1 cup sugar
- 1 cup brown sugar
- 2 eggs
- 1 teaspoon vanilla flavoring
- 2 cups plain flour, sifted
- 1 teaspoon baking soda
- ½ teaspoon baking powder
- ½ teaspoon salt
- 2 cups quick oatmeal
- 2 cups Rice Krispies cereal
- 1 cup coconut, shredded

Cream margarine, sugar, and brown sugar. Add eggs and vanilla. Mix until smooth. Slowly add flour, baking soda, baking powder, and salt. Mix well. By hand, mix in oatmeal, Rice Krispies, and coconut (dough will be stiff). Drop small balls onto greased cookie sheet. Bake at 350 degrees for 12–14 minutes or until golden brown.

Elizabeth White

Moravian Cookies

- ¾ pound lard
- 1 pound light brown sugar
- 1 quart molasses
- 2 tablespoons baking soda
- 2 tablespoons ground cinnamon
- 2 tablespoons ground ginger
- 2 tablespoons ground cloves
- 3 pounds all-purpose flour
- 1 teaspoon salt

Heat and stir together all ingredients except flour until warm. Mash out any lumps and be sure the lard has melted. Remove from heat and while still warm, stir in the flour. Mix well. Cover and refrigerate overnight or longer. Remove a small amount of dough, place on a lightly floured bake cloth, and roll until very paper thin. In the rolling process, use as little flour as possible. Too much flour will make the cookies tough. Cut into desired shapes. Bake on lightly greased cookie sheet at 300 degrees for about 7 minutes. Watch closely. After baking, brush with a clean cloth to remove excess flour. Let cool on cookie sheet. Remove and store in tightly covered tins.

Note: Cookies are better if dough has "mellowed" for awhile. The dough will keep several weeks if kept tightly covered in refrigerator. The baked cookies keep well and will remain crisp if kept in tight containers. Also, this recipe will make many cookies and perhaps you might want to cut the recipe in half.

Bro. Shep Johnson
Senior Pastor

Many First Baptist members have enjoyed these delicious cookies prepared by Bro. Shep's mother, Mrs. Gladys Johnson.

Peanut Butter Cookies

- 1 cup peanut butter
- 1 cup shortening or margarine
- 1 cup light brown sugar
- 1 cup granulated sugar
- 2 eggs
- 2 teaspoons baking powder
- 2½ cups all-purpose flour

In large bowl, cream peanut butter, shortening or margarine, brown sugar, and granulated sugar. Add eggs and continue to mix. Combine baking powder and flour, add to creamed mixture, and mix at highest speed. Roll dough into balls about the size of walnuts. Place on greased cookie sheet. Flatten in crisscross fashion with fork. Bake 350 degrees for 15 minutes. Watch carefully.

In Memory of Mrs. Ferne Roadcap

Peanut Butter Cornflake Cookies

- 3 cups sugar
- 1½ cups dark or light Karo syrup
- 3 cups peanut butter
- 15 cups cornflakes

Combine sugar and syrup in saucepan. Cook on medium heat until sugar is dissolved. Bring to a boil, stirring constantly. Remove from heat and add peanut butter and cornflakes. Mix well. Working quickly, spread in a pan and let cool. Cut into squares.

Margaret Lankford

Crunch Drops

- 2 cups plain flour
- 1 teaspoon baking soda
- ½ teaspoon salt
- 1 cup shortening
- 1 cup brown sugar
- 1 cup granulated sugar
- 2 eggs
- 1 teaspoon vanilla
- 2 cups quick-cooking oats
- 2 cups crisp rice cereal
- 1 cup coconut, shredded

Sift together flour, baking soda, and salt; set aside. Cream shortening until fluffy and add both sugars gradually. Add eggs one at a time and beat well. Stir in vanilla. Add flour mixture, combining well. Add oats, rice cereal, and coconut. Batter is stiff at this point so use clean hands to mix it thoroughly. Drop teaspoons of dough onto greased cookie sheet, placing about 2 inches apart. Cookies spread during baking. Bake for 12-15 minutes at 350 degrees.

Charlotte Bacon

Aunt Karen's No-Bakes

- 1 stick margarine
- 2 cups sugar
- 4 tablespoons cocoa
- ½ cup milk
- 1 teaspoon vanilla extract
- ½ cup peanut butter
- 3 cups oatmeal

Bring margarine, sugar, cocoa, and milk to a boil (no more than 2 minutes). Add vanilla, peanut butter, and oatmeal. Spoon onto wax paper.

Connie Bowers

Roll-Out Cookies

- 1 cup margarine or butter
- 1 cup sugar
- 1 large egg
- 2 teaspoons baking powder
- 1 teaspoon vanilla
- 2¾ cups plain flour

Preheat oven to 325-350 degrees. In a large bowl, cream butter and sugar. Beat in egg and vanilla. Add baking powder and flour one cup at a time, mixing after each addition. The dough will be very stiff. Blend last flour by hand. Do not chill dough. Divide dough in half. Work on a floured surface using half the dough. Roll out to ⅛ inch thickness. Dip cookie cutters in flour before using. Then repeat with second half of dough. Bake cookies on ungreased cookie sheets on top rack of oven for 6 to 7 minutes or until slightly brown. Take out and cool completely before decorating. Frosting or batter may be tinted with paste or liquid colors. (If you use liquid color in frosting, you may need to add a little more confectioners' sugar to have a good spreading consistency.) Spread thin layer of frosting and decorate with sprinkles or multiple colors. A cake decorating bag with a tip can be helpful for detail decorating. Have fun!

Butter Cream Frosting:

- ½ cup Crisco
- ½ cup margarine
- 1 teaspoon vanilla
- 1 box 10X confectioners' sugar
- 2 tablespoons milk (maybe more)

Mix all with electric mixer. If too stiff, add a little more milk.

Cathy Tatum

Sand Tarts

4 sticks of unsalted butter
3 cups self-rising flour
1½ cups pecans, chopped
1¾ cups powdered sugar

Mix together butter and powdered sugar. Add flour and mix well. Stir in pecans. Roll out dough into small balls and flatten slightly. They will flatten when baked. Bake at 350 degrees until slightly brown around edges. Do not over bake. When cool, dust with sifted powdered sugar. Store in airtight container.

Kelly Lastinger

Saltine-Chocolate Brittle Cookies

1 cup brown sugar, firmly packed
Saltine crackers
2 sticks real butter
1 (12 ounce) package chocolate chips, melted

Line cookie sheet with foil. Cover with 1 layer of saltine crackers. Mix butter and brown sugar, boil 3 minutes, stirring constantly. Pour over crackers and bake 5 minutes in 400 degree oven. Remove from oven, add melted chocolate, and smooth over top. Cool and place in refrigerator. When thoroughly cold, remove and break into cracker size. Store in airtight container.

Catherine Moodie

Old-Fashioned Sugar Cookies

- 3 cups White Lily plain flour
- 1½ teaspoons baking powder
- ½ teaspoon salt
- 1 cup sugar
- 1 cup butter, softened
- 1 beaten egg
- 3 tablespoons cream (or substitute milk)

Sift together flour, baking powder, salt, and sugar. Cut in butter. Add egg and milk. Roll out cookies on floured surface. Cut with favorite cookie cutters. Bake at 350 degrees for 8 to 10 minutes. Frost and decorate with buttercream frosting.

Theresa Wiggins

Gingersnaps

- ½ cup shortening
- ¼ teaspoon salt
- 1 cup sugar
- 1 egg, beaten
- ¼ cup molasses
- 2 cups plain flour
- 3 teaspoons soda
- 1½ teaspoons ginger
- ¾ teaspoon cloves
- 1½ teaspoons cinnamon
- 4X sugar, sifted
- 1 lemon, juiced

Mix in order given, omitting 4x sugar and lemon juice. Roll into ½ inch balls and place on greased baking sheet. Bake at 350 degrees for 10 to 12 minutes. Immediately press the center of each cookie down with finger to hold frosting. Remove from cookie sheet. Mix sifted 4X sugar with juice of one lemon. Make fairly stiff. Drop small amount in center of each cookie.

Dona Christopher

Mexican Wedding Cookies

2 cups butter
1 cup powdered sugar
1 cup pecans, chopped
4 cups all-purpose flour
1 teaspoon vanilla extract

Cream butter and sugar. Add flour and vanilla to this mixture. Add chopped pecans. Make into small balls about 1 inch in diameter. Bake at 350 degrees for 20 minutes. Cool and roll in powdered sugar.

Rose Williams

Wyoming Whopper Cookies

⅔ cup butter
1¼ cups brown sugar
¾ cup sugar
3 eggs, beaten
1½ cups chunky peanut butter
6 cups old-fashioned oats
2 teaspoons baking soda
1½ cups raisins
1 package chocolate chips

Cream butter and sugars. Add eggs, one at a time. Stir in remaining ingredients. Bake at 350 degrees for 15 minutes.

Suzanne Goodman

Hint: Shiny aluminum and stainless steel bakeware produce the best baked goods. They conduct heat evenly and encourage a brown crust. Dark pans can cause overbrowning.

Pecan Drop Cookies

1 cup pecans, chopped
½ cup butter or margarine
½ cup plus 2 tablespoons Crisco shortening
1 cup confectioners' sugar
2½ cups cake flour, sifted
2 teaspoons vanilla

Preheat oven to 325 degrees. Cream butter and Crisco until smooth. Beat in confectioners' sugar gradually. Stir in flour and mix thoroughly. Add vanilla and pecans; mix well. Drop by teaspoon on ungreased baking sheet. Makes a lot of cookies depending on how big you make them. Bake 15 to 20 minutes.

Lori Bradner

Butter Cookies

1 cup shortening
¾ cup sugar
1 egg
2¼ cups cake flour
1⅛ teaspoons salt
¼ teaspoon baking powder
1 teaspoon vanilla
1 tablespoon butter flavoring

Mix all ingredients. Put into cookie press and form cookies. Bake at 400 degrees for 10 to 12 minutes.

In Memory of Mrs. Jonell Garrett

Blonde Brownies

- 1 (1 pound) box light brown sugar
- 1⅓ sticks of margarine
- 3 eggs
- 3 scant cups plain flour
- 3 teaspoons baking powder
- 1 cup nuts, chopped

Mix all ingredients together and bake in a greased 9 x 13 inch pan at 325 degrees for 25 minutes.

Ellen Fitzgerald
Grandmother Drury

Blondies

- 1 stick butter
- 2 eggs, beaten well
- 1 package light brown sugar
- 2 cups self-rising flour
- 1 cup nuts, chopped

Melt butter over low heat. Remove from heat and add sugar. Stir until moist. Add eggs, flour, and nuts, mixing well after each added ingredient. Bake in 9 x 13 inch pan at 375 degrees until golden brown, 30-40 minutes or until a toothpick comes out clean. Oven temperatures vary so watch carefully. Add chocolate morsels instead of nuts or add both for a variety.

Nancy Roadcap

"All Scripture is inspired by God and profitable for teaching, for reproof, for correction, for training in righteousness."
2 Timothy 3:16
(NASB)

Chewies

- 2 cups light brown sugar
- 2 cups self-rising flour
- 2 cups pecans, chopped
- 1 stick salted butter
- 3 large eggs
- 2 teaspoons vanilla flavoring

Melt butter and add brown sugar. Add one egg at a time; stir. Slowly add flour until well mixed. Add vanilla flavoring and pecans. Grease pan and spread out batter. Bake at 325 degrees for 15 minutes. Let cool. Cut into pieces and enjoy.

Libba Burch

Coconut Bars

- 4 eggs
- 4 teaspoons vanilla
- 3 cups brown sugar, packed
- 4 cups self-rising flour
- 12 tablespoons margarine
- 3 cups pecans, chopped
- 2 cups of coconut

Mix all eggs, vanilla, sugar, flour, and margarine. Add nuts and coconut. Add 1 tablespoon of milk if needed. Spread ¼ inch thick in 2 oblong greased pans. Bake at 350 degrees for 25 minutes. Cut into bars.

Mirt Dockery

Date Nut Bars

- 1 box Pillsbury moist supreme cake mix
- ¾ cup brown sugar
- ¾ cup butter
- 2 cups walnuts, chopped
- 2 cups dates, chopped
- 2 eggs

Mix cake mix, butter, brown sugar, eggs, dates, and nuts. Spoon into 9 x 13 inch pan. Bake 35-45 minutes at 350 degrees. Cool and cut into bars.

Hattie Harkleroad

Brownies Deluxe

- 1 cup margarine or butter
- 3 squares baking chocolate
- 4 eggs
- 2 cups sugar
- 1 (12 ounce) package miniature marshmallows
- 1½ cups all-purpose flour
- 1 teaspoon baking powder
- 2 teaspoons vanilla extract
- 1 cup nuts, chopped

Melt 1 cup margarine or butter and 3 squares chocolate in top of double boiler. Beat 4 eggs and add 2 cups sugar gradually. Beat well. Sift together flour and baking powder. Add flour mixture to egg mixture along with chocolate. Mix thoroughly; add 2 teaspoons vanilla extract and 1 cup chopped pecans. Spread in a large sheet pan and bake at 325 degrees for 30 minutes. Do not overcook and do not wash chocolate pot but begin making icing at once.

Icing:

- ½ cup butter
- 3 squares baking chocolate
- ⅔ cup sugar
- 1 (5 fluid ounce) can evaporated milk
- 1 (1 pound) package powdered sugar
- 1 teaspoon vanilla extract

In the top of the double boiler mix icing ingredients except vanilla and powdered sugar, and cook over boiling water while brownies are baking. When brownies are done, cover with miniature marshmallows. Add box of powdered sugar to icing and beat well. More milk may be added if thinning is necessary. Add vanilla and pour over brownies and marshmallows while hot. Do not cut until the next day. Cover and leave overnight.

Note: With this recipe I use butter or ½ butter and ½ margarine. Some people call this "Mississippi Mud Cake" rather than brownies.

Bro. Shep Johnson
Senior Pastor

Fig Bars - Brown's Favorite

1	box Duncan Hines orange supreme moist cake mix	½	cup Crisco oil
1	egg	1	cup fig preserves
		1	cup pecans, chopped

Mix and bake in a greased 9½ x 13 pan at 325 degrees for 25-30 minutes. Bars will be chewy.

In Memory of Mrs. Virginia Brown

Pecan Balls

½	cup butter or margarine, softened	1	teaspoon vanilla
2	tablespoons sugar	1	cup cake flour
		1	cup pecans, finely chopped

Mix all ingredients. Roll into small bite-size balls. Bake on ungreased baking sheet for 25 minutes at 300 degrees. Roll in confectioners' sugar while warm.

Cindy Ward

Peanut Butter and Cornflake Snack

12 to 14	ounces peanut butter	1	cup Karo Syrup
1	cup sugar	6	cups cornflake cereal

Boil sugar and Karo syrup. Mixture is ready when a drop hardens in cold water. Stir in peanut butter and 6 cups cornflakes. Spoon onto wax paper and let cool.

Kay Fletcher

German Chocolate Pecan Pie Bars

- **3 cups pecan halves**
- **1¾ cups all-purpose flour**
- **¾ cup powdered sugar**
- **¾ cup cold butter, cubed**
- **¼ cup unsweetened cocoa**
- **1½ cups semi-sweet or milk chocolate morsels (your preference)**
- **¾ cup brown sugar, firmly packed**
- **¾ cup light corn syrup**
- **¼ cup butter, melted**
- **3 large eggs, lightly beaten**
- **1 cup sweetened flaked coconut**

Preheat oven to 350 degrees. Bake pecans in a single layer in a shallow pan for 8-10 minutes or until lightly toasted and fragrant, stirring halfway through. Line bottom and sides of a 9 x 13 inch pan with heavy-duty aluminum foil, allowing 2 to 3 inches to extend over the sides. Lightly grease foil. Pulse flour and next 3 ingredients in a food processor 5 or 6 times or until mixture resembles coarse meal. Press mixture on bottom and ¾ inch up sides of prepared pan. Bake crust at 350 degrees for 15 minutes. Remove from oven and sprinkle chocolate morsels over crust. Cool completely on a wire rack (about 30 minutes).

Whisk together brown sugar and next 3 ingredients until smooth. Stir in coconut and toasted pecans and spoon into prepared crust. Bake at 350 degrees for 25 to 30 minutes or until golden and set. Cool completely on a wire rack (about 1 hour). Chill for 1 hour. Lift baked bars from pan using foil sides as handles. Transfer to a cutting board and cut into bars.

Sonya Hendley

Salted Peanut Chews

Base:

- 1 package yellow cake mix
- ⅓ cup margarine or butter, softened
- 1 egg
- 3 cups miniature marshmallows

Topping:

- ⅔ cup corn syrup
- ¼ cup margarine or butter
- 2 teaspoons vanilla
- 1 (12 ounce) package peanut butter chips
- 2 cups crisp rice cereal
- 2 cups salted peanuts

Heat oven 350 degrees. In large bowl at low speed, combine all base ingredients except marshmallows until crumbly. Press in bottom of ungreased 9 x 13 inch pan. Bake at 350 degrees for 12-18 minutes or until golden brown. Remove from oven and immediately sprinkle with marshmallows. Return to oven for 1-2 minutes until marshmallows begin to puff. Cool while preparing topping.

In large saucepan, heat corn syrup, margarine, vanilla, and chips just until chips are melted and mixture is smooth, stirring constantly. Remove from heat and stir in cereal and nuts. Immediately spoon warm topping over marshmallows; spread to cover. Chill and cut into bars. Store covered. Reminiscent of favorite candy bar.

Audrey Wilkerson

Caramel Squares

- 1 cup brown sugar (dark, light, or mixture of both)
- 1 stick butter
- 1 egg
- 1 cup flour
- 1 teaspoon baking powder
- 1 teaspoon vanilla
- ⅛ teaspoon salt
- 1 cup nuts, chopped

Heat butter and sugar together until melted. Cool enough not to cook the egg when it is added. Beat egg in medium-sized bowl and add melted butter and sugar. Add salt to flour and stir flour and other ingredients into sugar mixture. Bake in a lightly greased square or rectangular pan at 350 degrees for 20-25 minutes. Do not over bake. Cool slightly and cut into squares.

Allison Cowart

Frosted Pumpkin Bars

- 4 eggs
- 2 cups sugar
- 1 (15 ounce) can pumpkin
- 1 cup vegetable oil
- 2 cups all-purpose flour
- ½ teaspoon salt
- 1 teaspoon soda
- 2 teaspoons baking powder
- 2 teaspoons cinnamon

In a mixing bowl, beat eggs by hand. Add sugar and beat well. Add pumpkin and oil; blend. Stir in dry ingredients. Pour in an ungreased 10½ x 15 x 1 inch jelly roll pan. Bake in a 350 degree oven 30 minutes. Cool.

Frosting:

- 1 (3 ounce) package cream cheese, softened
- 1 stick margarine, softened
- 1 tablespoon milk
- 1 teaspoon vanilla extract
- 2½ cups confectioners' sugar (approximately)

Cream all together until spreadable. Frost cooled bars and keep refrigerated. Cut into desired size bars.

Nell Sturgis

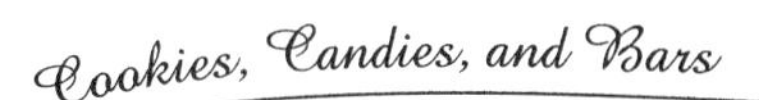

Pumpkin Supreme

½ gallon vanilla ice cream
1 cup light brown sugar
1 (16 ounce) can pumpkin
1 teaspoon allspice
1 teaspoon ginger
1 teaspoon nutmeg

Partially thaw ice cream. Mix all ingredients together with mixer.

Graham cracker crust:

2 stacks graham crackers
1 stick butter, melted
½ cup sugar

Crumble graham crackers, melted butter, and sugar. Mix well. Place in bottom of 9 x 13 inch glass dish. Pour pumpkin mixture into crust. Freeze until ready to use.

Note: Mix equal small amounts of sugar and cinnamon together. When serving, cut into squares, add some whipped cream, and then sprinkle a little of the sugar-cinnamon mixture on top of whipped cream. Makes for a pretty dessert.

Betty Taylor

Aunt Faye Gillis' Tea Cakes

2 cups self-rising flour
1 cup sugar
1 egg
½ teaspoon baking soda
¾ cup Crisco
1 cup milk
1 teaspoon vanilla flavoring

Sift flour in tray like making biscuits. Hollow out hole in flour. Add all other ingredients. Knead longer than you would making biscuits. Pinch off small amounts and pat out until thin. Put on greased cookie sheet and bake at 425 degrees for 10 minutes or until brown.

Alice Ward

Oreo Truffles

1 (18 ounce) package Oreo cookies (regular, not double stuffed), finely crushed
1 (8 ounce) package cream cheese, softened
1 pound white baking chocolate, melted

In large mixing bowl, combine crushed cookies and cream cheese. Beat with mixer on low speed until well blended. Form 1-inch balls by hand. I like to put the balls in the refrigerator to become firm before I dip them. Dip balls in white chocolate. Place on baking sheet covered with wax paper. Refrigerate 1 hour or until firm. To store, cover and refrigerate. Makes 50 truffles.

Kelly Lastinger

Peanut Brittle

1½ cups of sugar
½ cup Karo syrup (white)
½ cup of water
2 cups of peanuts
1 heaping teaspoon of baking soda

Cook sugar, syrup, and water until it comes to a rolling boil. Add peanuts. (Roast peanuts enough to get the skin off. Makes the candy better.) Cook until syrup turns cream colored. Remove from fire. Add heaping teaspoon of soda. Stir until syrup and peanuts are well mixed. Pour on a well-greased biscuit baker 12 x 14 inch. Pour it back and forth. Don't touch with spoon except to get it all out of the boiler. If you touch with the spoon you kill all the bubbles and it will make the candy hard.

Deidre Taft

Divinity Candy

2½ cups sugar
½ cup corn syrup
½ cup water
1½ cups pecans, chopped
1 teaspoon vanilla
2 egg whites, stiffly beaten
Pinch of salt

Cook sugar, corn syrup, water, and salt together until 260 degrees or hard-crack stage. Have 2 egg whites stiffly beaten. Pour syrup over egg whites slowly. Continue to beat until candy begins to lose glossiness. Add 1 teaspoon vanilla and 1½ cups of chopped pecans. Drop by spoon in 1 teaspoon mounds onto wax paper. Pick a cold clear day to cook divinity!

In Memory of Mrs. Virginia Brown

No-Cook Divinity Candy

1 jar marshmallow crème
3 tablespoons water
2 cups powdered sugar
1 teaspoon vanilla
½ cup nuts

Beat marshmallow crème, water, and vanilla at high speed until mixture stands in stiff peaks. Fold in sugar. Add nuts and drop by teaspoon onto waxed paper.

Nancy Roadcap

Granny's Oatmeal Fudge

2 cups sugar
4 tablespoons cocoa
½ cup evaporated milk
1 stick butter
1 teaspoon vanilla flavoring
1 cup pecans, chopped
2 cups quick oatmeal

Bring to a boil sugar, cocoa, milk, butter, and vanilla. Remove from heat. Add 1 cup pecans and 2 cups quick oatmeal. Stir and spoon onto wax paper.

Mary Ford Spivey

Divinity

2 cups sugar
½ cup water
Pinch salt
1 (7 ounce) jar marshmallow cream

Bring sugar, water, and pinch of salt to a rolling boil. Boil for 2 minutes. While beating with mixer, pour into marshmallow cream all at once. Beat until it starts to lose its gloss. Stir in nuts if desired. THIS RECIPE CANNOT BE DOUBLED!

Jan Lastinger

Pecan Pralines

2 cups sugar
¾ teaspoon soda
1 cup milk
1½ teaspoons butter
2 cups pecan halves

Combine sugar and soda. Add milk. Cook to soft-ball stage. Remove from heat. Add butter and pecans. Beat until it begins to thicken. Drop by spoonfuls onto wax paper. For best results always make candy on a good weather day; humidity in the air may cause candy to be sticky. Another good tip would be to place in cold oven until candy has set.

Debbie Fender

Date Nut Balls

- 1 stick butter
- 8 ounces dates, chopped
- 1 cup sugar
- 2 eggs, slightly beaten
- 1 teaspoon vanilla flavoring
- 2¼ cups crispy rice cereal
- ½ cup pecans, chopped
- Flaked coconut

Combine butter and dates in a saucepan and cook over low heat until dates dissolve. Add sugar and beaten eggs. Cook 10 minutes more. Remove from heat and add vanilla flavoring, cereal, and pecans. Cool. Roll in balls the size of a small nut. Roll in coconut.

In Memory of Mrs. Miriam White

Orange Coconut Balls

- 6 ounces orange juice concentrate, thawed
- 1 box vanilla wafers, crushed
- ½ cup pecans, chopped
- 1 pound 10X sugar or slightly less
- Shredded coconut

Mix all ingredients except coconut. Form into balls and roll in coconut. Keep in covered container in refrigerator.

In Memory of Mrs. Lou Ann Walker

Chocolate-Pecan Meringues

- **2 egg whites, room temperature**
- **1/8 teaspoon salt**
- **1/8 teaspoon cream of tartar**
- **3/4 cup sugar**
- **1 (6 ounce) package semi-sweet chocolate morsels**
- **2/3 cup pecans, chopped**
- **1 teaspoon vanilla extract**

Beat egg whites, salt, and cream of tartar until foamy; gradually add sugar, beating until stiff peaks form. Fold in chocolate, pecans, and vanilla.

Drop mixture by heaping teaspoonfuls 2 inches apart onto parchment-lined cookie sheets. Bake at 300 degrees for 25 minutes. Using a sharp spatula, remove meringues from parchment and cool on wire racks. Store in airtight container.

Lynn Schofield

Pecan Kiss Cakes

- **4 egg whites, room temperature**
- **1½ cups sugar**
- **1 teaspoon vanilla extract**
- **1 cup pecans, chopped**

Beat egg whites in a medium mixing bowl until foamy; add sugar, 2 tablespoons at a time, beating until stiff peaks form. Fold in vanilla and pecans.

Drop by heaping teaspoons 2 inches apart onto waxed paper-lined cookie sheets. Bake at 250 degrees for 55 minutes. Remove immediately by peeling from waxed paper, and cool on wire racks. Store immediately in airtight containers.

Lynn Schofield

Basic Table Setting

Informal Table Setting

Formal Table Setting

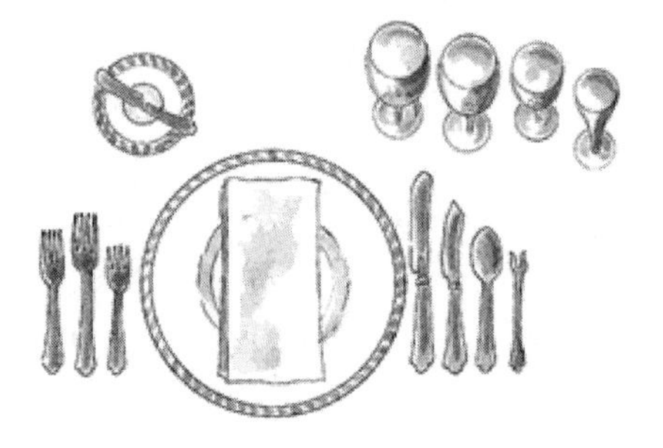

Place settings from Emily Post. www.emilypost.com

Desserts and Pies

"How sweet are Your words to my taste!
Yes, sweeter than honey to my mouth!"
Psalm 119:103
(NASB)

Desserts and Pies

Cheesecake

Crust:

- **2½ cups graham cracker crumbs**
- **1 stick butter**

Filling:

- **3 (8 ounce) packages cream cheese**
- **3 large eggs**
- **1 cup sugar**
- **1 teaspoon vanilla**

Topping:

- **½ pint sour cream**
- **3 tablespoons sugar**

To prepare crust, melt butter and add crumbs. Press into springform pan.

Mix all of the filling together and pour on top of crust. Bake at 350 degrees for 40 to 50 minutes. Mix together sour cream and sugar; add to top of cake for the last 10 minutes of baking time.

Paula Thomas

Bisquick Cheesecake

- **¾ cup milk**
- **2 teaspoons vanilla**
- **2 eggs**
- **1 cup sugar**
- **½ cup Bisquick baking mix**
- **2 (8 ounce) packages cream cheese, softened and cut into ½ inch cubes**

Topping:

- **1 cup sour cream combined with 2 tablespoons sugar**
- **2 teaspoons vanilla**

Blend milk, vanilla, eggs, sugar, and Bisquick in blender on high for 15 seconds. Add cream cheese and blend on high for another 2 minutes. Pour into a 9 x 1¼ inch pie plate, greased with cooking spray. Bake in preheated oven at 350 degrees for 40-45 minutes or until center is set. Allow to cool. Mix and spread topping over cheesecake. Chill and garnish with fruit before serving. Fresh peaches, blueberries, or frozen raspberries, thawed and thickened with a little confectioners' sugar, are good fruit toppings.

Becky Miller

Red Velvet Cheesecake

1½ cups chocolate graham crackers, crushed or crumbled
¼ cup butter, melted
1 tablespoon granulated sugar
3 (8 ounce) packages cream cheese, softened
1½ cups granulated sugar
4 large eggs, beaten
3 tablespoons unsweetened cocoa
1 cup sour cream
½ cup whole buttermilk
2 teaspoons vanilla extract
1 teaspoon distilled white vinegar
2 (1 ounce) bottles red food coloring
1 (3 ounce) package cream cheese, softened
¼ cup butter, softened
2 cups powdered sugar
1 teaspoon vanilla extract

Garnish: fresh mint sprigs

Stir together graham cracker crumbs, melted butter, and 1 tablespoon granulated sugar; press mixture into bottom of a 9-inch springform pan. Beat 3 (8 ounce) packages cream cheese and 1½ cups sugar at medium-low speed with an electric mixture for 1 minute. Add eggs and next 6 ingredients, mixing on low speed just until fully combined. Pour batter into prepared crust. Bake at 325 degrees for 10 minutes; reduce heat to 300 degrees and bake for 1 hour and 15 minutes or until center is firm. Run knife along outer edge of cheesecake. Turn off oven. Let cheesecake stand in oven for 30 minutes. Remove cheesecake from oven; cool in pan on wire rack 30 minutes. Cover and chill 8 hours. For topping, beat 1 (3 ounce) package cream cheese and ¼ cup butter at medium speed with an electric mixer until smooth; gradually add powdered sugar and vanilla, beating until smooth. Spread evenly over top of cheesecake. Remove sides of springform pan. Garnish, if desired.

Renee Roberson

Deluxe Cheesecake

5 (8 ounce) packages of cream cheese
1¾ cups sugar
3 tablespoons all-purpose flour
¼ teaspoon salt
5 eggs, plus 2 egg yolks
¼ cup heavy cream
Grated rind of 1 lemon and ½ orange

Prepare Cookie Dough Crust. Beat cream cheese until soft. Mix sugar, flour, and salt. Blend into cheese. Add grated rinds. Add eggs and egg yolks one at a time, beating after each. Blend in cream. Pour into crust and bake at 475 degrees for 15 minutes. Reduce heat to 225 and bake for 1 hour. Turn off heat and let stand in oven for 15 minutes. Remove from oven and cool.

Cookie Dough Crust:

1 cup all-purpose flour
¼ cup sugar
Grated rind of one lemon
1 egg yolk
1 cup butter or margarine, softened

Mix flour and sugar. Add remaining ingredients and mix well. Chill. Roll out dough and cover bottom of a 9-inch spring pan. Roll remaining dough into 2 strips. Butter sides of pan and press dough into sides of pan. Bake at 400 degrees for 8 minutes. Cool and add cream cheese mixture. Bake and serve with your favorite topping.

Cindy Williams

Key Lime Cheesecake Squares

- **2 cups graham cracker crumbs**
- **1 cup macadamia nuts, finely chopped**
- **2¾ cups sugar, divided**
- **6 tablespoons butter, melted**
- **1 egg white, lightly beaten**
- **2 (8 ounce) packages cream cheese, softened**
- **½ cup evaporated milk**
- **4 large eggs**
- **2 tablespoons key lime zest**
- **⅓ cup fresh key lime juice**
- **¼ cup all-purpose flour**
- **½ teaspoon baking powder**

Garnish: confectioners' sugar, key lime slices

Preheat oven to 350 degrees. In a medium bowl, combine graham cracker crumbs, macadamia nuts, ½ cup sugar, and butter. Add egg white, stirring to combine well. Lightly press mixture evenly into bottom of a 9 x 13 inch baking pan; bake for 8 minutes. In a medium bowl, combine cream cheese and ½ cup sugar; beat at medium speed with an electric mixer until smooth. Add evaporated milk, beating until well combined. Spoon cream cheese mixture evenly over crust. Bake for 15 minutes; remove from oven, and cool for 10 minutes. In a medium bowl, combine remaining 1¾ cups sugar, eggs, lime zest, and lime juice, whisking to combine well. In a small bowl, combine flour and baking powder; add to sugar mixture, whisking to combine. Pour sugar mixture over cream cheese mixture. Bake for 40 minutes or until a wooden pick inserted in center comes out slightly sticky. Cool completely. Garnish with confectioners' sugar and key lime slices, if desired.

Mary Lou Gillespie

Nutty Cheesecake Squares

- **2 cups all-purpose flour**
- **1 cup walnuts, finely chopped**
- **⅔ cup packed brown sugar**
- **½ teaspoon salt**
- **⅔ cup butter or margarine**

Filling:

- **2 (8 ounce) packages cream cheese, softened**
- **½ cup sugar**
- **2 eggs**
- **¼ cup milk**
- **1 teaspoon vanilla extract**

In a bowl, combine flour, walnuts, brown sugar, and salt; cut in butter until the mixture resembles coarse crumbs. Set half aside; press remaining crumb mixture onto the bottom of a greased 9 x 13 x 2 inch baking pan. Bake at 350 degrees for 10-15 minutes or until lightly browned. In a mixing bowl, beat filling ingredients until smooth; pour over crust. Sprinkle with reserved crumb mixture. Bake at 350 degrees for 20-25 minutes or until a knife inserted near the center comes out clean. Cool completely. Store in the refrigerator.

Nell Sturgis

Lucille's Heavenly Delight

- **1½ (20 ounces) cans sliced peaches (or fresh)**
- **¼ cup sugar**
- **1 stick butter, melted**
- **1 cup sugar**
- **½ cup flour**
- **2 eggs**

Boil peaches in a saucepan on low heat with ¼ cup sugar. Cream melted butter and 1 cup sugar. Add eggs one at a time, beating well after each egg. Add flour. Beat 1 minute. Place hot peaches into a 8 x 8 x 2 inch pan. Pour creamed mixture over peaches or drop by spoonfuls. Bake at 325 degrees for 25-30 minutes.

Linda Raybon

Granny's Blueberry Crisp

1 cup flour
1 cup sugar
1 stick margarine
¼ teaspoon salt
1 quart blueberries

Place berries in a 9 x 13 inch baking dish. In a bowl, mix sugar, flour, margarine, and salt with a fork and knife until mixed well. Sprinkle over berries and bake at 350 degrees for 1 hour.

Mary Ford Spivey

Holy Trinity Apple Crisp

Topping:

1½ cups old-fashioned oats
½ cup sugar
12 tablespoons cold butter
1 cup flour
2 tablespoons brown sugar
½ teaspoon salt

Filling:

2 tablespoons brown sugar
1 teaspoon cinnamon
1 tablespoon flour
¼ teaspoon nutmeg
½ teaspoon salt
⅛ teaspoon ground cloves
4 pounds apple (10) peeled, cored, and sliced

Combine topping ingredients until crumbly. To make filling, combine brown sugar, flour, cinnamon, salt, nutmeg, and cloves into large mixing bowl. Add apple slices and toss to coat. Spoon into 3-quart baking dish and cover with topping. Bake at 400 degrees for 50 minutes or until fruit bubbles and topping browns.

Allison Brice

Blueberry Crunch

- 1 (20 ounce) can undrained crushed pineapple
- 2 to 3 cups blueberries, fresh or frozen
- ¾ cup sugar
- 1 box yellow cake mix
- 2 sticks butter, melted
- 1 cup pecans, chopped
- ¼ cup sugar

Butter a 9 x 13 inch baking dish and spread the following in layers: pineapple, blueberries, ¾ cup sugar sprinkled on berries, dry cake mix, melted butter, pecans, and ¼ cup sugar sprinkled on top. Bake at 325 degrees for 1 hour or until brown on top. Serve warm or cold.

Dale Collins

Blackberry Dumpling Cobbler

- 2 (16 ounce) packages frozen blackberries
- 2 cups sugar, divided
- ¼ cup butter
- 3 (8 ounce) packages ⅓ less fat cream cheese, softened
- ⅔ cup fat-free milk
- 2¼ cups all-purpose baking mix
- ¾ cup uncooked oats

Bring blackberries, 1⅓ cups sugar, and butter to a boil in a large saucepan over medium heat. Stir gently until butter is melted and sugar dissolves; remove from heat. Beat cream cheese and remaining sugar until fluffy. Add milk and beat until smooth. Stir in baking mix and uncooked oats. Spread ⅔ of the cream cheese mixture onto bottom of a lightly greased 9 x 13 dish. Spoon blackberry mixture evenly over cream cheese mixture. Dollop remaining cream cheese mixture evenly over blackberry mixture. Bake at 350 degrees for 35 minutes or until golden brown.

Paula Thomas

Carlton's Blueberry Dessert

- 1 cup all-purpose flour
- 1 stick butter, softened
- ¼ cup dark brown sugar
- 1 cup pecans, chopped
- 2 (8 ounce) packages cream cheese, softened
- 1 (16 ounce) carton Cool Whip
- 1½ cups sugar
- 2 teaspoons vanilla extract
- 1 quart blueberries (Carlton adds extra blueberries)
- ⅓ cup sugar
- 2 heaping teaspoons cornstarch

Combine flour, butter, dark brown sugar, and pecans. Mix well. Lightly press into bottom of 9 x 13 inch baking dish. Bake for 15 to 20 minutes at 350 degrees or until lightly brown. Cool completely. Mix together cream cheese, Cool Whip, 1½ cups sugar, and vanilla. Spread over cooled base. In saucepan, combine blueberries, cornstarch, and ⅓ cup sugar. Cook over medium heat stirring often until thickened. Cool and spread over cream cheese layer. Refrigerate until served.

Note: The recipe is as Carlton makes it. If you prefer not to have the thicker filling, use only 1 (8 ounce) cream cheese, 1 (8 ounce) Cool Whip, ¾ cup sugar, and 1 teaspoon vanilla.

Mary Lou Gillespie

Hint: Do not wash blueberries when freezing. Place them in the freezer on a baking sheet. When frozen, transfer them into a freezer container. Keep frozen until ready to use.

Blueberry Supreme

Crust:

2½ cups self-rising flour
2 sticks margarine, melted
4 tablespoons sugar
1 cup pecans, chopped

Sift flour and sugar together and stir in nuts. Add melted margarine and mix. Knead into a ball, making sure all dry ingredients are moistened. Press into a 10 x 15 baking dish. Press tightly so that it bonds with the nuts. Bake at 350 degrees for 35 minutes. DON'T OVERBAKE THE CRUST. Cut crust into squares while still warm. (Cutting the cooled crust will cause it to crumble.) Let cool.

Center Filling:

1 (8 ounce) package cream cheese (room temperature)
1 cup powdered sugar or Splenda
2 (8 ounce) containers Cool Whip or Cool Whip Free

Cream powdered sugar (Splenda) and cream cheese together. Fold in Cool Whip. Mix well. Layer on cooled crust. Refrigerate until set.

Topping:

1 cup sugar
3 tablespoons cornstarch
¼ cup water
4 to 5 cups blueberries

Put the sugar and cornstarch in an empty (dry) Cool Whip container and shake well to mix. This prevents the cornstarch from clumping when added to the water. Bring water to a boil, add sugar mixture, and stir until it becomes almost clear. This takes only a few seconds. Add blueberries, mix and bring to a boil. Reduce heat a little. Continue to cook and stir until mixture thickens. Allow to cool to the touch, but not until firm. Layer blueberry topping on center filling. Keep refrigerated.

In Memory of Mrs. Emma Moore

Lemon Chiffon Dessert

- 1 large can evaporated milk, chilled
- 1 (3 ounce) package lemon Jell-O
- 1 cup boiling water
- 1 stick margarine
- 2 cups graham cracker crumbs
- 2 tablespoons sugar
- 1 (8 ounce) package cream cheese
- 3 tablespoons milk
- 1 teaspoon vanilla
- 1 cup sugar

Mix lemon Jell-O with 1 cup of boiling water and stir until dissolved. Put in refrigerator to chill until consistency of egg whites. Melt margarine and mix graham cracker crumbs and 2 tablespoons sugar. Line a 9 x 13 inch pan with this mixture (some may be saved for topping). Beat cream cheese with milk, vanilla, and 1 cup sugar. Beat until soft. Add thickened Jell-O to this mixture. Whip evaporated milk and fold into Jell-O mixture. (You can add a drop or two of yellow food coloring to give this a deeper color.) Pour over crust, sprinkle with reserved crumbs, and chill. To serve, cut in squares and garnish with a dollop of Cool Whip and a lemon twist.

Betty Jean Hurst

"The fruit of that righteousness will be peace; its effect will be quietness and confidence forever."

Isaiah 32:17
(NIV)

Butter Pecan Delight

- ½ bag Pecan Sandies
- 1 sleeve saltine crackers
- ½ cup butter, melted
- 1 large package instant vanilla pudding
- 2 cups whole milk
- 1 pint butter pecan ice cream, softened
- 1 (12 ounce) container Cool Whip
- 4 Heath candy bars, crushed

Crush together Pecan Sandies and saltine crackers. Mix together with ½ cup melted butter. Place mixture into 9 x 13 inch pan; press evenly as crust. Prepare pudding with milk; beat until thick. Fold in butter pecan ice cream and ½ portion of Cool Whip. Pour on top of crust. Allow to chill in refrigerator for 30 minutes. Remove and top with remaining Cool Whip. Sprinkle with crushed Heath candy bars. Refrigerate but do not freeze.

JoAnne Lewis

Million Dollar Dessert

- 1 cup plain flour
- 1 stick butter, softened
- ½ cup nuts, chopped
- 1 cup powdered sugar
- 1 (8 ounce) package cream cheese
- 1 large carton Cool Whip
- 2 small packages instant chocolate pudding
- 3 cups milk

Combine flour and butter until crumbly; press into 8 x 12 inch pan; sprinkle with part of nuts. Bake 15 minutes at 350 degrees. Let cool. Second layer: Combine sugar and cream cheese; mix well. Add ½ carton Cool Whip. Spread mix over baked crust. Third layer: Prepare pudding with 3 cups milk; spread over second layer. Fourth layer: Using remaining carton of Cool Whip, spread over top of chocolate pudding layer. Sprinkle with remaining chopped nuts. This can be made with other flavors of pudding.

In Memory of Mrs. Sarah Drew

Peach Delight

Crust:

- **1½ sticks margarine**
- **2 cups self-rising flour**
- **1 cup nuts, chopped**

Mix ingredients and press into 9 x 13 inch pan. Bake at 350 degrees for 25-30 minutes. Watch and don't let it get really brown. Cool.

Filling:

- **1 (8 ounce) cream cheese, softened**
- **2 cups powdered sugar, sifted**
- **1 (12 ounce) Cool Whip**

Beat with mixer and put over cooled crust.

Topping:

- **2 cups sugar**
- **2 cups water**
- **1 (3 ounce) box peach Jell-O**
- **6 tablespoons cornstarch**
- **5 to 6 peaches, sliced**

Microwave the first 4 ingredients on high until thick (4 to 8 minutes). Let cool. Slice 5 to 6 peaches and place on top of filling. Pour topping over peaches and chill.

Carolyn Norris

Chocolate Delight

- 1 cup all-purpose flour
- 1 stick butter
- 1 to 1½ cups pecans, chopped
- 1 (8 ounce) package cream cheese
- 1 cup powdered sugar
- 2 large tubs of Cool Whip
- 2 (8 ounce) packages of instant chocolate pudding
- 3 cups milk

First Layer:
Mix flour, butter, and ½ cup nuts together until lumpy. Pat into a 9 x 13 inch pan. Bake at 350 degrees for 15 minutes. Take out and let cool.

Second Layer:
Mix cream cheese, powdered sugar, and 1 large container of Cool Whip and spread onto first layer.

Third Layer:
Mix instant chocolate pudding and milk. Let set until thickened. Pour over second layer.

Fourth Layer:
Spread 1 large container of Cool Whip over third layer. Sprinkle with nuts. Refrigerate until serving time.

In Memory of Mrs. Doris Worrell

The Bible states that children are a reward from the Lord and that a woman of noble character is worth far more than rubies.

Psalm 127:3
Proverbs 31:10

Strawberry Cheese Pie

Crust:

To make crust, mix following ingredients and pat down in a 9 x 13 inch dish. Bake 10-15 minutes in 350 degree oven until light brown.

- **1 cup of pecans, chopped**
- **1½ cups self-rising flour**
- **2 tablespoons sugar**
- **¾ cup margarine**

First Layer:

To make first layer, mix following ingredients and pour over cooled crust.

- **1 (8 ounce) cream cheese, softened**
- **1 (9 ounce) Cool Whip**
- **1 (14 ounce) can Eagle Brand sweetened condensed milk**

Refrigerate while preparing second layer.

Second Layer:

- **2 (10 ounce) boxes of frozen strawberries**
- **½ cup water**
- **½ cup sugar**
- **3 tablespoons cornstarch**
- **3 tablespoons strawberry Jell-O**
- **3 drops of red food coloring**

Thaw strawberries, then drain, reserving the juice. Set aside strawberries. To strawberry juice add water, sugar, cornstarch, strawberry Jell-O, and food coloring. Cook in double boiler until juice is thick and clear. Cool. To this mixture, add strawberries and stir. Pour strawberry mixture over first layer and refrigerate for several hours or make a day ahead.

Archie Brown

Apple Dumplings

6 Granny Smith (or other variety of tart apples)
1 tablespoon butter
½ cup sugar
1½ teaspoons cinnamon
Pie crust dough (double crust)

Wash, peel, core, and slice apples. Mix butter, sugar, and cinnamon. Roll pastry and cut in squares large enough to cover stacked slices of apples (equivalent to about an apple). Wrap apple slices in pastry and seal. Arrange dumplings in a 9 x 9 x 2 inch greased baking dish.

Syrup:

1 cup sugar
1½ teaspoons cinnamon
2 cups water
4 tablespoons butter

Boil syrup ingredients for about 5 minutes. (I bring it to a boil and allow to simmer while I make the dumplings.) Pour syrup over the dumplings. Place in preheated 500 degree oven for 5 minutes. Reduce heat to 325 degrees and bake 35 to 40 additional minutes.

Bro. Shep Johnson
Senior Pastor

Apple Dumplings

2 large Granny Smith apples
2 cans of crescent rolls
2 sticks margarine, melted
2 teaspoons cinnamon
1 cup sugar
1 can Mountain Dew

Peel apples and slice into eight sections each (total 16 pieces). Wrap each piece of apple in one crescent roll starting with large end of roll. Place 16 dumplings into a 9 x 13 inch casserole dish or pan. Pour can of Mountain Dew over dumplings. Mix margarine, cinnamon, and sugar together and pour over dumplings. Bake at 350 degrees for 45 minutes. Serve with ice cream or Cool Whip, if desired.

Marsha Gilliard

Chocolate Éclair

1 cup sugar
¼ cup canned milk
⅓ cup cocoa
1 stick butter
2 small boxes vanilla instant pudding
3½ cups milk
1 (8 ounce) tub of Cool Whip
1 box Graham crackers

Melt butter in saucepan. Add cocoa and stir until smooth. Add sugar and canned milk. Bring to a boil for 1 minute and set aside. Blend vanilla pudding and whole milk. Fold Cool Whip in pudding mixture. Layer pan with graham crackers, ½ the pudding mixture, crackers, the rest of the pudding mixture, and then crackers on top. Pour and spread chocolate on top of crackers. Refrigerate for at least 8 hours.

Karrie LaRiccia

Lemon Mousse

1 can Carnation or Pet Milk
3 eggs
Juice of 3 lemons
1 cup sugar
1 box graham cracker crumbs

Pour milk in mixer bowl and put in freezer until icy. Whip with electric mixer until stiff. Add ½ of the lemon juice and ½ cup of sugar to mixture. Set aside. Beat 3 eggs until fluffy. Add rest of lemon juice and sugar to eggs. Fold egg mixture into milk mixture. Spread part of crumbs out over pan (about 9 x 12 inch) and spread mousse over crumbs. Sprinkle the rest of crumbs over top of mousse and freeze. Cut in squares and serve frozen.

In Memory of Mrs. Mamie Farrar

Banana Pudding

- ¾ cup sugar
- 4 tablespoons flour
- 2 cups milk
- 3 egg yolks
- 1 teaspoon vanilla
- 4 bananas
- Vanilla wafers

Mix sugar and flour together; add milk, stirring until there are no lumps. Add egg yolks and vanilla. Cook on medium heat, stirring constantly, until thickened.

Icing:

- 3 egg whites
- 6 tablespoons sugar

Beat egg whites until it forms peak; add sugar and beat until firm. Layer vanilla wafers, bananas, and pudding mixture; repeat layers. Spread icing on top and bake until golden brown. Serve warm!

Rosemary Brown

Easy Banana Pudding

- 1 box vanilla wafers
- 1 (8 ounce) Cool Whip
- 14 ounces sweetened condensed milk
- 1 (3 ounce) box instant vanilla pudding
- 2 cups milk
- Bananas

Mix pudding and milk, and then add sweetened condensed milk. Add ½ of the container of Cool Whip and stir until combined. Layer vanilla wafers, bananas, and pudding and repeat. Spread the rest of the Cool Whip on top and sprinkle with remaining vanilla wafers.

Kim Knight

Bread Pudding

2 sticks butter
3 eggs
2 cups sugar
8-10 slices cinnamon/raisin bread, cubed
1 (20 ounce) can crushed pineapple, undrained

Preheat oven to 350 degrees. Butter an 8 x 8 inch or 9 x 9 inch baking dish. (I usually just mist the pan with the vegetable oil spray.) Cream together butter, eggs, and sugar in a large bowl. Add cubed bread and pineapple. Stir to combine. Pour mixture into dish. Bake uncovered for 60 minutes. Serve warm or cold.

Note: This bread pudding keeps well in the refrigerator for up to 5 days.

Sherri M. Jenkins

Nabisco Famous Chocolate Refrigerator Roll

1 (9 ounce) package Nabisco Famous Chocolate Waters
2 cups heavy whipping cream
1 teaspoon vanilla extract
Sugar to taste
Chocolate curls, for garnish

Whip whipping cream with vanilla, adding sugar to taste. Spread 1½ teapoons whipped cream on each wafer. Begin stacking wafers together and stand on edge on serving platter to make fourteen inch log. Frost with remaining whipped cream. Better refrigerated overnight. To serve, garnish with chocolate curls; slice roll at 45 degree angle.

Note: I double this recipe and use a little more whipping cream than recipes states. Wafers are difficult to find. Look for them in most large chain grocery stores with the ice cream toppings and cones.

Mollie Morgan

White Chocolate Bread Pudding

- 9 large eggs, lightly beaten
- 2 quarts half-and-half
- 2 cups sugar
- 1 tablespoon vanilla
- 1 cup white chocolate ganache
- 1 loaf French bread, cut into 1-inch slices

Make white chocolate ganache and set aside. In a large mixing bowl, whisk together eggs, half-and-half, sugar, vanilla, and ganache. Add bread slices and let soak for at least 1 hour, stirring occasionally. Preheat oven to 325 degrees. Pour bread mixture into a lightly greased 4-quart baking dish. Bake until set and browned, about 1 hour. Serve warm with additional ganache or praline sauce.

White Chocolate Ganache:

- 1¾ cups heavy whipping cream
- 12 ounces white chocolate, chopped

Scald cream in heavy saucepan. Place white chocolate in mixing bowl. Pour cream over chocolate and stir until melted.

Praline Sauce:

- ½ cup butter
- 1 cup dark brown sugar, firmly packed
- 1 cup heavy whipping cream

Melt butter in heavy saucepan. Add brown sugar and stir. Bring to a boil. Add cream carefully. (Mixture may splatter at this point.) Stir until smooth. Serve warm over bread pudding.

Pam Gillis

Pumpkin Roll

- **3 eggs**
- **1 cup sugar**
- **2/3 cup pumpkin**
- **1 tablespoon lemon juice**
- **3/4 cup all-purpose flour**
- **1 teaspoon baking powder**
- **2 teaspoons cinnamon**
- **1 teaspoon ginger**
- **1 teaspoon pumpkin pie spice**
- **1/2 teaspoon salt**
- **1 cup pecans, chopped**
- **Powdered sugar**

Mix together first 4 ingredients. Stir together flour, baking powder, cinnamon, ginger, pumpkin pie spice, and salt. Mix with pumpkin mixture. Pour into a greased and floured 10 x 15 x 1 inch pan. Before baking, sprinkle nuts over flour mixture and pumpkin. Bake at 375 degrees for 15 minutes until done. Cool slightly and turn out on a tea towel dusted with powdered sugar. Roll up cake and towel together. Cool in refrigerator. Unroll and spread with filling mixture. Re-roll cake without towel and chill well.

Filling:

- **1 1/2 cups powdered sugar**
- **1 (8 ounce) cream cheese, softened**
- **5 tablespoons butter, softened**
- **1 teaspoon vanilla flavoring**
- **1/8 teaspoon salt**

Beat above ingredients until smooth and creamy.

In Memory of Mrs. Geneva Womack

Cocoa Torte

3 egg whites
½ teaspoon salt
½ teaspoon almond extract
¾ cup brown sugar, firmly packed
½ cup nuts, chopped

Filling:
1 (3 ounce) package cream cheese
1 teaspoon vanilla
1½ tablespoons water
⅔ cup instant cocoa mix (Quik)
1 carton whipping cream

Cut 4 (8-inch) circles from brown paper or parchment paper. Beat egg whites. Add almond extract and salt until foamy. Gradually add the brown sugar, about 2 tablespoons at a time, and beat until stiff glossy peaks are formed. Reserve 1 tablespoon chopped nuts. Fold remaining nuts into meringue. (I add nuts to all the layers.) Spread meringue on paper circles. Sprinkle top of circle with chopped nuts. Place on ungreased cookie sheet. Bake at 300 degrees for 35 minutes. Cool thoroughly; peel paper gently from meringue.

For filling:
Beat cream cheese, vanilla, and water until smooth. Add instant cocoa mix and whip cream. Whip until stiff. Spread about ½ cup filling on each of the layers, stacking on top of each other. Flute the top layer with remaining whipped cream. Chill several hours or overnight.

Catherine Moodie

Huguenot Torte

- 4 eggs
- 3 cups sugar
- 8 tablespoons flour
- 5 teaspoons baking powder
- ½ teaspoon salt
- 2 cups tart cooking apples, cored and chopped
- 2 cups pecans or walnuts, chopped
- 2 teaspoons vanilla flavoring
- Whipped cream, flavored and sweetened for topping

Beat eggs in electric mixer until very frothy and lemon-colored. Add other ingredients except the whipped cream in the above order. Pour into 2 well-buttered baking dishes about 8 x 12 inches. Bake in 325 degree oven about 45 minutes or until crusty and brown. To serve, scoop up with pancake turner (keeping crusty part on top). Pile on a large plate and cover with whipped cream and a sprinkling of the chopped nuts or make individual servings.

In Memory of Mrs. Rubye Phillips

Brownie Delight

- 2 boxes of brownies, baked per directions
- 1 package cream cheese
- 1 container Cool Whip
- 1 jar marshmallow cream
- 1 container caramel syrup (like for ice cream)
- Chopped nuts

Bake brownies according to directions. Cream Cool Whip, cream cheese, and marshmallow cream. In a trifle dish, place a layer of crumbled brownies, cream mixture, caramel syrup, and nuts. Repeat layers. Top with Cool Whip and chopped nuts. May add cherries and chocolate sprinkles, if desired.

Jan Tyre

Strawberry Trifle

1 angel food cake
1 (8 ounce) package cream cheese
1 (8 ounce) Cool Whip
1 cup powdered sugar (or to taste)
2 cartons of sweetened frozen strawberries, thawed

Mix softened cream cheese, Cool Whip, and powdered sugar. In a trifle bowl, place chunks of cake, a layer of strawberries, and a layer of cream cheese mixture. Repeat the layers until all ingredients are used. End up with cream cheese layer on top.

Faye Ray

Angel Fluff

1 Duncan Hines angel food cake mix, bake and cool
1 large can pineapple
1 (12 ounce) Cool Whip
10 ounces frozen sliced strawberries
3 tablespoons fresh lemon juice
2 envelopes Knox gelatin
4 tablespoons cold water
1 cup boiling water
1 cup sugar
1 can Angel Flake coconut

Dissolve gelatin in cold water. Add to boiling water. Add sugar, fruit, and lemon juice to mixture. Fold in ½ of Cool Whip. Break angel food cake into pieces and put ½ of cake in long, oblong casserole. Pour ½ fruit mixture on cake. Add other ½ of cake on top, and the remainder of fruit mixture. Put rest of Cool Whip and coconut on top. Chill.

In Memory of Lou Ann Walker

Mom's Apple Pie

3 cans apples, diced
1¼ cups sugar
1 teaspoon cinnamon
1 teaspoon cloves
1 teaspoon apple pie spice
2 sticks butter
Biscuit dough (thin)

Combine first 5 ingredients and pour into a 9 x 13 casserole dish. Layer biscuit dough on top. Top with butter slices. Sprinkle more cinnamon and cloves on top. Bake on 350 degrees until brown.

Teresa Holliday
Wife of Bro. B. J. Holliday
Minister of Music

Almond Chiffon Pie

4 egg yolks
¼ teaspoon salt
½ cup sugar
1 cup hot milk
1 envelope Knox gelatin (plain)
¼ cup water
1 teaspoon almond flavoring
4 egg whites, whip-stir
½ cup sugar
1 cup almonds, sliced and toasted
1 pie shell, baked
Cool Whip or Dream Whip

Cook egg yolks, salt, sugar, and milk to a custard in a saucepan. Dissolve Knox gelatin in water and add to custard. Stir in almond flavoring and set aside to cool. When cooled, fold in ¾ cup toasted almonds. Whip egg whites and sugar until a stiff peak forms and fold into custard. Pour into baked pie shell. Top the pie with Cool Whip or Dream Whip. Use back of spoon to make peaks. Garnish top with remaining toasted almonds.

Janet K. Wade

Blueberry Cream Pie

- 1 egg
- 1 cup sour cream
- 2 teaspoons all-purpose flour
- ¾ cup sugar
- 1 teaspoon vanilla
- ¼ teaspoon salt
- 2½ cups blueberries
- 1 unbaked pie shell
- 3 teaspoons all-purpose flour
- 3 teaspoons oleo (margarine), softened
- 3 teaspoons pecans, chopped

Combine first 6 ingredients; beat 5 minutes at medium speed until smooth. Fold in blueberries. Pour into crust and bake at 400 degrees for 25 minutes. Combine remaining ingredients, stirring well. Sprinkle over top of pie. Bake 10 additional minutes. Chill before serving.

In Memory of Mrs. Pat Goodman

Mama's Sweet Potato Pie

- 2 cups sweet potatoes, boiled, peeled, and mashed
- ¾ cup sugar
- 1 can evaporated milk (use only enough to make batter thick, but runny)
- 2 tablespoons self-rising flour
- 1 teaspoon lemon
- 1 tablespoon vanilla
- 2 eggs
- 1 tablespoon margarine
- 2 pie crusts, unbaked

Mix together all ingredients and pour into 2 pie crusts. Bake 350 degrees until knife put in center of pie comes out clean (or when you jiggle the pie it doesn't run).

Patsy Herlocker

Caramel Coconut Pie

(Batten Family Favorite)

¼ cup butter or margarine
1 (7 ounce) package flaked coconut
½ cup pecans, chopped
1 (8 ounce) cream cheese, softened
1 (14 ounce) sweetened condensed milk
1 (16 ounce) Cool Whip, thawed
2 deep pastry shells, baked
1 (12 ounce) jar caramel ice cream topping

Melt butter in large skillet. Add coconut and pecans. Cook until golden, stirring frequently. In mixing bowl, combine cream cheese and condensed milk. Beat on medium speed until smooth. Fold in Cool Whip. Layer ¼ of pie mixture into each cooked and cooled pie shell. Drizzle ¼ of caramel over the pie. Sprinkle ¼ of coconut and pecan mixture on top of caramel. Repeat layering sequence ending with coconut and pecan mixture. Freeze at least 8 hours. Serve frozen. Makes 2 deep-dish pies. I substitute low-fat or fat-free items when available. I use the caramel fruit dip located in the vegetable section instead of the ice cream topping.

Note: Wednesday night supper has been a tradition at First Baptist Church for many years. Mrs. Mary Thacker prepared many meals, and this was one of her most popular desserts.

Terry Cook

"For by grace you have been saved through faith; and that not of yourselves, it is the gift of God; not as a result of works, so that no one may boast."

Ephesians 2:8-9
(NASB)

Praline Pie

For Graham cracker crust:

Mix together 1¼ cups graham crackers, ¼ cup sugar, and 5 tablespoons butter or margarine, melted. Pat in bottom of 9 x 13 inch pan or 2 round pie plates. Let cool.

For gingersnap crust:

Use 2 cups of crushed gingersnaps (I put them in food processor), ½ cup sugar, and 1 stick butter, melted. Pat in bottom of 9 x 13 inch baking dish or 2 round pie plates. Bake crust at 350 degrees for 8 to 10 minutes. Let cool.

For Filling:

- **1 (8 ounce) cream cheese**
- **1 cup pecans, chopped**
- **1 cup coconut**
- **1 can condensed sweetened milk**
- **1 (16 ounce) Cool Whip**
- **Caramel syrup**

Mix cream cheese and sweetened condensed milk together with mixer, and then fold in Cool Whip. Toast coconut and pecans in oven. (Spread them in a shallow pan and bake in oven at 400 degrees for 4 to 5 minutes or until golden brown. Watch carefully and stir coconut frequently to avoid burning on the edges.) Layer on top of crust, ½ cream cheese mixture, then sprinkle with ½ of toasted coconut and ½ of pecans, and drizzle with caramel on the top. Repeat layers. Freeze several hours before serving.

Terri Bailey

Chocolate Pie

- 1 cup sugar
- 3 tablespoons cocoa, rounded
- 3 tablespoons plain flour, rounded
- 1 egg
- 2 cups milk
- 1 teaspoon vanilla flavoring
- 1 (9 inch) prebaked pie crust
- Pinch of salt

Stir sugar, flour, cocoa, and salt together in a thick saucepan or boiler. Add egg to dry ingredients and mix together well. Add milk slowly. Cook slowly on medium-low heat until thick and boiling, stirring constantly. Add vanilla. Pour into a prebaked pie crust. Chill and serve.

JoAnn Worrell

Chocolate Pie

- 2 cups milk
- 2 squares chocolate, melted
- ⅓ cup plain flour
- ⅛ teaspoon salt
- 1 to 2 tablespoons butter, added before removing from heat
- 1 cup sugar
- 3 eggs, separated
- ½ teaspoon vanilla
- 1 pie shell, baked

Scald milk. Blend sugar, flour, and salt. Add to milk and stir until smooth and thick. Add chocolate. (Cocoa can be used instead of chocolate squares; Mrs. Maude Gillis liked cocoa better.) Separate eggs and beat yolks until thick. Add gradually to the hot mixture. Continue to cook until smooth, about 5 minutes. Add vanilla and butter, remove from heat, and allow to cool slightly. Pour into baked pie shell. Top with meringue made from egg whites. Bake under broiler until lightly browned.

Note: Mrs. Maude Gillis was a teacher at Satilla and Coffee County High. This recipe was a favorite of many members and guests of Stokesville Baptist Church.

Laura Mell Pope

Andy's Chocolate Pie

- 1 cup sugar
- 2 tablespoons flour
- 3 teaspoons heaping cocoa
- 3 eggs, separated
- 1 cup milk
- 1 teaspoon vanilla
- 3 tablespoons sugar
- 1 pie crust, baked

Mix first 3 ingredients together. Stir in with 3 egg yolks, milk, and vanilla. Cook over medium heat, stirring often. Pour into pie crust and cover with meringue. To make meringue, beat 3 egg whites until stiff, and then add sugar. Put meringue on pie and bake under broiler until lightly browned.

Sara Davis Tift

Amazing Coconut Pie

- 2 cups milk
- ¾ cup sugar
- ½ cup biscuit mix
- 4 eggs
- ¼ cup butter or margarine, softened
- 1½ teaspoons vanilla
- 1 cup Baker's angel flake coconut

Combine biscuit mix, milk, sugar, eggs, butter, and vanilla. Blend in blender on low for 3 minutes. Pour in a greased 9-inch pie pan. Let sit 5 minutes. Sprinkle coconut on top and bake at 350 for 40 minutes. Serve warm or cool.

Ruth Griggs

Coconut Cream Pie

- 1⅓ cups whipped Carnation evaporated milk, chill and whip
- 2 egg whites, beaten
- 2 egg yolks
- ⅓ cup sugar
- 1 teaspoon vanilla
- 2 teaspoons clear gelatin
- ¼ cup Carnation milk
- ¼ teaspoon salt
- ½ cup moist coconut
- 1 pie crust, baked

Beat egg yolks lightly and add sugar, salt, and vanilla. Soak gelatin in ¼ cup milk about 5 minutes. Dissolve over hot water and add to yolk mixture. Fold whipped milk, beaten egg whites, and coconut into yolk mixture and put into baked pie crust. Refrigerate to congeal.

Meringue:

- 2 egg whites
- 4 tablespoons sugar
- ½ cup coconut

Beat egg whites stiff. Add sugar and coconut. Put on pie and put under broiler until lightly browned.

In Memory of Mrs. Lou Ann Walker

Easy Coconut Pie

- ½ cup self-rising flour
- 2 cups sweet milk
- 1¾ cups sugar
- ½ stick margarine, melted
- 4 eggs
- 1 teaspoon vanilla
- 1 (7 ounce) can flaked coconut

Beat eggs. Mix flour and sugar and add to eggs. Add all other ingredients. Beat well and pour into 2 greased pie pans. This recipe makes its own crust. Bake at 350 degrees for 30-40 minutes.

Melanie Marshall

Egg Pie

- 2 cups milk
- 2 cups sugar
- 2 cups eggs
- 6 tablespoons self-rising flour
- 2 tablespoons butter, melted
- 1 tablespoon vanilla

Mix all above in blender. Pour in 2 pie plates that are greased. Bake at 300 degrees until done. This recipe makes its own crust.

In Memory of Mrs. Othalyne Gillis

Grandmother's Egg Custard

- 4 eggs
- 1 pint sweet milk
- 1 pinch nutmeg (½ teaspoon)
- 1 thumb butter (1 tablespoon)
- 1 pinch salt (½ teaspoon)
- 1 scoop sugar (1 cup)
- 1 tad of flour (1 tablespoon)
- 1 pie shell, unbaked

Beat eggs together with sugar, nutmeg, salt, butter, and flour. Warm milk but do not boil. Add to above ingredients and pour in uncooked pastry shell. Bake for 10 minutes at 450 degrees, reduce oven to 350 degrees, and cook for 30 minutes or until custard is set. (You can add flaked coconut to this for a variation.)

Faye Ray

Japanese Fruit Pie

- 1 cup sugar
- 3 eggs
- ½ stick oleo (margarine), melted
- ¾ cup raisins, chopped
- ¾ cup pecans, chopped
- ¾ cup coconut, chopped
- 1 tablespoon vinegar

Mix together and add vinegar. Bake in 300 degree oven 30-40 minutes or until brown.

In Memory of Mrs. Dot Sparks

Fruit Pie

- 4 ounces cream cheese
- ½ cup powdered sugar
- ½ cup thawed Cool Whip
- 1 graham cracker pie crust
- 1 (4 ounce) package Jell-O (strawberry or peach)
- 1 (4 ounce) package vanilla cook and serve pie filling
- 1¼ cups water
- 2 cups sliced fruit (strawberries or peaches)

Mix Jell-O, pie filling, and water on medium heat until smooth. Cool in refrigerator until it begins to thicken. Stir occasionally. Mix cream cheese, powdered sugar, and Cool Whip. Spread on bottom of pie crust. (Do this while the Jell-O mixture is cooling.) When Jell-O mixture is cool, mix in the fruit and place over cream cheese mixture. Refrigerate until set.

Note: Strawberries with strawberry Jell-O or peaches with peach Jell-O — both are good.

Kim Knight

Rose Bud's Fruit Pie

- **1 large can crushed pineapple (with juice)**
- **1 can sour pitted cherries, drained**
- **1¼ cups sugar**
- **¼ cup flour**
- **1 package of orange Jell-O**
- **1 cup pecans, chopped**
- **5 bananas, sliced or chopped**
- **2 (9 or 10 inch) pie shells or 3 (8 inch) pie shells, baked**

Cook pineapple, cherries, sugar, and flour until thickened. Add orange Jell-O and cool for 10 minutes. Add pecans and bananas. Pour into prebaked pie crusts. Chill and cover with whipped cream.

Joy Paulk

Key Lime Pie

- **1 can sweetened condensed milk**
- **1 large container Cool Whip**
- **⅓ cup key lime juice**
- **1 graham cracker crust pie shell**

Mix condensed milk, Cool Whip, and lime juice. Pour into graham cracker crust. Chill until ready to eat.

Debbie Fender

Lemon Pie

- **3 eggs, separated**
- **1½ cups sugar (mixed with 4 tablespoons flour)**
- **1½ cups milk**
- **3 tablespoons butter, melted**
- **1 teaspoon vanilla**
- **2 large lemons, juiced**

Mix all together except egg whites and bake at 450 degrees for 10 minutes; 325 degrees for 25 minutes. It will be done when it is firm and doesn't shake. When done, top with meringue and put in oven to brown.

Ruth Griggs
Alice Geiger

Lemon Icebox Pie

(My daddy's favorite)

Graham pie crust:

- **1¼ cups Nabisco graham crackers**
- **¼ cup granulated sugar**
- **5 tablespoons of butter or margarine**

Mix together and bake at 350 degrees for 6-8 minutes. Let cool.

Pie filling:

- **1 can condensed milk**
- **1 (8 ounce) cream cheese**
- **⅓ cup lemon juice**

Mix ingredients and pour over graham crust.

Meringue topping:

- **3 egg whites, at room temperature**
- **6 tablespoons sugar**
- **¼ teaspoon cream of tartar**
- **¼ teaspoon vanilla flavoring**

Beat egg whites until foamy. Add cream of tartar and beat until stiff. Beat in sugar until well blended; add vanilla. Spread evenly over top of pie and brown meringue for 15 minutes at 325 degrees. Refrigerate.

Joy Paulk

Million Dollar Pie

- **1 can condensed milk**
- **¼ cup lemon juice**
- **1 medium can sliced peaches, drained and diced**
- **1 medium can mandarin oranges, diced**
- **1 can crushed pineapple, drained**
- **1 large carton Cool Whip**
- **2 ready-made graham cracker crusts**

Mix together and put in two ready-made graham cracker crusts. Makes 2 large pies. Can be made the day before or ready to serve immediately.

Christa Norris Turner

Lemon Chess Pie

- **3 eggs, beaten until light**
- **1 cup sugar**
- **1 lemon, juiced**
- **½ stick butter, melted**
- **1 pastry shell, unbaked**

Preheat oven to 400 degrees. Combine ingredients and pour into pie shell. Bake about 25 minutes. Watch carefully. May have to reduce heat.

Sara Davis Tift

Hint: For extremely flaky pie pastry, measure the flour and shortening into a bowl and chill at least an hour before mixing.

Mud Pie

- 1 box German chocolate cake mix
- 1 stick margarine or butter, cut into pieces
- 1 (8 ounce) package cream cheese, cut into pieces
- 1 cup brown sugar, packed
- 2 cups walnuts, chopped
- 1 (3½ ounce) can flake coconut

Grease (2) 9-inch pie pans. Prepare cake batter according to package directions and spread evenly in pans. In a saucepan over low heat, soften the cream cheese and margarine; combine well. Remove from heat and add brown sugar, mixing well. Add the walnuts and coconut, stirring to mix. Using a spoon, place the cream cheese mixture evenly over the cake batter. Bake at 350 degrees for 30-35 minutes.

Terry Cook

Peach Pie

- 3 cups peaches or any fruit (add ½ cup sugar if fresh fruit - if needed)
- ¾ cup sugar
- ¾ cup self-rising flour
- ¾ cup milk
- ½ stick butter

Preheat oven to 350 degrees. Melt butter in baking dish in oven. Mix flour, sugar, and milk. Pour into melted butter; add fruit. Bake 45 minutes until crust is golden brown. Simple and easy quick dessert.

Cathy Tatum

Mom's Crumbly Peach Pie

Pie shell:

- **1½ cups flour**
- **½ cup Crisco shortening**
- **¾ teaspoon salt**
- **2 - 3 tablespoons ice cold water**

Combine all ingredients and roll into a circle to fit bottom and sides of a pie plate that has been lightly sprayed with nonstick cooking spray. Crimp edges of shell to pie plate so that no dough hangs over.

Filling for Pie:

- **1 cup sugar**
- **2 tablespoons flour**
- **½ cup butter, softened**
- **2 - 3 tablespoons water (unless peaches are juicy)**
- **Enough peeled peaches to fill pie shell, cut in thick wedges**
- **Nutmeg to taste, about ¼ to ½ teaspoon (whole nutmeg freshly grated is best)**

Mix together sugar, flour, butter, and nutmeg into a crumbly mixture. Sprinkle half of mixture in bottom of pie shell. Add sliced peaches. Sprinkle remainder of crumbly mixture on top. Add the water. Bake at 450 degrees for 10 minutes. Reduce heat to 350 degrees and bake until peaches are tender, about 1 hour. Tent edges of pie shell with foil if crust is getting too brown. This pie is best served warm with fresh whipped cream or vanilla ice cream.

Note: Pillsbury Ready Crust refrigerated pie crust may be substituted to save time. Follow box directions for fruit pies.

Allison Cowart

Cast-Iron-Skillet Southern Pecan Pie

- ½ (14.1 ounce) packaged refrigerated pie crust
- 1 tablespoon powdered sugar
- 4 large eggs
- 1½ cups light brown sugar, firmly packed
- ½ cup butter, melted and cooled to room temperature
- ½ cup granulated sugar
- ½ cup pecans, chopped
- 2 tablespoons all-purpose flour
- 2 tablespoons milk
- 1½ teaspoons vanilla extract
- 1½ cups pecan halves

Preheat oven to 325 degrees. Fit pie crust in 10-inch cast iron skillet. Sprinkle pie crust with powdered sugar. Whisk eggs in bowl until foamy. Whisk in brown sugar and next 6 ingredients. Pour mixture in pie crust and top with pecan halves.

Bake at 325 degrees for 30 minutes; reduce oven temperature to 300 degrees and bake 30 more minutes. Turn oven off and let pie stand for 3 hours with oven door closed.

Joy Paulk

Mama's Southern Pecan Pie

- 1 cup sugar
- ¼ cup corn syrup
- ¼ cup butter, melted
- 4 eggs, well beaten
- 1 cup pecans
- 1 unbaked pie shell

Mix sugar, syrup, and butter together. Add eggs and nuts. Pour into unbaked pie shell. Bake at 400 degrees for 10 minutes. Reduce heat to 350 degrees and continue to bake for 30-35 minutes.

Melanie Marshall

Pecan Pie

- ½ cup butter, melted
- 1 cup Karo syrup
- ½ cup sugar
- 1 tablespoon flour
- 1 teaspoon vanilla
- 3 eggs, beaten slightly
- 1 cup pecans, chopped
- 1 pie crust, unbaked

Mix sugar and flour. Add eggs and vanilla flavoring; stir. Add syrup, melted butter, and pecans. Mix thoroughly. Put in unbaked pie crust. Bake at 350 degrees for 30 minutes.

In Memory of Mrs. Virginia Norris

Pecan Pie

- 2 eggs
- ½ cup sugar
- ¾ cup white Karo syrup
- Pinch of salt
- ½ stick butter, melted
- 1 teaspoon vanilla
- 1 cup pecans, chopped
- 1 regular frozen pie crust

Beat eggs with the salt and sugar. Add Karo syrup and melted butter. Add vanilla and pecans. Put in frozen pie crust and bake at 350 degrees for 50 to 55 minutes. You can double the recipe to make 3 pies or you can triple recipe to make 4 pies.

Note: I never bake just one pie. I make these for family reunions and there is never any left. In fact, I make 8 or 10 pies at a time. My oven will bake six pies, but I usually only cook 4 pies at one time. These pies have been a family tradition for 50 years. I call it a "Skinny Pecan Pie."

Charlotte Bacon

Lucy's Pecan Pie

- **¼ cup margarine, melted**
- **1 tablespoon self-rising flour**
- **⅔ cup white syrup**
- **½ cup sugar**
- **2 eggs beaten**
- **1 cup pecans, chopped**
- **1 teaspoon vanilla**
- **1 frozen pie shell**

Mix all ingredients in order listed then pour into pie shell. Bake at 350 degrees for 55-60 minutes. Pie is done when you touch top and it bounces back up.

In Memory of Mrs. Lucy McLeroy

Peanut Butter Pie

- **1 (8 ounce) cream cheese**
- **¾ cup powdered sugar**
- **1 (8 ounce) Cool Whip**
- **⅓ cup peanut butter**
- **1 teaspoon vanilla**
- **2 teaspoons milk**
- **1 graham cracker crust**

Combine peanut butter, cream cheese, powdered sugar, milk, and vanilla. Beat until smooth. Fold in Cool Whip. Pour into crust. Freeze for 2 hours or until firm.

Jennifer Kirkland

Chocolate Chess Pie

- **1½ cups sugar**
- **3½ tablespoons cocoa**
- **2 eggs**
- **1 stick butter, melted**
- **1 teaspoon vanilla flavoring**
- **1 small can Pet milk**
- **1 pie crust, unbaked**

Stir together sugar and cocoa. Add remaining ingredients. Mix and pour into unbaked pie shell. Bake at 325 degrees for 45 to 55 minutes.

Charline McElroy

Peanut Butter Ice Cream Pie

- ½ gallon vanilla ice cream
- 10 ounces peanut butter
- 3 tablespoons brown sugar
- 1 stick oleo (margarine)
- 3 tablespoons cocoa
- 6 tablespoons milk
- 1 box 4X sugar
- 1 teaspoon vanilla
- 3 graham cracker pie crusts

Mix together ice cream, peanut butter, and brown sugar with hand mixer. Pour into 3 graham cracker crusts and place in freezer until frozen. Combine oleo, cocoa, and milk; bring to a boil. Add 4X sugar and vanilla. Pour over frozen pies. Return pies to freezer. Remove from freezer 10 minutes before serving.

Mirt Dockery

Pineapple Chiffon Pie

- 1¼ cups sugar
- 2 whole eggs
- 1¼ cups pineapple juice
- 1 large can frozen evaporated milk
- 1 box of orange Jell-O (or choice)
- 1 (8 ounce) container Cool Whip
- 1 graham cracker crust

Mix sugar, eggs, and pineapple juice. Cook until eggs are done. Add Jell-O, Cool Whip, and can of milk to other ingredients and pour into graham cracker crust.

Faye Ray

Pumpkin Pie

- 1 can pumpkin
- 2 eggs
- 1 can condensed milk
- ¼ cup sugar
- 1 teaspoon pumpkin pie spice
- 2 tablespoons butter, melted
- 1 pie crust, unbaked

Mix ingrdients well and pour in pie crust. Preheat oven to 425 degrees and bake pie for 15 minutes. Reduce heat to 350 degrees and bake 30 minutes or until done.

Topping:

- 1 carton Cool Whip
- 1 teaspoon vanilla

Mix together and top pie. Sprinkle with pumpkin pie spice.

Joyia Lanier

Pumpkin Pie

- 2 cups pumpkin, freshly cooked
- 1 cup sugar
- ½ stick butter
- 1 teaspoon lemon flavoring
- 1 egg
- 1 tablespoon flour
- Cool Whip or whipped cream
- Optional: Coconut and pie crust

Mash fresh pumpkin and mix with remaining ingredients except Cool Whip or whipped cream. Bake at 350 degrees for approximately 30 minutes. Serve pie warm topped with whipped cream or Cool Whip.

Note: This is our favorite family traditional holiday recipe.

Dot McKinnon

Fresh Strawberry Pie

- 6 tablespoons cornstarch
- 2¼ cups boiling water
- 2¼ cups sugar
- 1 (3 ounce) package strawberry Jell-O
- 1 quart fresh strawberries, washed and well drained
- 2 or 3 pie crust, prebaked

Mix sugar and cornstarch. Add boiling water. Cook until clear and begins to thicken. On low heat, add Jell-O and remove from heat; let cool. Add strawberries and pour into cooled, baked crusts. Top with Dream Whip or whipped cream. Makes 2 large or 3 medium pies.

Dale Collins

Mama's Fresh Strawberry Pie

- 1 cup sugar
- 1 cup water
- 2 tablespoons cornstarch
- 1 (3 ounce) package strawberry gelatin
- 1 pint fresh strawberries, sliced
- 1 (9-inch) pastry shell, prebaked

Combine sugar, water, cornstarch, and gelatin in saucepan. Bring to a boil and cook until mixture is thick. Remove from heat and cool. Stir in strawberries and spoon into crust. Chill and top with whipped cream.

Cindy Williams

Pie Crust

- ⅓ cup Wesson oil
- ¼ cup water
- 1 cup self-rising flour

Bring oil and water to a boil. Remove from heat and add flour. Mix with a fork and press into pan.

Dot McKinnon

Crepes

1 cup all-purpose flour
3 tablespoons butter, melted
3 eggs
⅔ cup milk
⅔ cup water
Melted butter or vegetable oil for frying
Pinch salt

Blend the flour, butter, eggs, milk, salt, and water in a blender or food processor. Refrigerate about 1 hour before making the crepes. Place a 7-inch skillet over medium heat and brush lightly with melted butter or oil. Add several tablespoons of batter. Quickly tilt the pan so the batter covers the bottom evenly in the thinnest possible layer. Quickly pour any excess batter back into the bowl. Cook for just a few minutes or until the bottom of the crepe is lightly browned and the edges lift easily. Turn with a spatula or lift by the edge with your fingers and flip over; brown lightly on the other side. Remove the finished crepe to a platter. Brush the pan with more melted butter and repeat. Makes 24 crepes. Top with your favorite topping.

Toby Smith

Hint: Crepes have become breakfast, brunch, a light lunch, dessert, a hearty dinner entrée, or a wonderful snack. They may be eaten on a diet, sweetened or unsweetened, vegetarian or stuffed with a variety of meat mixtures. The filling is limited only to your imagination.

All the Rest

"How lovely on the mountains are the feet of him who brings good news,
who announces peace and brings good news of happiness, who announces
salvation, and says to Zion, 'Your God reigns!'"

Isaiah 52:7
(NASB)

Glorifying…Growing…Going

Oklahoma Missions to Native American Indians

All the Rest

Blueberry Chutney

- 1 large Granny Smith apple, peeled and diced
- ½ cup sugar
- ½ cup orange juice
- 1 tablespoon orange rind
- 1 teaspoon ground ginger
- ¼ to ½ teaspoon dried crushed red pepper
- ¼ teaspoon ground black pepper
- 4 cups blueberries (fresh or frozen)
- 3 tablespoons balsamic vinegar

Bring first 7 ingredients to a boil in a medium saucepan. Reduce heat to low; simmer, stirring occasionally for 15 minutes or until apple is tender. Stir in blueberries and vinegar and bring to a boil. Reduce heat to medium; cook, stirring occasionally for 40 minutes or until thickened.

In Memory of Mrs. Geneva Womack

Pepper Relish

- 12 red bell peppers
- 12 green bell peppers
- 6 hot peppers
- 6 medium onions
- 1 quart vinegar
- 3 teaspoons salt
- 2 cups sugar

Grind bell peppers, hot peppers, and onions. Cover with boiling water. Let stand 5 minutes. Drain. Add other 3 ingredients which have been mixed and boiled. Boil vinegar, salt and sugar until dissolved. Add to cooked pepper and onion mixture and boil for 25 minutes. Pack in hot jars.

In Memory of Mrs. Virginia Brown

Refrigerator Cukes

- **7 cups cukes, sliced**
- **1 cup onion, sliced**
- **1 cup bell pepper, sliced**
- **2 tablespoons salt**
- **1 teaspoon celery salt**
- **2 cups sugar**
- **1 cup white vinegar**

Mix. Keep in refrigerator in large glass container.

In Memory of Mr. Harry Walker

Easy Dill Pickles

- **4 dozen pickling cucumbers (about 3 inches in length)**
- **1 bunch fresh dill**
- **1 quart apple cider vinegar**
- **8 cups water**
- **1 cup pickling salt or kosher salt (do not use table salt)**
- **12 to 16 garlic cloves, peeled (quantity according to taste)**

Wash the cucumbers and remove any stems. Cut a thin slice from end of each cucumber and discard. Cover with cold water and refrigerate overnight or for several hours. Pack the cucumber (whole or sliced) into pint jars as tightly as possible. Poke in 2 sprigs of dill per jar. Bring the vinegar, water, salt, and garlic cloves to a boil. Boil for 2 minutes. Fish out the garlic cloves with a slotted spoon and put one in each jar (or to taste) while the brine cools slightly. Pour the hot brine into the jars and seal. Makes 12 pints.

Debbie Fender

Squash Pickles

8 cups small squash, sliced
2 cups onions, coarsely chopped
2 cups green and red peppers, chopped
Salt

Salt and let stand in ice water for 3 hours. Drain and dry on paper towels.

Make syrup for vegetables:
2 cups cider vinegar
3 cups sugar
2 teaspoons mustard seeds
2 teaspoons celery seeds
1 tablespoon turmeric

Combine syrup ingredients and bring to a boil. Add vegetables and boil again. Turn to low so vegetables cook thoroughly but do not become mushy. Put into jars and seal.

In Memory of Mrs. Martha Belger

Muscadine Preserves

Muscadine grapes (4 cups juice)
3 cups sugar

Select grapes and wash. Separate pulp from skins by squeezing. Cook pulp until done. Press through a sieve or ricer to remove seeds. Add a small amount of water to the skins and cook until tender. Pour skins and pulp together and measure. Bring mixture to a boil, adding 3 cups of sugar to every 4 cups of mixture. Cook until it reaches the jelly test — flakes at 220 degrees. Pour while hot into hot jars and seal. If you use ½ pint jars, recipe will make 3. This is sweet but, oh, so good!

Charlotte Bacon

Applesauce

1 quart apples, tart
½ cup sugar (more if needed)
1 teaspoon lemon juice
⅛ teaspoon lemon rind, grated
Dash of salt
1 cup water
⅛ teaspoon nutmeg
⅛ teaspoon cinnamon

Simmer apples and salt in water until tender. Stir in remaining ingredients and cook 1 minute more. Serve hot or cold.

Catherine Moodie

Swimmer's Ear Solution

1 teaspoon vinegar
1 teaspoon rubbing alcohol

Mix vinegar and alcohol in a small, clean medicine bottle with dropper. After swimming or bathing, dry ears well and add a few drops to each ear canal.

Note: This is a recipe given to us by a doctor. We have used it for years with very good results.

Mary Jo Radosevich
Wife of Bro. Paul Radosevich
Former Youth Minister

Mac Mac's Play Dough

- 2 cups all-purpose flour
- 2 cups cold water
- 1 cup salt
- 2 tablespoons vegetable oil
- 1 tablespoon cream of tartar
- Food coloring

Spray electric skillet with Pam and put in all ingredients except food coloring. Stir until thoroughly mixed. Turn on heat and stir as mixture thickens. Remove as soon as all moisture is gone and mixture forms a ball. (You will be surprised how quickly this happens.) Knead in the food coloring of your choice. Play dough is ready for immediate use. Store in an airtight plastic bag or container in the refrigerator.

Note: My mom, nicknamed Mac Mac, had her own day care center for many years, and she never bought a container of play dough. Her version stays soft and pliable for an incredibly long time.

Glennis Coleman
Wife of Rev. Ray Coleman
Smyrna Baptist Association

Orange Pineapple Sherbet

- 72 ounces orange soda
- 1 can sweetened condensed milk
- 1 large can crushed pineapple

Add condensed milk, pineapple, and enough orange soda to fill churn to "fill line." Stir until condensed milk is dissolved. Churn as directed.

Kate Walker

Aunt Kathy's Chocolate Ice Cream

- 1 (16 ounce) Cool Whip
- 1 (14 ounce) can sweetened condensed milk
- 1 gallon chocolate milk

Pour condensed milk and Cool Whip in an ice cream freezer. Fill to "fill line" with chocolate milk. Stir all ingredients, then turn on machine, and let it freeze!

Note: This tastes like Wendy's Frosty!

Rosemary Brown

Chocolate Ice Cream

- 2 cans sweetened condensed milk
- 1 cup chocolate syrup, to taste
- 2 pints half-and-half
- Whole milk (enough to finish filling ice cream freezer)

Mix all ingredients thoroughly. Pour into a 1-gallon ice cream freezer. Freeze according to freezer directions.

Kathy B. Stone

Peach Fizz Ice Cream

- 1 (2 liter) peach drink
- 1 can sweetened condensed milk
- 1 can peaches, diced

Mix together and put in ice cream freezer. Variations: Use orange pineapple drink with crushed pineapple or strawberry drink with fresh strawberries.

Linda Raybon

Lemon Ice Cream

- **1 quart whipping cream**
- **1 quart half-and-half**
- **1 pint milk**
- **3-4 cups sugar**
- **1 tablespoon lemon rind, grated**
- **2 teaspoons lemon extract**
- **Juice of 8 lemons (¾ cup)**

Combine all ingredients in large bowl. Mix well, stirring to dissolve as much sugar as possible. Pour into ice cream freezer. Freeze according to manufacturer's directions. Let ripen for 30 minutes. Yields about 1½ gallons.

Note: So refreshing! This ice cream is much better made in advance and put in freezer. I have the best luck using a wooden churn. White Mountain is the best!

Mollie Morgan

Milky Way Ice Cream

- **8 Milky Way bars**
- **2 cups milk**
- **6 eggs, well-beaten**
- **1½ cups sugar**
- **2 teaspoons vanilla**
- **2 large cans evaporated milk**

In a double boiler, melt Milky Way bars in 2 cups of milk. Cool. Mix sugar and eggs and beat well. Add vanilla and evaporated milk. Add Milky Way mixture and mix well. Pour into one-gallon freezer container and add enough milk to fill within two inches of top.

In Memory of Mrs. Eunice Traynham

Vanilla Ice Cream

- 3 to 3½ cups sugar
- 3 to 4 eggs
- 2 cans evaporated milk
- 1 pint heavy whipping cream
- 1 tablespoon vanilla flavoring
- Pinch of salt
- Whole milk

In a mixer, beat eggs and then add sugar. Beat until creamy, about 3 minutes. Turn mixer to low and add the evaporated milk and heavy whipping cream. Add salt and vanilla flavoring. Pour into a 6-quart churn. Fill churn with whole milk to level on churn. Freeze.

Note: Can add any fruit but may need to add more sugar. If I use a 4-quart churn, I use 3 eggs and 3 cups sugar; 6-quart churn, 4 eggs and 3½ cups sugar.

Pam Gillis

Mint-Chocolate Chip Ice Cream

- 1 large egg
- 1 cup half-and-half milk
- 3 cups heavy cream
- ¾ cup sugar
- ½ to ¾ cup semi-sweet chocolate chips
- ¼ teaspoon peppermint oil
- 6 drops green food coloring (optional)

Put egg, half-and-half, heavy cream, sugar, peppermint oil, and food coloring in blender. Blend on medium until sugar is dissolved and mixture is smooth, about 30 seconds. Freeze in churn according to churn instructions. When mixture is half frozen, stir in chocolate chips and continue to freeze. Makes slightly more than 1 quart.

Becky Miller

Index

Appetizers and Beverages

Breakfast and Brunch

Salads and Dressings

Soups

Breads

Pasta

Vegetables and Casseroles

Entrées

Seafood

Cakes and Frostings

Cookies, Candies, and Bars

Desserts and Pies

All the Rest